THE LITERATURE OF WAR

THE LITERATURE OF WAR

Five Studies in Heroic Virtue

ANDREW RUTHERFORD

Regius Professor of English
University of Aberdeen

BOOKS
10 East 53d St. New York 10022
(a division of Harper & Row Publishers, Inc.)

First published 1978 by
THE MACMILLAN PRESS LTD
London and Basingstoke

Published in the U.S.A. 1978 by
HARPER & ROW PUBLISHERS, INC.
BARNES & NOBLE IMPORT DIVISION

Printed in Hong Kong

Library of Congress Cataloging in Publication Data

Rutherford, Andrew
   The literature of war.

   Bibliography: p.
   Includes index.
    1.   English fiction—20th century—History and
criticism.   2. Heroes in literature.   3. War in
literature.   I. Title.
PR888. H4R87   823' .03   78—244
ISBN 0—06—49033—1

TO RICHARD, JOHN AND ALISON

Contents

Acknowledgements   ix

1 Introduction   1

2 The Subaltern as Hero: Kipling and Frontier War   11

3 The Intellectual as Hero: Lawrence of Arabia   38

4 The Common Man as Hero: Literature of the Western
  Front   64

5 The Christian as Hero: Waugh's *Sword of Honour*   113

6 The Spy as Hero: Le Carré and the Cold War   135

  Notes   157

  Bibliography   168

  Index   174

Acknowledgements

My thanks are due to Stanford University Press and Oliver and Boyd Ltd. for permission to include a revised version of my essay 'Officers and Gentlemen,' first published in *Kipling's Mind and Art*, ed. Andrew Rutherford; and to Methuen and Co. Ltd. for permission to include a revised version of my essay 'Waugh's *Sword of Honour*,' first published in *Imagined Worlds*, ed. Maynard Mack and Ian Gregor.

The publishers and I also wish to thank the following who have kindly given permission for the use of copyright material:

Jonathan Cape Limited and The Letters of T. E. Lawrence Trust for quotations from *The Letters of T. E. Lawrence*, ed. David Garnett.

Jonathan Cape Limited and Seven Pillars of Wisdom Trust for quotations from *Seven Pillars of Wisdom*, by T. E. Lawrence.

Chatto and Windus Limited and The Estate of Wilfred Owen for extracts from the poem 'Apologia Pro Poemate Meo', from *Collected Poems*, ed. C. Day Lewis.

Rosica Colin Limited on behalf of Catherine Guillaume for quotations from *Death of a Hero*, by Richard Aldington.

Peter Davies Limited for quotations from *The Middle Parts of Fortune*, by Frederic Manning.

Every effort has been made to trace all the copyright holders, but if any have been inadvertently overlooked the publishers will be pleased to make the necessary arrangement at the first opportunity.

The works of history, biography and criticism to which I am most consciously indebted are acknowledged in the bibliography, which is, however, of necessity selective. I should also like to record my gratitude to the officers and men of the Seaforth Highlanders and the Somaliland Scouts, from whom I learned much that has proved relevant to war literature and life.

'"My dear young friend," said Mustapha Mond, "civilization has absolutely no need of nobility or heroism. These things are symptoms of political inefficiency. In a properly organized society like ours, nobody has any opportunities for being noble or heroic. Conditions have got to be thoroughly unstable before the occasion can arise. Where there are wars, where there are divided allegiances, where there are temptations to be resisted, objects of love to be fought for or defended—there, obviously, nobility and heroism have some sense. But there aren't any wars nowadays. The greatest care is taken to prevent you from loving any one too much. There's no such thing as a divided allegiance; you're so conditioned that you can't help doing what you ought to do. And what you ought to do is on the whole so pleasant, so many of the natural impulses are allowed free play, that there really aren't any temptations to resist. And if ever, by some unlucky chance, anything unpleasant should somehow happen, why, there's always *soma* to give you a holiday from the facts."' Aldous Huxley, *Brave New World* (London, 1932), pp. 280-1.

'The danger is that those who see the falseness of many outmoded concepts of "glory" may persuade themselves and others to believe that courage is no longer a virtue. In fact courage in the face of adversity remains the supreme human quality. Nothing will ever be built, or last, without it. A society that loses its courage can only fade and crumble away.' John Baynes, *Morale: A Study of Men and Courage* (London, 1967), p. 13.

1 Introduction

'The "hero" is one of humanity's ideals, like the saint and the sage.' E. R. Curtius, *European Literature and the Latin Middle Ages*, trans. W. R. Trask (London, 1953), p. 167.

'We talked of war. JOHNSON. "Every man thinks meanly of himself for not having been a soldier, or not having been at sea. . . . Mankind reverence those who have got over fear, which is so general a weakness."' *Boswell's Life of Johnson*, ed. R. W. Chapman (London, 1953), pp. 926–7.

' "Let's just have some down-to-earth men for a change, shall we? No more heroes, Bumbo, they're on the shelf, in the nursery with Winnie the Pooh and the Beatrix Potters."' Andrew Sinclair, *The Breaking of Bumbo* (London, 1959), p. 102.

The assumption that heroism, like saintliness, is obsolete as an ideal, and that the literature of heroism belongs to the childhood of the individual or of the race, seems typical of current intellectual opinion. Fortitude is out of fashion as a virtue. Indeed the portrayal of courage in the face of adversity, suffering or danger is now positively suspect in the eyes of many readers, whose unexamined ethical assumptions often predetermine their aesthetic judgments on the literature of war (leading them, for example, to see Falstaff's views on Honour as more normative than Hal's, or to discount war poetry when it is not anti-war). The deflation of specifically chivalric folly in *Don Quixote* has been extended to the whole profession of Arms—which Cervantes himself rated higher than that of Letters—and thence to all varieties of courage and self-sacrifice. Such cynicism can issue in exhilarating and cathartic comedy; it can also function—as in *Arms and the Man* or *The Good Soldier Schweik*—to expose false sentiment, hypocrisy or error; but it fails disablingly to take account of the basic dualism of human nature analysed by Orwell in 'The Art of Donald McGill':

There is one part of you [he wrote in 1941] that wishes to be a hero
or a saint, but another part of you is a little fat man who sees very
clearly the advantages of staying alive with a whole skin. He is your
unofficial self, the voice of the belly protesting against the soul. His
tastes lie towards safety, soft beds, no work, pots of beer and
women with 'voluptuous' figures. He it is who punctures your fine
attitudes and urges you to look after Number One, to be unfaithful
to your wife, to bilk your debts, and so on and so forth. Whether
you allow yourself to be influenced by him is a different question.
But it is simply a lie to say that he is not part of you, just as it is a lie
to say that Don Quixote is not part of you either, though most of
what is said or written consists of one lie or the other, usually the
first. . . . Nevertheless the high sentiments always win in the end,
leaders who offer blood, toil, tears and sweat always get more out
of their followers than those who offer safety and a good time.
When it comes to the pinch, human beings are heroic. Women face
childbed and the scrubbing brush, revolutionaries keep their
mouths shut in the torture chamber, battleships go down with their
guns still firing when their decks are awash. It is only that the other
element in man, the lazy, cowardly, debt-bilking adulterer who is
inside all of us, can never be suppressed altogether and needs a
hearing occasionally. [1]

Since then he has graduated from the occasional hearing to frequent
appearances as an official spokesman for our culture; but it seems all
the more important that his half-truths should not pass for wisdom.
'The refusal to be heroic may be very human,' as Arnold Kettle
remarks, 'but it is also less than human';[2] and literature which
explores this paradox deserves more critical attention than it
currently receives.

*   *   *

The anti-heroic bias of so many modern readers is attributable at
one level to a general and very understandable revulsion from war;
but more fundamentally it seems to stem from three main theoretical
assumptions, aesthetic, moral and historical.

Its aesthetic basis might be defined initially as an antipathy to the
ideal in art, though this will need some qualification and expansion.
The addiction to realism in one form or another has certainly led to a
naive dismissal of 'ideal' art as untrue to life: in a significant semantic
shift the term 'idealised' itself has been debased to a mere synonym for

'falsified' or 'sentimentalised'. Hence readers tend now to have little time for *pius* Aeneas, Chaucer's 'verray parfit gentle knight', Spenser's exemplary protagonists, Wordsworth's Happy Warrior, Tennyson's hero-king, or indeed beautiful idealisms of moral excellence of any kind. This can shade, moreover, into a suspicion of Frye's high mimetic mode, with its epic or tragic heroes who are fully human, fallible therefore, but 'superior in degree to other men', with 'authority, passions and powers of expression greater than our own.'[3] Realism prefers the commonplace, if not the sordid or aberrant; and the quintessentially modern tragic hero, Willie Loman, is significantly classified by his own surname. Visions of nobility, however flawed, begin to seem archaic even when their origins are near-contemporary. Yeats's praise of Major Robert Gregory ('Soldier, scholar, horseman, he,/As 'twere all life's epitome'[4]) tends therefore to evoke a sceptical response, and this kind of scepticism has become endemic in our culture. Leavis's impatience with Othello's nobility ('if he went down [at sea]—and we know he won't—he would go down magnificently'[5]) seems symptomatic of changed values independent of his literary argument. Even more significant is the debunking of 'real-life' heroes by revisionist biographers like Lytton Strachey and his followers, in works which seem to imply that vices are, in some unexamined sense, more real than virtues—that vanity, hypocrisy and self-deception, for example, somehow constitute a truer reality than altruism, self-sacrifice and heroism, *even when these are known to have existed.* This reinterpretation of historical and psychological reality by art involves an opposition not only between high and low mimetic modes (Victorian/Edwardian hagiography *versus* modern realism), but between the low mimetic, with its realistic characters much like ourselves, and the 'ironic', which in terms of Frye's useful definition portrays characters 'inferior in power or intelligence to ourselves, so that we have the sense of looking down on a scene of bondage, frustration, or absurdity'.[6] This, rather than the realistic, has become the dominant mode of literary vision in our time; and the implications for war literature, both past and present, are profound. Even when an heroic reality, imitated realistically in art, can be shown to have existed, biographically or historically, readers may well feel uneasily that it affronts their expectations of both literature and life—that Richard Hillary's truth, for example, is embarrassingly incompatible with Heller's fiction, or that soldiers are more properly portrayed as victims, brutes or fools, or as a mixture of the three, than as conscious and effective moral agents. (This is probably why the virtuosic blend of pathos and absurdity in

Slaughterhouse Five has been more widely acclaimed than the tragic profundity of David Piper's great war novel, *Trial by Battle*.)

A disbelief in the psychological probability of the ideal underlies this aesthetic objection to the heroic in literature. The moral objection rests on a disbelief in the ethical validity of the ideal itself. That disbelief is not, of course, peculiarly modern. Michael in *Paradise Lost*, to cite only one example, had condemned pride in war and conquest as one of the worst perversions of spiritual value—one of the saddest consequences of the Fall of Man:

> For in those days might only shall be admired,
> And valour and heroic virtue called;
> To overcome in battle, and subdue
> Nations, and bring home spoils with infinite
> Manslaughter, shall be held the highest pitch
> Of human glory, and for glory done
> Of triumph, to be styled great conquerors,
> Patrons of mankind, gods, and sons of gods,
> Destroyers rightlier called and plagues of men.
> Thus fame shall be achieved, renown on earth,
> And what most merits fame in silence hid. [7]

The perennial tension between Christianity and military codes of conduct is, however, less significant today than the wide prevalence of what T. E. Hulme calls the rationalist-humanitarian ethic, with its supreme values of life and personality. This helps to account for the neglect or distrust of literature which embodies his 'more heroic or tragic system of ethical values'— which accepts the necessity, and indeed the propriety, of the sacrifice of life for appropriate causes. [8]

> The notions of glory, honor, and courage [comments Leslie Fiedler] lose all meaning when in the West men, still nominally Christian, come to believe that the worst thing of all is to die— when, for the first time in a thousand years, it is possible to admit that no cause is worth dying for. There are various mitigated forms of this new article of faith—that no cause is worth the death of all humanity, or a whole nation, or simply many lives; but inevitably it approaches the formulation: no cause is worth the death of a man, no cause is worth the death of *me*! [9]

In its extreme form this is the moral cynicism for which Solzhenitsyn has denounced the West: a readiness to condone any evil, any tyranny, any degradation of the human spirit, rather than risk our comfort and prosperity—far less our lives—for values we professedly believe in. This spiritual malaise (epitomised for him in the slogan 'Better red than dead') was thrown off, he admits, in Britain's war with Nazi Germany, when for once she took 'a moral stance . . . [which] inspired her to one of the most heroic acts of resistance in her history'.[10] And whatever one thinks of his polemic as a whole, extreme examples of oppression, cruelty or aggression—like Hitler's—make it plain that there *can* be a moral case for actively resisting evil. Yet there remains the moral problem about how to do so without being contaminated by the means one must employ.

That problem may well be insoluble; but there is a suggestive comment in Hulme's attack on the rationalist–humanitarian ethic: 'As *life* is its fundamental value,' he wrote on his return from the trenches in 1915, 'it leads naturally to pacifism, and tends to regard conceptions like Honour, etc., as empty words, which cannot deceive the *emancipated.*'[11] Honour, however, is a concept not so easily dismissed. A code of honour itself implies a system of ethics, however simplified or specialised, which provides guidance on the minutiae of conduct in ordinary life, but which deals also, characteristically, with extremes of experience—with crises that may pass beyond normality, with death and the danger of death as well as life—so that it offers patterns of not just domestic but heroic virtue. An important function of such a code is to enable or at least encourage men to act courageously in crises, but also to impose restraints so that they are not calloused or corrupted morally by what they do. This is why it is important that armies (and police forces) should have a keen sense of honour, and why those who deride the concept increase the probable incidence of brutalities they would themselves condemn. It was Ruskin's perception of this that made him stigmatise Cervantes as the author who had, perhaps, wrought more harm to the human race than any other powerful and popular writer in the cause of error— although Byron and Voltaire were rival candidates—since by his scorn for chivalric, generous ideals 'he, of all men, most helped forward the terrible change in the soldiers of Europe, from the spirit of Bayard to the spirit of Bonaparte, helped to change loyalty into licence, protection into plunder, truth into treachery, chivalry into selfishness. . . . '[12] The historical change hypothesised here is illusory, since Ruskin ignores the frequent contrast between theory and practice in medieval warfare—not least in the Crusades; but he is justified in stressing the genuine ethical content of chivalric ideals, which aimed essentially at 'the humanising of the fighting man'.[13] And in view of aberrations more sinister even than the Napoleonic—those of the Knights of Bushido, the Waffen SS, and the Americans at My Lai—one can hardly see this aim as ethically negligible.

Closely associated with moral objections to the heroic is the assumption that historical progress has made its values and its subject-matter obsolete. The relative security of modern society, especially for the prosperous classes, has been a major factor in this change of outlook.

> One of the most characteristic features of a modern age [Arnold wrote in 1857], of an age of advanced civilization, is the banishment of the ensigns of war and bloodshed from the intercourse of civil life. Crime still exists, and wars are still carried on; but within the limits of civil life, a circle has been formed within which man can move securely, and develop the arts of peace uninterruptedly. The private man does not go forth to his daily occupation prepared to assail the life of his neighbour or to have to defend his own. With the disappearance of the constant means of offence the occasions of offence diminish; society at last acquires repose, confidence, and free activity.[14]

In Victorian Britain there was an increasing tendency for the finest literature to focus on those aspects of experience that fell within the limits of civil life, in which man can move securely, though wars and crime figured largely in historical and sensational fiction, and there was a copious sub-literature of heroism. The emergence of the realistic novel, that 'characteristic expression of bourgeois society',[15] involved not only a rejection of earlier conventions, epic and romantic, but a redefinition of reality in terms of essentially middle-class ideals and experience. This may have been originally a matter of generic convention, and even in the mid-Victorian period the domestic realism of Dickens, Thackeray, George Eliot and Trollope co-existed with Carlyle's hero-worship and the high romance of *Idylls of the King*; but the former soon became the dominant literary mode. Eneas Sweetland Dallas could declare in 1866 that the salient characteristic of their time was 'the withering of the hero and the flourishing of the private individual':

> We dwell far more than we used to do on the private side of human

life. We have learned to feel that there is as much greatness in the family as in the state, in love as in strife, in the shedding of ink as in the shedding of blood, in finessing the pips at whist as in counting the chances of endless division lists. . . . This elevation of the private life and the private man to the place of honour in art and literature, over the public life and the historical man that have hitherto held the chief rank in our regards, amounts to a revolution. The fact of such a revolution having taken place may perhaps be seen most distinctly in the pictorial art, where it is impossible not to be struck with the almost entire subsidence of historical painting. Instead of craving for historical pictures, we glory in genre and landscape; and even a simple bird's-nest by William Hunt has more attractions for us than any pictorial attempt which could now be made at a battle or a martyrdom, the crowning of kings or the conference of heroes.[16]

This bourgeois–domestic version of reality is still widely current, with appropriate variations; but it never went unchallenged, and in our century of wars, revolution, terrorism and civil strife, its selective nature is much more apparent, its normative status much more questionable.

Cruelty, violence, anarchy, tyranny, oppression and war have proved to be recurrent historical phenomena, and society's 'repose, confidence and free activity' seem much more vulnerable than was once supposed. The dream of progress and security ended for one generation in 1914, and Kipling registered its passing with bleak stoicism:

> Comfort, content, delight,
> The ages' slow-bought gain,
> They shrivelled in a night.
> Only ourselves remain
> To face the naked days
> In silent fortitude,
> Through perils and dismays
> Renewed and re-renewed.[17]

Such perils and dismays have been renewed and re-renewed throughout our century. Yeats's 'Nineteen Hundred and Nineteen' is an anguished recognition of the change—hideously quick and easy—from the rule of law to anarchy, from peace to violence and terror:

Now days are dragon-ridden, the nightmare
Rides upon sleep: a drunken soldiery
Can leave the mother, murdered at her door,
To crawl in her own blood, and go scot-free;
The night can sweat with terror as before
We pieced our thoughts into philosophy,
And planned to bring the world under a rule,
Who are but weasels fighting in a hole. [18]

The rise of Fascism presented Europe with a near-absolute of evil, which *had* to be fought, as Auden urged, rather histrionically, in 'Spain':

To-morrow the rediscovery of romantic love,
The photographing of ravens; all the fun under
       Liberty's masterful shadow;
To-morrow the hour of the pageant-master and the musician,

The beautiful roar of the chorus under the dome;
To-morrow the exchanging of tips on the breeding of terriers,
       The eager election of chairmen
By the sudden forest of hands. But to-day the struggle.

To-morrow for the young poets exploding like bombs,
The walks by the lake, the weeks of perfect communion;
       To-morrow the bicycle races
Through the suburbs on summer evenings. But to-day the
                                                  struggle. [19]

'A little injustice in the heart can be drowned by wine,' runs one of the epigraphs to Waugh's *Put Out More Flags* (1942); 'but a great injustice in the world can be drowned only by the sword.' The great injustices have proved, unfortunately, to be Hydra-headed: Edwin Muir sadly compares Communist with Nazi tyranny in Czechoslovakia; and Vera Brittain comes to see 'the belief that individuals were entitled to expect peace and happiness as their normal fate' as a late-Victorian illusion. In reality, she suggests, 'the normal experience of mortal life has been one of war and catastrophe'. [20]

   Perceptions like these, however partial, modify fundamentally the sense of what is typical or representative in human experience—and hence in literature. When Robert Graves went up to Oxford after the

Great War, he found Anglo-Saxon heroic poetry more congenial than the Augustans, because its subject-matter matched his own experiences: 'Beowulf lying wrapped in a blanket among his platoon of drunken thanes in the Gothland billet; Judith going for a *promenade* to Holofernes's staff-tent; and *Brunanburgh* with its bayonet-and-cosh fighting—all this was closer to most of us at the time than the drawing-room and deer-park atmosphere of the eighteenth century.'[21] The argument could, however, be pressed further: Grendel's repeated irruptions into Heorot might well symbolise for us the continual threat of evils that must be resisted—and resisted heroically—if the 'normal' life we value is to be protected and sustained.

This is indeed a favourite theme of popular art, which often reasserts values out of fashion with a literary public alienated from the culture as a whole. ('The evidence suggests,' notes Kermode in a somewhat different context, 'that the lack of any common language in matters of aesthetic is a measure also of enormous ethical differences.'[22]) There are, however, unexpected links or analogies with great art of the past. *The Faerie Queene*, Book VI, and *Shane*— that quintessential Western—are alike in their juxtaposition of the pastoral and the heroic, their endorsement of the values of the former, and their subsequent recognition of the need for the latter—Calidore resuming his armour, Shane his gun-belt, since the heroic virtues are needed to protect the innocence of the pastoral world from the violence and evil which would otherwise destroy it. Similar perceptions inform the *roman policier* and its TV derivatives: Barlow and his colleagues of *Z Cars* and *Softly, Softly*, Kojak and the other heroes of American police series, can be seen as contemporary equivalents of Arthur and his knights, who 'rode abroad redressing human wrongs', and who, in the continual conflict between Order and Anarchy,

> Cleared the dark places and let in the law,
> And broke the bandit holds and cleansed the land.[23]

In a comparable mode, though with more literary sophistication, Raymond Chandler confronted his corrupt urban civilisation with a hero ('a man of honour') who refused to despair in face of its corruption, who concentrated instead on righting some selected portion of the mass of wrong, and whose proud integrity had itself a redemptive quality. The analogy of epic was often invoked by war films, in which the external threat of Nazism, and its horrors, seemed to justify all those shown fighting against it; while the subsequent menace of the Cold War authorised for a vast public the more questionable activities of James Bond and his successors, lineal descendants of the heroes of romance.

Such recurrent figures—gunfighters, police detectives, private eyes, and secret agents—form part of the heroic mythology of modern urban man; but the art which celebrates their actions tends to over-simplify the social-political context, the psychological realities, and the moral issues involved. Sometimes, as in certain classic Westerns, this is in the interest of a stylisation as deliberate as that of pastoral; but all too often entertainment art approximates to the heroic simplicity of boys' adventure stories, permeated by childish assumptions like those Graham Greene diagnoses in *The Ministry of Fear*:

> Behind the complicated details of the world stand the simplicities: God is good, the grown-up man or woman knows the answer to every question, there is such a thing as truth, and justice is as measured and faultless as a clock. Our heroes are simple: they are brave, they tell the truth, they are good swordsmen, and they are never in the long run really defeated. That is why no later books satisfy us like those which were read to us in childhood—for those promised a world of great simplicity of which we knew the rules, but the later books are complicated and contradictory with experience; they are formed out of our own disappointing memories—of the V.C. in the police-court dock, of the faked income tax return, the sins in corners, and the hollow voice of the man we despise talking to us of courage and purity. The Little Duke is dead and betrayed and forgotten; we cannot recognize the villain and we suspect the hero and the world is a small cramped place.[24]

This book, however, is concerned with authors who at their best take full account of the complicated, contradictory nature of adult experience—who eschew ethical and psychological simplicities—but who none the less choose to treat heroic themes and reinvestigate heroic values. It is a study of works of literary art which, basing themselves on different aspects of British national experience, explore the possibility, the worth, the human cost, of heroism in the modern world.

2 The Subaltern as Hero: Kipling and Frontier War

'Surely in all places your writing genius ought to rejoice over an acting genius, when he falls-in with such; and say to himself: "Here or nowhere is the thing for me to write of! Why do I keep pen-and-ink at all, if not to apprize men of this singular acting genius, and the like of him? My fine-arts and aesthetics, my epics, literatures, poetics, if I will think of it, do all at bottom mean either that or else nothing whatever!"' *The Works of Thomas Carlyle*, ed. H. D. Traill (London, 1896—9) vol. xxix, pp. 273—4.

'In the quarrels of civilised nations, great armies, many thousands strong, collide. Brigades and battalions are hurried forward, and come perhaps within some fire zone, swept by concentrated batteries, or massed musketry. Hundreds or thousands fall, killed and wounded. The survivors struggle on blindly, dazed and dumfoundered [*sic*], to the nearest cover. Fresh troops are continually poured on from behind. At length one side or the other gives way. In all this tumult, this wholesale slaughter, the individual and his feelings are utterly lost, only the army has a tale to tell. With events on such a scale, the hopes and fears, the strength and weakness of man are alike indistinguishable. Amid the din and dust little but destruction can be discerned. But on the frontier, in the clear light of morning, when the mountain side is dotted with smoke puffs, and every ridge sparkles with bright sword blades, the spectator may observe and accurately appreciate all grades of human courage.' Winston L. S. Churchill, *The Story of the Malakand Field Force* (London, 1898), pp. 12—13.

Henry James confessed in print in 1891 to having 'wept profusely' over 'The Drums of the Fore and Aft'

the history of the 'Dutch courage' of two dreadful dirty little boys, who, in the face of Afghans scarcely more dreadful, saved the reputation of their regiment and perished, the least mawkishly in the world, in a squalor of battle incomparably expressed. People who know how peaceful they are themselves [he went on] and have no bloodshed to reproach themselves with needn't scruple to mention the glamour that Mr Kipling's intense militarism has for them and how astonishingly contagious they find it, in spite of the unromantic complexion of it—the way it bristles with all sorts of uglinesses and technicalities. [1]

The very novelty of Kipling's subject-matter in such stories was a source of fascination for contemporary readers. Correlli Barnett has shown how strikingly detached the Army was, throughout the eighteenth and nineteenth centuries, from the mainstream of national life. [2] In Victorian England 'Tommy Atkins', and to a lesser extent his officers, were sociologically unfamiliar breeds; and literature had done little to illuminate their ways of life.

It is a curious reflection [Lionel Johnson wrote in 1892, in a review of *Barrack-Room Ballads*] that the British Army at large, and the British soldier in particular, have received so little attention in literature of any excellence. We have plenty of heroic poems . . . ; plenty of verse alive with the martial spirit, with the 'pomp and circumstance of glorious war'; plenty of things hardly less great than Wordsworth's 'Happy Warrior', or the Laureate's 'Ode on Wellington'. But of the British Army, as a way of daily life, as composed of individual men, as full of marked personal character-istics and peculiarities, our poets great and small have had little conception. What Smollett in prose, and Dibdin in verse, did for the Navy, no one has yet done for the Army. [3]

Kipling's stories and poems of frontier, mess and barrack-room came therefore as a revelation to the reading public. He was unique in his own day in being a man of letters with direct, personal knowledge of soldiers and some aspects at least of soldiering. As a young journalist he had been consulted by Lord Roberts, as they rode up Simla Mall, about 'what the men thought about their accommodation, entertainment-rooms and the like'; [4] and as an author he strove for years, with varying success, to interpret the realities of Army life to the public at large.

This chimed with his conception of his wider mission as an artist.

At an early stage in his career he set out 'to tell to the English something of the world outside England—not directly but by implication'—a notion which grew bit by bit 'into a vast, vague conspectus—Army and Navy Stores List, if you like—of the whole sweep and meaning of things and efforts and origins throughout the Empire.'[5] This programme was not primarily political, since his main interest was in people rather than in policies, but it was interpenetrated by political assumptions; and he wished as part of it to celebrate the admirable, indeed the heroic qualities he had observed in the British overseas—to convey to a public living, as it seemed to him, in ignoble comfort and security some sense of the hardships and dangers willingly endured by their compatriots in the service of Empire.

This aim, particularly as it affected soldiers actively engaged on the imperial frontiers, involved a break with the main tradition of serious prose fiction in England in the nineteenth century.

Heroic endeavour had been traditionally dealt with by epic and romance, but these *genres* were associated with particular historical periods and earlier states of society, and they seemed increasingly remote from life as it was lived in nineteenth-century England.

We admire Homer deservedly [Southey had written in 1814] (and undeservedly too, as might very easily be shown by a good analysis of the two poems), but if Homer were living now, he would write very differently. Book after book of butchery, however skilfully performed, is unsuitable to the European state of mind at present. . . . In this age Homer would address himself more to our feelings and reflecting faculties.[6]

This sense of anachronism could coexist with admiration, and both epic and romance continued to enjoy high esteem; but their changing status is suggested by the doubts Tennyson felt in offering the public his *Morte d'Arthur*—doubts expressed, self-protectively, through 'the poet Everard Hall', who is said to have destroyed all the remainder of his twelve-book epic:

> 'Nay, nay,' said Hall,
> 'Why take the style of those heroic times?
> For nature brings not back the Mastodon,
> Nor we those times . . .'[7]

And the *Idylls of the King*, as they afterwards developed, suggest that these early doubts of Tennyson's were only too well founded, since his great theme of Sense at war with Soul is distanced, and to some extent obscured, by the subject-matter, only half congenial to him, of 'a time/That hovered between war and wantonness'.[8]

It seems plain in retrospect that epic and romance, although still cultivated by Victorian poets, were obsolescent forms, in process of being superseded by the anti-heroic, anti-romantic novel, which dealt characteristically with very different areas of experience. Scott had indeed established the historical romance as an important sub-*genre*, and in his best novels he had used rather unheroic heroes to chart his own reactions to the world of action and adventure to which he was imaginatively drawn. Yet even for him that world was in the past, and it hardly figures in the other major novelists, who normally portray their characters in domestic, social and professional settings which give little scope for heroism. None of them had the range, the inclusive vision, of a Tolstoy, who could portray the crises and testings of War as well as those of Peace: none gives, in E. M. Forster's phrase, 'so complete a picture of man's life, both on its domestic and heroic side'.[9] Thackeray is typical in seeing his place as being with the non-combatants in Brussels when the gallant —th march out to Waterloo; and his sour reflections on traditional poetic treatments of war show his awareness of the novel as a *genre* committed not only to different subject-matter, but to a different kind of vision and a truer sense of values:

> Time out of mind [he writes] strength and courage have been the theme of bards and romances; and from the story of Troy down to today, poetry has always chosen a soldier for a hero. I wonder is it because men are cowards in heart that they admire bravery so much, and place military valour so far beyond every other quality for reward and worship?[10]

His dissatisfaction with such conventional estimates would have been shared by the most important English novelists of his century. Common to all of them, except Conrad, is the assumption which Daiches attributes to Scott—the belief that 'heroic action . . . is, in the last analysis, neither heroic nor useful, and that man's destiny, at least in the modern world, is to find his testing time not amid the sound of trumpets but in the daily struggles and recurring crises of personal and social life'.[11]

This assumption was, however, rooted in local and temporary circumstances—in the national security of Victorian England, which can hardly be taken as representative of the human lot. Nor was the assumption universal even then: the nature and necessity of heroism were treated by Carlyle throughout his *oeuvre*, and less apocalyptically by Macaulay in his immensely popular *History of England*. Furthermore, an important aspect of Victorian culture was the widespread popular interest in war, comfortably detached from an awareness of its actuality. 'How many people,' Bagehot reflected in 1859, 'read the account of a war when it is brought to them in the newspaper, who read nothing else there!' [12] It is surely significant that Creasy's *Fifteen Decisive Battles of the World* was a best-seller; and in the preface he acknowledges both the evil of war and its perennial fascination:

> It is an honourable characteristic of the Spirit of this Age [he wrote in 1851], that projects of violence and warfare are regarded among civilized states with gradually increasing aversion. . . . For a writer, therefore, of the present day to choose battles as his favourite topic, merely because they were battles; merely because so many myriads of troops were arrayed in them, and so many hundreds or thousands of human beings stabbed, hewed, or shot to death during them, would argue strange weakness or depravity of mind. Yet it cannot be denied that a fearful and wonderful interest is attached to these scenes of carnage. There is undeniable greatness in the disciplined courage, and in the love of honour, which makes the combatants confront agony and destruction. . . . [13]

It is symptomatic of the narratives which follow, and, it might be argued, of the period itself, that the abstractions 'disciplined courage', 'love of honour', 'agony and destruction' obscure the reality of 'hundreds or thousands of human beings stabbed, hewed, or shot to death'. There does seem to have been a general reluctance in Victorian England to face the full realities of war, though Russell's dispatches from the Crimea form an honourable exception. There was an abundance of verse, as Lionel Johnson acknowledged, celebrating deeds of heroism, past and present, but nothing to compare even remotely with Byron's ironically inclusive treatment of the siege of Ismail in *Don Juan*. Nor was the dream of martial glory ever subjected—except incidentally, as in *Henry Esmond*—to the realistic and imaginative scrutiny of the great novelists. Instead it was abandoned to a sub-literature, often of best-sellers, extending from *Westward Ho!* and the works of Marryat and Lever to Charlotte M. Yonge's *Book of Golden Deeds*, James Grant's *Romance of War*, and straightforward adventure stories for boys. This last category was raised to a higher literary status by the much acclaimed revival of Romance, as a category of the Novel, in the 1880s; but that movement involved so doctrinaire an hostility to realism that the Novel of Adventure presented itself less as an account of actual though unusual experience than as an apotheosis of escape. ('We are all homesick,' wrote Andrew Lang, one of its main advocates, 'in the dark days and black towns, for the land of blue skies and brave adventures in forests, and in lonely inns, on the battle-field, in the prison, on the desert isle';[14] and it was these yearnings that Stevenson and Haggard seemed to satisfy.)

For Kipling this meant that in portraying courage and devotion to duty, or for that matter cowardice and negligence, on the imperial frontiers, he had to start from scratch, evolving his own methods without any adequate models to assist him. His solution involved the immediate reconciliation of 'the crocodile of Realism and the catawampus of Romance', which Lang had seen as embattled opposites.[15] In his new synthesis he celebrated the romance of reality—the genuinely heroic qualities shown in the everyday, routine, apparently humdrum work of administrators, engineers, or even journalists; but he also demonstrated the reality of romance, by showing that in an imperial setting heroic adventures were not anachronistic or fantastic inventions (as they might seem in Stevenson and Haggard respectively), but facts of contemporary life.

'A Conference of the Powers' (1890) forms a useful starting point for an enquiry into his achievement in this new heroic vein. Kipling as narrator, and as character within the story, acts as mediator here between the world of action and Empire, represented by three subalterns on leave from India, and the 'civilised' world of London, represented by the novelist Eustace Cleever. The opposition thus established is less crude than the contrasts he was sometimes tempted to draw between these worlds. The subalterns are not the low-browed extroverts he often holds up for our admiration—they have at least read Cleever's book, and enjoyed it in their unsophisticated way. While he, in spite of some 'pundit caste' affectations of speech, is presented to us as no despicable aesthete but a great novelist, whose greatness, often insisted on, lies in his deep understanding of the

English countryside and people. His knowledge does not extend, however, to the English overseas:

> He could not altogether understand the boys who hung upon his words so reverently. The line of the chin-strap, that still showed white and untanned on cheek-bone and jaw, the steadfast young eyes puckered at the corners of the lids with much staring through red-hot sunshine, the slow, untroubled breathing, and the curious, crisp, curt speech seemed to puzzle him equally. He could create men and women, and send them to the uttermost ends of the earth, to help delight and comfort; he knew every mood of the fields, and could interpret them to the cities, and he knew the hearts of many in cities and the country, but he had hardly, in forty years, come into contact with the thing which is called a Subaltern of the Line.[16]

This description, with its pervasive tendency to over-writing, generates a certain uneasiness in the reader—an uneasiness which is at its most acute over the phrase 'steadfast young eyes': their steadfastness would hardly be apparent on a social occasion like this, any more than 'slow untroubled breathing' would be a matter for remark, and one realises that Kipling is infiltrating a term of quasi-moral praise into what purports to be simple description of 'the boys' as they first appear to Cleever. Hence the passage suggests an emotional commitment which the author is not prepared to acknowledge openly—which indeed he seeks to conceal by his pretence of anthropological detachment in the phrase '*the thing which is called* a Subaltern of the Line'.

He goes on to show excellent qualities in Cleever as well as in the subalterns, but whereas they already know the novelist's work and admire it, he must be taught to know and admire theirs. His admittedly finer sensibility was in Kipling's view a hot-house plant of civilisation, which had flourished by being insulated from basic realities of life, including those that sustain civilisation itself. ' "To me," said Cleever softly, "The whole idea of warfare seems so foreign and unnatural, so essentially vulgar, if I may say so, that I can hardly appreciate your sensations." '[17] To force readers—even readers as refined as Cleever—into an awareness of soldiers' 'sensations' was one of Kipling's primary aims, not least in the dramatic lyrics and monologues of *Barrack-Room Ballads*; and the primitivism apparent in his choice of subject-matter and persona there was based ultimately on his conviction that the activities and consciousness of coarser but more useful 'people who do things' provide richer material for art than do the delicate perceptions of the highbrow. In the present instance Cleever's ignorance of the Army 'whose toils enabled him to enjoy his many-sided life in peace' is dispelled largely through the Infant's story of war in Upper Burma, which opens his eyes to conditions of life outside the sheltered world in which he moves:

> 'The dacoits were having a first-class time, y'know—filling women up with kerosene and setting 'em alight, and burning villages, and crucifying people.'
> The wonder in Eustace Cleever's eyes deepened. He could not quite realise that the Cross still existed in any form.
> 'Have you ever seen a crucifixion?' said he.
> 'Of course not. Shouldn't have allowed it if I had; but I've seen the corpses. . . .'[18]

The passage, like the story as a whole, points to a major difference between the preoccupations of Kipling's age and those of our own. Our recurrent political nightmares are of tyranny—the horrors of Fascist or Communist police-states, or of repressive colonial or post-colonial régimes—whereas Kipling was much more aware of the horrors of anarchy. The wanton violence which so often raged beyond the frontiers of the Empire was to him an emotional and moral justification for extending those frontiers; though in 'A Conference of the Powers' he is less concerned with justifying the (rather unscrupulous) annexation of Burma than with displaying the qualities of the men engaged in bringing law and order to the wretched villagers of the Hlinedatalone and Shan States.

His account of the process involves no arrogant assertion of British superiority, no simple antithesis of black or brown and white. We hear from the Infant of his C.O.—' "*Pukka* Bounderby; more Bounder than *Pukka*" '—and his fussy incompetence; also of his fellow subaltern, overbearing and too prone to fever; and the private soldiers, who enjoyed the fun of dacoit-hunting, but expected to live on fresh meat and full rations as though they were in barracks. As a contrast we have the Burmese mounted police with whom he then worked: ' "nippy little devils, keen as mustard" ', though they told their wives too much and all his plans got known, till he learned to give false marching orders over-night, and take the men to quite a different village in the morning. There was also his friend Hicksey of the Police—' "the best man that ever stepped on earth; a first-class man" '—praise which is clearly meant to draw its strength from the Infant's usual habit of understatement, and from the contrast with all the other Englishmen mentioned, including the Civil Officer (' " . . . he was awf'ly clever. He knew a lot of things, but I don't think he was quite steady enough for dacoit-hunting" '). The climax of his story is the capture of Boh Na-ghee—an episode in which violence and farce intermingle; and the Boh himself turns out to be a sportsman in spite of his villainies, a good loser who begs only to be hanged on the spot instead of sent for trial. ' "If I'm sent to Rangoon," said he, "they'll keep me in jail all my life, and that is a death every time the sun gets up or the wind blows." But we had to send him to Rangoon, and, of course, he was let off down there, and given penal servitude for life.'[19]

Up to this point in the story Kipling's own role has been largely that of *compère*, introducing the subalterns, but letting them reveal themselves almost unconsciously in conversation and monologue, while he intervened occasionally to interpret some piece of army slang, with a rather ostentatious display of inside knowledge. Now, however, he feels impelled to point the moral, and if we sensed his thumb in the scale in his earlier descriptions of the boys, its pressure is unmistakable in the conclusion. Cleever, whose admiration for them is by now unbounded, spends the whole evening delighting in their company; they, for their part, consider him ' "as good a man as they make" '; and when he leaves Kipling asks him his opinion of things generally:

He replied with [a] quotation, to the effect that though singing was a remarkably fine performance, I was to be quite sure that few lips would be moved to song if they could find a sufficiency of kissing.

Whereby I understood that Eustace Cleever, decorator and colourman in words, was blaspheming his own Art and would be sorry for it in the morning.[20]

Earlier in the story Kipling had himself drawn an antithesis between action and expression: ' "How can he speak?" ' he had said of the Infant. ' "He's done the work. The two don't go together." ' And the implication is that an author, even of stories like this, is inferior to a man of action: those who can, do; those who can't, write. Now that Cleever has come to the same conclusion, however, Kipling rebukes him for blaspheming his own art—yet even while delivering the rebuke he seems to endorse the blasphemy. Cleever's art is dignified with a capital A, which might have been ironical were it not for the earlier unequivocal praise, but subtly devalued by the description of him as 'decorator and colourman in words'. The artistry which this phrase suggests is something very different from the greatness as a novelist previously attributed to Cleever, so that Kipling seems to be evading the question he himself has posed, about the relative value of great art and heroic action: he evades it by cooking the experiment, and diminishing the allegedly great art, with its insights into human nature, to a mere aesthete's preoccupation with beauties of language. The phrase also discounts Cleever's deep knowledge of the English countryside; and indeed, although he shows a certain generosity of spirit and a readiness to have his ideas enlarged, his knowledge of England is not *shown* to extend beyond the coteries of London. Kipling thus seems to be avoiding serious consideration of his own implied question 'What should they know of England/Who only England know?'—a question which as far as this story is concerned remains merely rhetorical. It is as if he were unwilling to explore fully and freely the case he has presented—as if, too, he did not trust his artistic vision to correspond at all points to his intention, so that he intervenes himself to make sure that the tale comes out at the right conclusion.

This artistic dishonesty is the more regrettable since the story, apart from these unfortunate manipulations, is undoubtedly successful in its minor way. Its success lies in his presentation of the subalterns—in his use of their speech with all its slang, colloquialisms, banalities, and *clichés*, to reveal their characters and the nature of their experiences. And in this we see one of Kipling's characteristic strengths. He had a remarkable faculty of observation, which had been sharpened, he thought, like Fra Lippo Lippi's by the hardships and sufferings of his childhood; and an extraordinary ability to profit from other people's observation— to get as vivid a picture of a scene from someone else's account as he could have got at firsthand. Nor was it simply a matter of getting the gist of what anyone told him: he was also fascinated by the manner of the telling, and his ear for speech habits and variations was as remarkable as his gift for visual observation. He realised that the best way 'to think in another man's skin'[21] was through a study of the other's use of language; and he therefore regarded men's conversation as one of the best clues to their character. 'They were direct of speech among each other,' he wrote of the middle-aged politicians he met in Australia, 'and talked a political slang new to me. One learned, as one always does, more from what they said to each other or took for granted in their talk, than one could have got at from a hundred questions.'[22] In his fiction Kipling aimed at dialogue and monologue which would be equally revealing without ceasing to be authentic. At best this was not just a matter of dialect (which could be a snare for him, as it was in the Mulvaney stories), but rather of catching the very idioms and rhythms proper to a character's modes of thought as well as speech. To take only one example: when the Boh was pleading to be hanged, ' "If I'm sent to Rangoon", said he, "they'll keep me in jail all my life, *and that is a death every time the sun gets up or the wind blows.*" ' This phrase strikes a poetic-philosophic note quite alien to the Infant's own slangy colloquial discourse. Whether or not it is true to what a Burmese dacoit might have said, it *sounds* convincing, and establishes him as a definite personality expressing itself in idioms and speech-rhythms quite distinct from the Infant's or the narrator's; so that we glimpse through this request itself and the manner in which it is made a world of feeling and experience as remote from the Infant's as the Infant's was from Eustace Cleever's.

The subalterns' own use of language, however, which gives the tale its documentary and imaginative validity, also betrays their limitations. In the Infant's references to kerosene and crucifixions there is no attempt at recreating the atrocities imaginatively, yet paradoxically we do apprehend them through the deliberately inadequate medium of the subaltern's discourse; and his very curtness—the discrepancy between the horrors themselves and his casual, matter-of-fact statements—helps to establish Kipling's ideal of men who express themselves characteristically in deeds rather than words. But this is a technique which brings diminishing returns. Casual references to horrors may lead *us* to take them casually; or if our moral sensibility remains unblunted, we shall find ourselves condemning the speaker for his imperception or brutality. This is indeed a recurrent problem in Kipling's presentation of soldier-heroes: in too many of his portraits we see an abandonment of the centuries-old European attempt to combine courage and military skill with culture, intelligence, and sensitivity. Not that he can himself be blamed for the failure of what one might see as the Renaissance synthesis, since this failure was an historical as well as a literary phenomenon. The specialisation of functions in nineteenth-century English society had already led to the growth of a professional officer caste which had little contact with or interest in the world of letters; so that in portraying men like the Infant and bestowing on them the crude *patois* of a minor public school, Kipling was not inventing a type, but recording facts as he had observed them. In presenting such men for our admiration, however, he seems at best unaware of their limitations, while at worst he glories in them. Thus his praise of courage is too often associated with a denigration of intelligence: he sneered at 'brittle intellectuals/Who crack beneath a strain',[23] and there was for him a significant correlation between the Civil Officer's cleverness and his cowardice, between his moral sensitivity and his weakness of character; just as in a later story, 'The Honours of War', one of the main counts against an unpleasant and unpopular subaltern was the fact that he talked too much and had a university degree. This aggressive anti-intellectualism was no doubt Kipling's response to contemporary provocations: conscious of the lack of sympathy with which many intellectuals viewed the men and values he admired, he carried the war into the enemies' camp—the more eagerly since he was deeply committed emotionally to the defence of his officer and administrator heroes. Quite apart from their unquestionable virtues, these were the men by whom he had first been accepted into manhood; more important, perhaps, these had been the boys among whom he first found friendship, and comradeship against adult oppression after the isolated suffering of his childhood. Hence he could never view them with the sympathetic detachment which Waugh brings to his Halberdiers, and which Kipling himself brought to other races, other classes, Other Ranks. Sentimentality such as he lavished on Bobby Wicks in 'Only a Subaltern' is rare—it is usually precluded by a sharper awareness of social realities; but he does tend to accord such men his undiscriminating admiration, while sometimes his prejudices lead him to play up their least attractive features as if these were merits. Hence Dunsterville, the original Stalky, emerges from his own *Reminiscences* as a much more intelligent and humane personality than his *alter ego* does in Kipling's fiction. It is, for example, impossible to imagine Kipling's Stalky making friends with an Hungarian musician, however aristocratic, and persuading him to spend a winter as his guest in the Mess at Lahore. Yet Dunsterville played host in just this way to the consumptive Sigismund de Justh.[24]

The last chapter of *Stalky & Co.* (1899) exemplifies the dangers for Kipling of over-emphasis shading into propagandist over-statement. Here the same Infant, some years older, has resigned from the service, having inherited a baronetcy and an estate; and he is entertaining a group of his old school-mates, most of them on leave from India.

From their talk we learn of another notable frontier action—on the North-West Frontier this time—and there is what seems at first sight the same kind of army jargon, slang, colloquialisms, the same kind of authentic detail in the narrative; yet here the whole effect is curiously off-key.

For one thing, the action described seems unnaturally neat. In the Infant's expedition courage and planning had combined convincingly with elements of cowardice, muddle, and good luck. Here everything is much simpler: the Politicals have landed the troops in a mess from which Stalky proceeds to extricate them, by means of his superb fieldcraft and tactical sense, his heroism, and his unrivalled knowledge of the native mind. There is nothing impossible in what he does, but our sense of its improbability is increased by the fact that this adventure does not stand alone: it is the culmination of a series every item of which has shown comparable triumphs stemming from comparable qualities in the hero. This recurrent pattern has been explained by Edmund Wilson as 'an hysterical outpouring of emotions kept over from schooldays', revenge-fantasies replacing the realities of schoolboy experience,[25] but it is also a result of Kipling's heavily didactic intentions. *Stalky & Co.* developed from his 'idea of beginning some tracts or parables on the education of the young', and in 1935 he still felt that in its finished state it was 'a truly valuable collection of tracts'[26]—presumably because it demonstrated the continuity of school and adult experience, and showed so clearly the qualities he thought most worth developing in boys and men. Yet the very tract-like nature of these tales—the remorselessly recurring pattern of 'stalkiness' bringing its own reward—strains our credulity, especially when in this last episode the praise of the hero becomes too unanimous and hyperbolic: ' "Stalky is the Great Man of his Century" '—' "Stalky *is* a Sikh" ' Don't you remember how Rutton Singh grabbed his boots and grovelled in the snow, and how our men shouted?" '[27] Even the saturnine M'Turk is described as 'swelling with pride' at having seen Stalky more recently than the others, almost as if he were a disciple favoured with the last glimpse of his departing deity. This particular inflation is symptomatic: whereas the Infant in the earlier story had been a first-rate subaltern, Stalky is now spoken of as a kind of superman, almost a demi-god. And even when Kipling-Beetle denies his uniqueness—' "India's full of Stalkies— Cheltenham and Haileybury and Marlborough chaps—that we don't know anything about" '—the effect is not to detract from this quasi-mythical status but to enhance it, by suggesting that Stalky is less an individual portrait than a symbolic figure—the living embodiment of the British officer-ideal as Kipling conceived it.

This tendency to overstate the actuality observed accounts for much that one finds distasteful in the book—its local faults in tone as well as the structuring of the narrative as a whole. There is a curiously hectic note, for example, in passages like 'Luckily the baize doors of the bachelors' wing fitted tight, for we dressed promiscuously in the corridor or in each other's rooms, talking, calling, shouting, and anon waltzing by pairs to songs of Dick Four's own devising.'[28] However authentic this may have been as a description of the behaviour of ex-public-schoolboys, the last detail, coloured as it is by the oddly challenging 'promiscuously', has for us overtones of abnormality which were certainly no part of Kipling's intention, but which result from his over-insistence on the cult of self-sufficient masculinity. Our embarrassment is not, however, simply embarrassment at the behaviour portrayed, for Kipling's style on such occasions generates an acute discomfort of its own: when, for example, he tells how 'we had to sing the old song through twice, again and once more, and subsequently, in order to repeat it', or how Dick Four at the climax of his story had to wait until 'the roaring, the shouting, the laughter, and, I think, the tears, had subsided'.[29] Here it is clearer that Kipling is not writing realistically so much as working his material up to give us the quintessence of reunions and the emotions they evoke. The trouble is that he works it up to a point where it seems not only offensive in itself but at variance with the realistic mode in which most of the narrative is cast: we doubt very much whether men of this type would in fact have wept on such an occasion, and Kipling's own doubt is suggested by the coyness of 'I think, the tears'.

The same process of working up affects the language of the characters themselves. Indeed a sophisticated Philistinism, a deliberate brutality of speech, is one of the least pleasant features of *Stalky & Co.* The Infant's references to death and violence in the earlier story had been genuinely laconic in a boyish way—matter-of-fact, without any trace of self-conscious Hemingwayan toughness. (Though there was perhaps a touch of this in Nevin's reply to Cleever's question about how he had felt after killing a man: ' "Thirsty, I wanted a smoke, too." ') Such toughness, however, with its disturbing suggestions of connoisseurship in violence, is exactly what repels us in remarks like Dick Four's: ' "One of our men, a young fellow from Dera Ismail . . . jumped down, blubbing like a child. He'd been hit smack in the middle of the hand. Never saw a man yet who could stand a hit

in the hand without weepin' bitterly. It tickles up all the nerves." '30
The Infant's understatements, again, had been part of the genuine
speech habits of a semi-articulate subaltern: in *Stalky & Co.*
understatement becomes part of the mystique of British heroism, and
is therefore overemphasised, sometimes to the point of caricature.
(' "Adequate chap. Infernally adequate", said Tertius, pulling his
moustache and staring into the fire'; and his utterance is obviously
meant to have the force of many superlatives.)

In passing from 'A Conference of the Powers' to *Stalky*, then, we
see how genuine experience and observations can be crudened and
distorted by their conversion or partial conversion into propagandist
fable—a process all too frequent in Kipling's art. He tends often to
discredit his original perceptions, which may have had a real validity
of their own, by an over-emphasis manifesting itself in both the style
and structuring of his stories, and provoking us to incredulity,
irritation, or disgust. (The closest parallel that comes to mind is the
Lawrence of 'St. Mawr' or 'The Virgin and the Gipsy'.) And a related
weakness in his narrative technique is his tendency to intervene as
ineptly and disastrously as Thackeray at his worst, with comments—
sententious, brutal, sentimental, or facetious—that antagonise the
reader by their vulgarity of tone as much as by their content.

The myth-making tendency of his mind, however, operates to
very different effect in *The Jungle Books* (1894, 1895) and *Puck of
Pook's Hill* (1906). These have an imaginative potency and a
profundity of unstated meaning which set them apart from his mere
elaborated anecdotes (and 'A Conference of the Powers' is not much
more than this); yet they differ from his more obvious fables or
allegories like 'A Walking Delegate' or 'The Ship that Found
Herself', in that their significance is not exhausted by a simple
transposition of the narrative into conceptual terms. Their success is
due largely to a happier blending of the myth-making with the
realistic impulses in Kipling's imagination— also to his abstracting his
plots from the contemporary circumstances and contemporary
pressures which were often responsible for the distortions and
excesses I have noted.

Parnesius' tale, like *Puck of Pook's Hill* as a whole, emerges from
Kipling's sense of his country's history and traditions. It refers also to
circumstances of his own day: the parallel between the Great Wall
and the North-West Frontier has often been remarked on, as has the
resemblance between the Winged Hats and the Prussian menace. But
the story is more than the imaginative recreation of an historical

event, and more than an allegory of contemporary problems: it is Kipling's supreme presentation of one of the major themes that fired his imagination—the defence of civilisation against savagery by men whose chosen duty it is to spend themselves in such a cause. The notion had cropped up in 'A Conference of the Powers' when we were told that it was the Army 'whose toils enabled [Eustace Cleever] to enjoy his many-sided life in peace'; but the absence of a European threat and the remoteness of the imperial frontiers in that story kept us from taking the claim very seriously. What did make an impact was the picture of the Infant, servant of an expanding empire, dealing with violence outside the pale, or just within it, and bringing the *Pax Britannica* to areas where it had never before reigned. The underlying assumptions are optimistic: progress is demonstrably taking place, and the values of law and order are confidently asserted, even though Kipling is more interested in the process of pacification and the heroic action this involves, than in the ends to which that action is directed. This bias is intensified in *Stalky & Co.*, where the ultimate aims of heroic activity have receded still further into the background. We are never told why deeper penetration into Afghanistan should be thought desirable, or why we should despise the Viceroy for discountenancing it. The answers could be found in contemporary strategic and political disputes, but they are not embodied in Kipling's fiction; and it begins to look as if he approves of empire-building not for the sake of empire so much as for the qualities which it develops in the empire-builders: frontier soldiering seems so admirable as a way of life that it becomes virtually an end in itself. Soon after the publication of *Stalky & Co.*, however, the Boer War jolted Kipling into a sharper awareness of military and imperial realities. Along with the revelation of incompetence at so many levels throughout the Army, came a sudden realisation of the hostility of the major European powers, and from now on Kipling's thoughts turned more and more to problems of defence. In bitter polemical verses like 'The Islanders' and 'The Dykes', in impassioned pamphleteering like 'The Parable of Boy Jones' or 'The Army of a Dream', he warned Britain of the need to prepare for Armageddon, to make ready to defend herself against dangers of invasion and defeat which she had not had to face since the overthrow of Napoleon. This gave a more pessimistic turn to his own imaginings. He could still write a confident tale of the expanding Empire in 'A Deal in Cotton' (1907), where the suppression of the slave-trade, the establishment of peace, and the development of the country's natural resources all serve to justify the efforts, the heroic endurance, of the soldier-administrators. We do not doubt that the Sheshaheli will be better off growing cotton under Strickland junior than cannibalising and being hacked to pieces by Ibn Makarrah's young men. Kipling's Law and Order are unquestionable values when asserted in such contexts, and the progress the tale celebrates is real. (Yet it is oddly qualified by the kinship young Strickland feels with the Arab slaver, which closely resembles the earlier kinship between the Infant and Boh Na-ghee. The friendship of two such strong men, such 'Great Ones', obscures the moral antitheses which the tale assumes; it also emerges as more important than anything pertaining to the lesser beings for whom the *Pax Britannica* is nominally being secured. Kipling was not the first writer to find epic values more inspiring than those of pastoral, but he found it peculiarly difficult to evolve a synthesis appropriate to his imperial theme.)[31]

In Parnesius' story, on the other hand, the tide is flowing the other way: the Roman Empire, prototype and symbolic equivalent of the British, is declining, contracting—the old province of Valentia is lost irrecoverably, and the tribes beyond the pale now constitute a threat to peace and order within the Empire itself. Only the Wall and its custodians stand between civilisation and the anarchy that would destroy it. This makes for a grimmer heroism than Stalky's or the Infant's: the weight of responsibility, the greatness of the issues, and the fierceness of the fighting soon banish the notion, tenable in mere frontier scuffles, of war as a game. And the tale is more deeply satisfying than those of the Indian frontier— partly because heroism always seems greater when the odds are unfavourable, as at Thermopylae, Maldon, and Roncevalles, partly because the situations symbolically presented are closer to our own national experience in the twentieth century, but also because the distancing of these events in time has had a purifying effect on Kipling's vision. This hero has a finer, fuller humanity than his nineteenth-century equivalents, and the values which he represents are asserted with new tact, new subtlety, and an imaginative power that has no trace of propagandist zeal.

Parnesius at the beginning of his story is an Infant of those days, and when he sets out on his long march north he comes up against difficulties very like those the Infant had met with in Burma:

'I was grubbing on fowls and boiled corn [the Infant had reported], but my Tommies wanted their pound of fresh meat, and their half-ounce of this, and their two ounces of t'other thing, and they used to come to me and badger me for plug-tobacco when we were four days in jungle. . . . They wanted all the luxuries of the season, confound 'em.'

'Their very first day out [Parnesius now recalls], my men complained of our water-ground British corn. They said it wasn't so filling as the rough stuff that is ground in the Roman ox-mills. However, they had to fetch and eat it. . . . [But they] looked at the flour in their helmets as though it had been a nest of adders.'32

Although Kipling is intensely aware here of the parallels between past and present—of the similarity of the tests young officers have to face throughout the centuries—he does not try to bring this out by making Parnesius speak like the Infant. That would have had a disastrously anachronistic effect. Instead he gives us, simultaneously, a sense of the difference of the past, partly by means of vividly imagined detail—that touch, for example, about the men bringing flour from the mill in their helmets— and partly by the manner of Parnesius' speech. In phrases like 'the rough stuff that is ground' or 'as though it had been a nest of adders', the slight but unmistakable formality of syntax and rhythm superimposed on his easy colloquial speech sets him off from the contemporary; and the cumulative effect of such details is to suggest convincingly the Roman dignity and higher intelligence which differentiate him from Kipling's nineteenth-century subalterns.

Miss Tompkins, however, draws our attention to still further stylistic variations in Parnesius' tale:

When he describes his home in Vectis he uses language entirely familiar to the children who question him, but, as he moves into the longer laps of unbroken narrative, the rhythm strengthens, and the language, without ceasing to be entirely speakable—we never question the authenticity of the narrating voice—acquires a precision and an order which is strictly outside colloquial usage. 'Red-hot in summer, freezing in winter, is that big, purple heather country of broken stone.' At the height of the story, when the Winged Hats bring the Emperor's letter to the Captains of the Wall, they show Parnesius 'a dark stain on the outer roll that my heavy heart perceived was the valiant blood of Maximus', and the deliberate, dragging cadence, the stately artifice of the words, commend themselves to the hearer as what the event requires.[33]

Clearly, this goes beyond establishing the narrator's personality, period, and race: it amounts to a richer orchestration of the whole story. And that richer orchestration is called for by the story's richer meaning, which requires in the narrator a more flexible and eloquent mode of speech than Kipling's British officers could ever attain to. They had all, like Major Cottar of 'The Brushwood Boy', been taught 'not . . . to dwell on [their] emotions, but rather to keep in hard condition'—to keep their pores open and their mouths shut—with the result that they are incapable of expressing intense emotions such as love or grief, which render them tongue-tied or maudlin. The sentimentalities of 'The Brushwood Boy' are an embarrassing attempt to give a new dimension of uninhibited private emotion to what is essentially a public type; at the opposite extreme, but equally embarrassing, are the clipped, restrained love-passages of 'William the Conqueror'. In 'The Head of the District', on the other hand, the dying Yardley-Orde speaks movingly and without inhibitions of his wife and district, yet this is an exceptional case, where approaching death has loosened the taboos of his class and service. Generally, therefore, such men make good heroes but inadequate narrators.

This is one aspect of a wider problem involved in treating the life of action: men who excel in it are often unaware of the values which the author perceives in them—their own consciousness is not adequate for rendering his sense of what they are. To bestow *his* own consciousness on one of them, as Conrad did on Marlow, is to evade rather than solve the problem: more to the point is the virtuosic narrative technique by which he brings us to a full appreciation of the qualities of the inarticulate MacWhirr. Kipling, writing as omniscient narrator, can make us similarly aware of heroism in his Scotts, Ordes, Tallantires; but he was drawn characteristically to the use of fictional narrators, who speak either directly to Kipling himself or to other auditors within the tale. This may be regarded as a journalistic technique, of securing copy through interviews or conversation, which has been converted to the purposes of art. It was certainly a device which by its demands for dramatic propriety in speech often helped him to a surer stylistic control than he could guarantee when writing in his own person (although at times it brought temptations of its own). In *Puck of Pook's Hill* this device is central. Kipling himself does not share the children's experiences—significantly, their father is kept firmly in the background—so that they and we are spared his knowing interpretative comments. When some comments *are* required to modify the *naïveté* of Dan and Una's reactions, these are provided pungently and economically by Puck, while Kipling preserves his role of impersonal narrator, leaving the main burden of the story to his fictional creations. A Roman centurion was the obvious choice for the narrator-hero of this episode, dealing as it does with service on another, more ancient imperial frontier; but in order to bring out the full significance of his story Kipling had to bestow on him a more adequate consciousness—one capable of apprehending and communicating deeper truths and a wider range of emotions than the Infant or Stalky could ever discern or experience. Yet he did not make the mistake of letting Parnesius perceive too much—of making him a mere mouthpiece for the author. This hero can render his own experience superbly, but he has the limitations of vision inherent in any genuinely fictional narrator; and Puck's comments, the framing narrative, and the intervening poems all help to create new perspectives of which he is unaware, but which form an important part of Kipling's meaning.

The story opens with Una making ready to meet Lars Porsena's invading army, and chanting verses from 'Horatius'—whose defence of the bridge foreshadows, though in childishly simple terms, the theme of Parnesius' tale. The high-pitched rhetoric of her defiance is soon deflated, however; and the explanations when Parnesius reveals himself are in familiar friendly vein, so that we pass quickly from the melodramatic to the domestic. Any relapse into heroics is precluded by Parnesius' own modesty and sureness of tone, reinforced by Puck's friendly mockery—'Let the hero tell his own tale'—and the ready irony Puck brings to any touch of excess in the narration. In response to Una's questions Parnesius now describes his childhood in Vectis, and this evocation, uninhibited by any cult of the inarticulate, does more than sketch in his own background. The picture of happy family life, the warm affection, the glimpses of society beyond the island—the expedition to Aquae Sulis, his sister married to the son of a magistrate in the west, and his brother now settled on the estate—all these domestic details, with their suggestions of simple, peaceful happy lives, give warm reality to the elusive concept of civilisation, and make the defence of the Wall meaningful in human terms.

This is all the more important in view of the political uncertainties of Parnesius' world. Born and bred in Britain, he resents the arrogance of the Roman-born, and though his father reminds him that their duty is to the Empire, this can no longer command unquestioning allegiance: it is already showing signs of disintegration; several Provinces have tried to set up Emperors of their own; while the present ruler, Gratian, is said to have 'turned himself into a raw-beef-eating Scythian'. This awareness of decadence at the heart of the Empire is expressed still more strongly by Parnesius' father; and although his son listens with a young man's impatience—touches like this give the tale its fictional vitality—he accepts the conclusion that Britain may yet be saved, in spite of Rome's corruption—that Rome's northern frontier must be guarded, therefore, as a national frontier, whatever the condition of Rome herself.

The issue is still further complicated, however, by the intervention of Maximus, a figure at once beneficent and sinister, through whom Kipling suggests the ambiguous nature of power and the inhumanity that lies at the heart of imperial greatness. Parnesius has just quelled an incipient mutiny in the draft he is conducting to the Wall:

'Then, quietly as a cloud, Maximus rode out of the fern (my Father behind him), and reined up across the road. He wore the Purple, as though he were already Emperor; his leggings were of white buckskin laced with gold.

My men dropped like—like partridges.

He said nothing for some time, only looked, with his eyes puckered. Then he crooked his fore-finger, and my men walked—crawled, I mean—to one side.

"Stand in the sun, children," he said, and they formed up on the hard road.

"What would you have done," he said to me, "If I had not been here?"

"I should have killed that man," I answered.

"Kill him now," he said. "He will not move a limb."

"No," I said, "You've taken my men out of my command. I should only be your butcher if I killed him now. . . ."'[34]

The episode is of profound importance. 'Don't think yourself Emperor of Britain already,' the mutineer had shouted at Parnesius, and the insult showed how disorder in the draft mirrored disorder in the Empire as a whole. In his new garb Maximus might seem to embody this spirit of rebellion, yet his personal authority is so great that we feel he has simply assumed the role for which he is best fitted. It is not the imperial purple that quells the soldiers, but the sense of Maximus' own latent power, communicated by the dramatic quietness of his approach, and the way his threats manifest themselves only in an economy of gesture and deceptive mildness of speech. We realise that this is a man born to rule, and that although he is himself a rebel he is likely to suppress disorders in the Empire as readily and as ruthlessly as in this draft of legionaries. For ruthlessness is what he will employ if necessary—hence his command to kill the offending soldier. And Parnesius' refusal to obey such an order, even when it comes from his commander-in-chief, marks the essential differences between them. Parnesius exemplifies the soldier's code, but it is far removed from that of Nazi Germany or the centurions of Lartéguy: for him a sense of basic human decency overrules strict military or political obligations, and he emerges from the test with increased stature in our eyes. But success to us is failure in the eyes of Maximus:

'. . . Maximus frowned. "You'll never be an Emperor," he said. "Not even a General will you be."
    I was silent, but my Father seemed pleased.
    "I came here to see the last of you," he said.
    "You have seen it," said Maximus. "I shall never need your son any more. He will live and he will die an officer of a Legion—and he might have been Prefect of one of my Provinces . . ."'[35]

For Kipling supreme power involved inhumanity, or at least a complete detachment from humanity in the making of decisions; but his whole-hearted admiration was reserved for the subordinate commanders like Sir Richard or Parnesius, deeply involved with their fellow men, and defining their sense of duty in terms of a fully personal integrity. Yet Maximus has great potentialities for good: paradoxically, his cold-blooded self-seeking ambition might well be the motive force which would restore the Empire's greatness. 'It is always one man's work,' he mutters later in the story, establishing a parallel as well as a contrast between his battles in Gaul and Parnesius' duties on the frontier. But finally the insatiable egotistic nature of his ambition brings him to the ruin Parnesius' father had foretold; and although the deep loyalty he inspires in the young men is never devalued, we see more clearly than they do the inhumanity involved in his kind of greatness. 'Only a life,' he exclaimed, when Pertinax asked for justice against his uncle: 'I thought it would be money or an office. Certainly you shall have him.'[36] Clearly, there is a kind of poetic justice, tacitly endorsed by the author, in his now dying, however bravely, the death he had meted out so ruthlessly to others.

Ironically, the Captains who had held the Wall while Maximus gambled and lost have now to defend it knowing that even if they succeed they may meet the same fate at the hands of the victorious Emperor. But the uncertainty that this breeds for the future—the uncertainty indeed that it breeds about political values in the present—serves only to emphasise, to isolate in even greater clarity, the soldier's code, the soldier's virtues of courage, endurance, loyalty, friendship, honour, sense of duty.

    ' "It concerns us to defend the Wall, no matter what Emperor dies, or makes die," I said.
    "That is worthy of your brother the philosopher," said Pertinax. "Myself I am without hope, so I do not say solemn and stupid things!" '37

Pertinax's jesting tone contrasts, as it often does, with Parnesius' solemnity, but his testing irony finds no weakness here—indeed, it is itself discredited as it plays against Parnesius' statement without undermining it; and the two men now unite in a stoical acceptance of their professional military ethic.

    The success with which this is presented derives from Kipling's imaginative awareness of the actual complexities of soldiering in any age, as opposed to the heroic simplicities he sometimes inclined to. Thus he is simultaneously conscious of the Wall's symbolic value and of the squalid realities of garrison life: Parnesius passes directly from his magnificent description of the Wall itself to an account of the vicious and corrupting town that lies behind it. There is also the shock of realising that this great defensive line is manned by troops and officers of doubtful quality—of finding, too, even here on the frontier, a cynical disregard of duty which recalls the decadence of Rome herself. 'Oh, you'll soon outgrow that sort of nonsense', Parnesius is told when he refuses to accept a drink before handing over his men; and he sees all round him signs of professional disintegration. Kipling's rejection here of the facile City/Frontier opposition is symptomatic of the story's strength: so is the vividness with which the hero's bitter loneliness and disillusion are conveyed to us, though they are beyond the children's comprehension. The narrative carries conviction by its refusal to oversimplify, morally, politically, or psychologically, though certain reticences are inevitable in a book written partly at least for children. Rutilianus, the old general commanding the garrison, is an easy-going glutton, but

Kipling shows genuine insight and avoids the temptation to caricature by making him fight bravely when the fighting comes. The
futility of his heather-burning policy is clear to Parnesius: this is in
itself is nothing unusual, since Kipling's officers can nearly always see
the faults of their superiors; yet here the perception has its roots in an
understanding of the Picts which enables Parnesius to see the Empire
itself from the point of view of those outside it—to look at the Wall, as
it were, from the other side. Thus Maximus asks him, when they meet
again, whether he could hold and govern the old province of
Valentia:

> ' "No," I said. "You cannot remake that Province. The Picts
> have been free too long."
> "Leave them their village councils, and let them furnish their
> own soldiers," he said. "You, I am sure, would hold the reins very
> lightly."
> "Even then, no," I said. "At least not now. They have been too
> oppressed by us to trust anything with a Roman name for years
> and years." '[38]

Parnesius is no anti-imperialist—he remains throughout a Roman
centurion: 'You little painted beast!' were the first words we heard
him utter—'I'll teach you to sling your masters.' But his kindly, if
paternalistic, concern for the Picts' welfare, and still more, this ability
to see things from their point of view, humanise his imperialism and
keep it from ever becoming oppressive or expansionist. He will fight
the Picts and the Winged Hats only if they attack the Wall which it is
his duty to defend, and his relationship with Amal shows his respect
for Rome's enemies as human beings in their own right. The last episode, moreover, which deals with the actual fighting, is far removed
from the light-hearted boy-scoutery of Stalky and the Infant. This
tale is told in a different part of Far Wood, 'sadder and darker
than the Volaterrae end because of an old marlpit full of black water,
where weepy, hairy moss hangs round the stumps of the willows
and alders. But the birds come to perch on the dead branches, and
Hobden says that the bitter willow-water is a sort of medicine for sick
animals.'[39] To impose a strictly allegorical interpretation here would
be to falsify, but the sadness and darkness of this setting clearly
foreshadow the nature of the tale itself. And while the last sentence
suggests that Kipling finds redeeming qualities in the bitterness of
war, the paradox is fully acknowledged on this symbolic level—just

as in the literal narrative there is no attempt to minimise the bitterness of the experiences which made Parnesius seem old before his time. It is a measure of the tale's success—of the 'economy of implication' which Kipling aimed at[40]—that the intensity of the fictional experience lived through makes it easy for us to accept this change in the hero's appearance. The emphasis throughout is neither on adventures nor on violence, but on the psychological effects of war and command: the burden of responsibility, the strain, the sense of unreality, the exhaustion—all the pressures which by testing bring out the full value of men's courage and preserved integrity.

Paradoxically, these redeeming qualities which shine out from the darkness of Parnesius' tale are set in a context which seems at first sight to reduce them to insignificance. 'Trouble no more . . . Rome's arm is long,' says the ambassador from Theodosius, whose fresh legions re-establish the crumbling frontier, while behind it the Empire is unified under this new Emperor as it might have been under Maximus. Yet *we* know that this success could only be temporary—that Rome was in fact doomed and the Wall's days numbered. Nor is this just a matter of historical hindsight, for the point is made fictionally by the structuring of the book, as well as by details in the tales themselves. Before we ever meet Parnesius we have the whole life-cycle of Sir Richard, who is himself remote from us in time, as he passes from youth, love, and adventure to old age and loneliness. To be then transported still further back through the centuries to Parnesius' world gives us a poignant sense of transience. For his world, we know, is soon to pass away: he himself can still speak of Rome as 'Eternal', yet the very language of his Empire is now 'dead'—it has become the 'beastly Latin' of a schoolboy's imposition, references to which frame the first instalment of his tale. This is itself preceded by a poem which makes the point explicitly, in a quasi-Elizabethan lyric mode:

> Cities and Thrones and Powers,
>   Stand in Time's eye,
> Almost as long as flowers,
>   Which daily die. . . .

And the same theme is later transposed into the sombre cadences of a medieval hymn, as Puck chants the '*Cur mundus militat sub vana gloria*' of Jacopone da Todi. This, coming where it does in the story, seems to pass judgment not only on the ambitions of Maximus ('*Quo Caesar abiit celsus imperio?*'), but on most human activities, including Parnesius' self-dedication to service on the Wall. Indeed the verbal similarity of 'militat' and 'military' draws soldiering unmistakably into the category of 'vana gloria'. And the futility of heroic endeavour is suggested again by the 'Pict Song' at the close of his tale, in which the mutability theme is restated in political terms, foretelling the fall of Rome and of the Wall Parnesius had successfully defended.

This recognition of time's destructive power gives an added resonance to the tale. It also plays against the optimistic theory of history implied by Puck's 'Weland gave the Sword! The Sword gave the Treasure, and the Treasure gave the Law'. Modern England is certainly seen as heir to the whole of her own past, but the deliberate dislocation of chronology in the arrangement of the stories seems to deny any simple pattern of progress, as does this sense of the impermanence of human achievement. Yet each age does leave something to posterity, even if the contributors are long forgotten. Parnesius, it might be said, leaves nothing but an example, yet his defence of the Wall is as satisfying and praiseworthy an achievement in its way as Hal o' the Draft's rebuilding of St Barnabas'. The heroic qualities which were acknowledged in his own day by a well-earned Triumph are celebrated again in Kipling's story, and epitomised, though with less subtlety, in the hymn to Mithras which precedes the Winged Hats episode. This poem confines itself to the limited time-span of a single day: Morning, Noontide, Sunset, and Midnight symbolise the crises of a soldier's life, and less immediately phases of human life itself, which can be imaged in its brevity in terms of a day. Yet the hymn—and the story—assert not the futility and evanescence, but the value of an individual life well-lived, well-spent in service. For Kipling's awareness of the mutability inherent in a wider time-scale does not lead him to a nihilistic denial of significance to human endeavour. In 'The White Man's Burden' he foresees that the only reward for imperial effort will be 'The blame of those ye better,/The hate of those ye guard', and that in the long run 'Sloth and heathen Folly' will 'bring all your hope to nought'.[41] Yet this does not detract in the slightest from the immediate duty, as he sees it, of self-sacrifice and labour: the work must be undertaken for the good that can be done now, even if it ultimately comes to ruin. Similarly, Findlayson's achievement in 'The Bridge-Builders' is dwarfed by the temporal perspectives in which it is placed: when many centuries have passed it *will* seem like the shifting of a little dirt; yet when the vision ends the bridge still stands against the flood, and we rejoice in the great qualities that went to its creation. Kipling's sombre secular vision of change and decay saves him on such occasions from any tendency to brash progressive optimism, but it does not lead him to despair. The dark background serves rather as a foil to his conception of human greatness, as he shows men like Parnesius doing their duty regardless of encroaching mutability and death. Their achievements are none the less because they must ultimately perish: this is simply the condition of life on earth, and Kipling recognises the existence of no other. Yet that condition can be transcended, not through religion but through art, for the celebration of such men and their works by the artist-creator is itself a triumph—the only possible triumph— over Time the destroyer.

Time was, however, to provide a bitterly ironic postscript to the tale. The Western Front became the modern counterpart to Kipling's Wall; and his only son (the 'Dan' of *Puck of Pook's Hill*) was commissioned in the Irish Guards before he was eighteen, only to be killed next year at Loos in his first action. His body was never found, and his parents endured many months of agonised uncertainty before they finally gave up all hope. Kipling's intense grief is reflected in much of his later fiction, but it was characteristic of him that he should also establish a memorial to the courage, the endurance and the sufferings of his son's regiment, in his history of *The Irish Guards in the Great War*; and characteristic too that in the Introduction he should allow himself a single sad allusion to the 'many, almost children, of whom no record remains':

They came out from Warley with the constantly renewed drafts, lived the span of a Second Lieutenant's life and were spent. Their intimates might preserve, perhaps, memories of a promise cut short, recollections of a phrase that stuck, a chance-seen act of bravery or of kindness. The Diaries give their names and fates with the conventional expressions of regret. In most instances, the compiler [of this History] has let the mere fact suffice; since, to his mind, it did not seem fit to heap words on the doom.[42]

3 The Intellectual as Hero: Lawrence of Arabia

'Now [having read the *Seven Pillars of Wisdom*] . . . I am able to view your vast war-work near at hand, with its almost daily multifarious terrible & difficult haps, experiences, physical and mental strains, & sufferings & dark chances that must needs be taken, in meeting & circumventing enemies, in the anxious Leadership of an Armada of discordant elements, as often naturally hostile among themselves of Arab Tribes; until, after two years, you won through to the triumph of Damascus, after enduring all that human life can endure to the end.' C. M. Doughty, in *Letters to T. E. Lawrence*, ed. A. W. Lawrence (London, 1962), p. 54.

'As autobiography *The Seven Pillars of Wisdom* is veiled, ambiguous, misleading: less a direct revelation than a performance from which the truth can be wrenched. Nor can it be taken as formal history, since it focusses too subjectively, too obsessively, perhaps too passionately on its theme. . . . Primarily the book is a work of art, the model for a genre that would become all too characteristic of the age: a personal narrative through which a terrible experience is relived, burned out, perhaps transcended.' Irving Howe, 'T. E. Lawrence: The Problem of Heroism', *The Hudson Review*, vol.15 (1962–3), p. 356.

'*The Seven Pillars* is a sort of introspection epic. . . .' *The Letters of T. E. Lawrence*, ed. David Garnett (London, 1938), p. 621.

Lawrence once told Wyndham Lewis that 'Rudyard Kipling did not like what he had written, because he considered "he had let the man of action down"';[1] and whatever the truth of the story, it shows Lawrence's awareness that he was himself a man of action of a very different kind from Kipling's heroes. There are some unexpected similarities, however. Lawrence was patriotic, with 'a pugnacious wish to win the war' and to establish most of the Middle East as an

Arab dominion within the Empire. ('It will be a sorry day,' he subsequently wrote to Robert Graves, 'when our estate stops growing.'[2]) He gave innumerable proofs of his courage in action, his stoical endurance of hardships, and his charismatic leadership. He had a gift amounting to genius for irregular warfare; and fighting in what E. M. Forster called 'the last of the picturesque wars'[3]—a war, moreover, in which individuals could still have a decisive influence— he seems at times like a glorified Stalky let loose in Arabia. Yet the comparison has only to be made to be at once repudiated, for Lawrence was both a brilliantly successful man of action and an intellectual—sensitive, scholarly, self-analytical and self-tormenting; and it is his combination of these two roles that gives the *Seven Pillars of Wisdom* its unique distinction.

As an amateur soldier, he applied his keen intelligence to the successful prosecution of the war, the necessity or justice of which he never questioned. He rebelled instead against current military orthodoxies, which led in his view to the 'murder battles' of the Western Front, and he formulated an alternative approach of his own for the Arabian campaign:

I began idly to calculate how many square miles [we wished to liberate]: sixty: eighty: one hundred: perhaps one hundred and forty thousand square miles. And how would the Turks defend all that? No doubt by a trench line across the bottom, if we came like an army with banners; but suppose we were (as we might be) an influence, an idea, a thing intangible, invulnerable, without front or back, drifting about like a gas? Armies were like plants, immobile, firm-rooted, nourished through long stems to the head. We might be a vapour, blowing where we listed. Our kingdoms lay in each man's mind; and as we wanted nothing material to live on, so we might offer nothing material to the killing. It seemed a regular soldier might be helpless without a target, owning only what he sat on, and subjugating only what, by order, he could poke his rifle at.[4]

His essay on 'The Evolution of a Revolt,' published in the first number of *The Army Quarterly* in 1920,[5] showed a sophisticated awareness of the strategic, political and psychological factors involved in this new kind of people's war. And his originality was nourished by his extensive reading in military history: it was with reference to this essay, later incorporated in the *Seven Pillars*, that he

said, years afterwards, that he had written only a few pages on the art
of war, but that in them he had levied contributions from his
predecessors in five languages.[6] He ranks as one of the great exponents
of guerilla warfare in both theory and practice, partly because his
approach to military problems was so cerebral and analytical. His
generalship, he told Liddell Hart in 1933, 'came of understanding, of
hard study and brainwork and concentration':

> I was not an instinctive soldier, automatic with intuitions and
> happy ideas. When I took a decision, or adopted an alternative, it
> was after studying every relevant—and many an irrelevant—
> factor. Geography, tribal structure, religion, social customs,
> language, appetites, standards—all were at my finger-ends.

Whereas he criticised 'a fundamental, crippling incuriousness' in
many British officers ('Too much body and too little head'); and he
pleaded for more 'hard work and thinking' on their part—'more
study of books and history, a greater seriousness in military art'.[7] That
seriousness had to include the technical as well as the historical and
theoretical: his article on 'Demolitions under Fire', published in the
Royal Engineers' Journal for January 1919,[8] shows his own technical
expertise on the subject of explosives; and he claimed subsequently
that he had mastered every weapon used in his command, in order to
know how to employ them best.

This professionalism involved of necessity a certain ruthlessness.
('The noise of dynamite explosions,' he wrote to General Clayton in
July 1917, 'we find everywhere the most effective propagandist
measure possible.'[9]) Yet it coexisted with literary sensibility and
moral scruples. His imagination was steeped in Homer, French
chansons de geste, medieval and modern romances, and manuals of
chivalry,[10] all of which encouraged an acceptance and idealisation of
battle, and it is significant that he carried Malory's *Morte Darthur* in
his saddle-bags throughout the Arabian campaign. His other choices,
however, were the *Oxford Book of English Verse* and the plays of
Aristophanes (in the original); and he told D. G. Hogarth that he had
'read all the *Peace*, very gratefully'[11]—hinting here at a revulsion
from the war which he had expressed more openly in a letter of
September 1917:

> I'm not going to last out this game much longer: nerves going and
> temper wearing thin. . . . I hope when the nightmare ends that I

will wake up and become alive again. This killing and killing of
Turks is horrible. When you charge in at the finish and find them
all over the place in bits, and still alive many of them, and know
that you have done hundreds in the same way before and must do
hundreds more if you can. . . .[12]

Equally revealing in its own way, however, is the cheerful callousness
with which he described the same experiences to another cor-
respondent, or the combination of zest, frivolity and distaste in a letter
of July 1918 to an old Oxford friend:

My bodyguard of fifty Arab tribesmen, picked riders from the
young men of the deserts, are more splendid than a tulip garden,
and we ride like lunatics and with our Bedouins pounce on
unsuspecting Turks and destroy them in heaps: and it is all very
gory and nasty after we close grips. I love the preparation, and the
journey, and loathe the physical fighting. Disguises, and prices on
one's head, and fancy exploits are all part of the pose: how to
reconcile it with the Oxford pose I know not.[13]

Lawrence notoriously liked to present different aspects of himself to
different acquaintances; but there is also a basic instability in his
responses here, stemming from fundamental conflicts in his own
attitude to war experience. His youngest brother wrote years
afterwards that in Arabia Lawrence 'had anaesthetized his emotions,
and turned himself from a man into an instrument of victory', but his
emotions would not stay anaesthetised. 'The war shattered his
sensitive nature,' writes Richard Meinertzhagen, who had known
him since 1917: 'He was shaken off balance by the stresses, hardships
and responsibilities of his campaign';[14] and though Lawrence held
himself to his appointed task by sustained, heroic efforts of the will,
his self-questionings and inner conflicts grew increasingly acute.

Particularly agonising was his conviction that he was betraying the
Arabs whom he helped to lead, by persuading them that Britain's
promises of independence were to be relied upon, when he himself
believed that they were worthless. 'We are calling them to fight for us
on a lie,' he wrote as early as June 1917, 'and I can't stand it.'[15] Yet he
deliberately sacrificed his personal integrity to his patriotism: for the
sake of Britain's final victory he connived in the deceit, although,
tormented by his own duplicity, he tried to salve his conscience
by the hope

that by leading these Arabs madly in the final victory I would
establish them, with arms in their hands, in a position so assured (if
not dominant) that expediency would counsel to the Great Powers
a fair settlement of their claims. In other words, I presumed (seeing
no other leader with the will and power) that I would survive the
campaigns and be able to defeat not merely the Turks on the
battlefield, but my own country and its allies in the council-
chamber.[16]

This programme he adhered to in spite of war-weariness and deep
psychological distress, complex in origin. With the fall of Damascus
in October 1918 his war came to an end, whereupon he strove to
expiate his guilt by vigorous political action. After helping to
establish an Arab administration in Syria, under Feisal, he argued the
case for Arab independence first in London, then at the Peace
Conference in Paris in 1919; and his sincerity is not in any way
impaired by his belief that independent Arab states would affiliate
themselves voluntarily to the British Empire, to become 'not our last
brown colony' but 'our first brown dominion', in a new com-
monwealth which he envisaged based on racial equality.[17]
     These hopes, however, were soon shattered by the triumph of a
more traditional imperialism. The French, who had always been
impatient of Arab claims to independence, secured a mandate over
Syria and the Lebanon, and proceeded to depose and banish Feisal;
while the British, imposing their direct and heavy-handed rule on
Iraq, provoked a large-scale rebellion which was bloodily repressed.
For Lawrence it was a time of disillusion and despair. All he could do
was to fight on, as he did in 1920, with articles and letters to the press
denouncing Allied policies throughout the Middle East; until
suddenly things changed for the better. Early in 1921 Winston
Churchill, newly appointed to the Colonial Office, enlisted
Lawrence's help as an adviser; and in the course of one hectic year they
succeeded in reversing Britain's policy, establishing autonomous
Arab states in Iraq and Transjordan, under Feisal and Abdulla
respectively, with Lawrence playing a leading role in the neg-
otiations. Although this settlement was and remains highly controversial, and although, excluding as it did Palestine and all 'French'
territory in Syria and Lebanon, it fell far short of Lawrence's original
idea, he believed that it satisfied both national and personal honour:

     . . . Mr Winston Churchill [he writes in a footnote to the *Seven*

Pillars] was entrusted by our harassed Cabinet with the settlement of the Middle East; and . . . he made straight all the tangle, finding solutions fulfilling (I think) our promises in letter and spirit (where humanly possible) without sacrificing any interest of our Empire or any interest of the peoples concerned. So we were quit of the war-time Eastern adventure, with clean hands, but three years too late to earn the gratitude which peoples, if not states, can pay.[18]

Whereupon he himself, exhausted now and spiritually broken by his war experiences and their aftermath, enlisted in the R.A.F. in August 1922, to spend the next thirteen years—almost the whole remainder of his life—in the self-imposed degradation of the ranks. He saw it as 'the nearest modern equivalent of going into a monastery in the Middle Ages'.[19] It was, among other things, a masochistic seeking for humiliation, a deliberate self-punishment for his own sins of flesh and spirit, an abandonment of all responsibility (of which he had had more than enough), and a renunciation of authority (which he had both loved and hated exercising). It was also a complete repudiation of his former life of heroic action—which, however, he still valued as the raw material for art.

Having an almost superstitious reverence for art and artists, but lacking creative power, Lawrence saw his war-time experience as a *donnée* which he must use to the full. He longed to produce a literary masterpiece, and the textual history of the *Seven Pillars* documents his long quest for perfection—though with intermittent lapses into haste, despair, and irresponsibility. The first version, based partly on his wartime despatches and diaries, was written in 1919, allegedly lost (most of it) at Reading railway station, and then replaced by a second, reconstructed version, written in 1919–20. This was in its turn replaced by a third, longer version, completed in 1922, of which eight copies were printed for Lawrence by the *Oxford Times*. This was the text circulated among his friends and advisers; it is the one constantly referred to in his correspondence of 1922–3; but it was then completely rewritten, much reduced in length, and heavily revised— with Bernard Shaw's help—over the next few years, while he was serving in the Tank Corps and the R.A.F. The main (though not as he claimed the sole) criteria for change were literary. Lawrence had been deeply dissatisfied with the Oxford text: 'The thing is spotted in nearly every line with blemishes of style,' he wrote to Edward Garnett in August 1922, 'and while my critical sense doesn't reach as far as subject matter and construction, I judge them equally bad, by analogy.'[20] In 1926 he condemned that version as 'diffuse and unsatisfactory': the revisions, which shortened it by some fifteen per cent, resulted (he thought) in a 'swifter and more pungent' narrative.[21] The suppression, on Shaw's advice, of the original first chapter made for a more dramatic opening; and Lawrence also aimed at purging the text of stylistic imprecision and excess. ('Beginners in literature are inclined to fumble with a handful of adjectives around the outline of what they want to describe: but by 1924 I had learnt my first lessons in writing, and was often able to combine two or three of my 1921 phrases into one'.[22]) The final version which emerged from this laborious yet oddly haphazard reworking was eventually published in the limited subscribers' edition of 1926, the only edition of the *Seven Pillars* to appear in Lawrence's own lifetime.

It is undoubtedly one of the most ambitious works in English to emerge from the Great War. 'Confession is in the air,' Lawrence wrote to Edward Garnett in August 1922: 'Do you remember my telling you that I collected a shelf of "Titanic" books (those distinguished by greatness of spirit, "sublimity" as Longinus would call it): and that they were *The Karamazovs, Zarathustra,* and *Moby Dick*. Well, my ambition was to make an English fourth.'[23] He believed, or professed to believe, that he had failed; but his disclaimers sometimes appear disingenuous—designed in part at least to evoke contradictions, praise and reassurance from his correspondents. 'Damn you,' wrote Siegfried Sassoon in November 1923, 'how long do you expect me to go on reassuring you about your bloody masterpiece? It is a GREAT BOOK, blast you. Are you satisfied?, you tank-vestigating eremite. . . .'[24]) More often his depreciatory comments seem defensive—attempts to forestall and disarm the adverse criticism he feared:

> You see [he wrote to Shaw in August 1922] the war was, for us who were in it, an overwrought time, in which we lost our normal footing. I wrote this thing in the war atmosphere, and believe that it is stinking with it. Also there is a good deal of cruelty, and some excitement. All these things, in a beginner's hands, tend to force him over the edge, and I suspect there is much over-writing. . . .[25]

Lawrence could be a shrewd and penetrating critic of other men's work, but he was miserably lacking in artistic confidence about his own. 'I've wished all my life,' he told Robert Graves in 1927, 'to have the power of creating something imaginative: sculpture, painting,

Literature: and I've always found my gift of expression ludicrously inadequate to the conception I felt.'[26] Hence the recurrent agonising doubts he expressed while working on the *Seven Pillars*, sweating himself blind (in his own words) trying to make it as good as possible. He vacillated in his own assessment of the book, admitting once that he would like, in secret, to believe it good, and that his weathercock of a judgment blew round that way whenever it found a fine wind from someone else; but ultimately he saw it as a failure, and there is something neurotic, something obsessive, in his total repudiation of his own achievement. Nevertheless, the splendour of the 1926 edition, on which he lavished vast expense and care, belies many of his disclaimers and suggests an unacknowledged pride in the work which had already been judged a masterpiece by writers as eminent and varied as Sassoon, Shaw, Hardy, E. M. Forster, and which was soon to be acclaimed by Churchill as a 'grand & permanent contribution to English literature'.[27]

Yet this grand and permanent contribution—the description is a just one—has proved oddly resistant to literary criticism, existing as it does in a generic limbo for which we seem to lack an appropriate methodology. Its autonomy as art is not self-evident. For the historian and biographer it is simply one source among many—a highly personal, potentially biassed statement, to be validated by its degree of correspondence with a more objective truth established by external evidence. For the literary critic it seems easier and more appropriate to take the work on its own terms, but there is unusual difficulty in determining just what these are. The boundary line between life and art can be drawn only by a conscious effort, since the *Seven Pillars* blends history, autobiography and epic—many commentators would add fiction—in a strange amalgam; and Lawrence's own statements of intention are only fitfully illuminating, varying as they do with different moods, correspondents and occasions. They tend indeed to blur the outlines of the work itself with a haze of half-truths, contradictions and exaggerations, which reflect his own uncertainty about the essential relationship of fact, truth and imagination. Meinertzhagen, for example, claims that Lawrence surprised him in 1919 'by saying that little of his book was strict truth, though most of it was based on fact': 'He . . . admitted to me that though it purports to be the truth, a great deal of it is fancy, what might have happened, what should have happened and dull little incidents embroidered into hair-breadth escapes.' Meinertzhagen strongly advised him to write 'a straightforward account of his

Arabian exploits . . . omitting all glorification and embroidery';[28] and Lawrence was later to claim that this was exactly what he had done. Having written a history of the Arab Revolt, he sometimes maintained that that was his sole purpose, over-stating the factual, documentary, non-imaginative nature of the book. Sometimes, too, he responded to criticism of the *Seven Pillars* as literature by denying, characteristically though disingenuously, that it had any claim whatever to that status:

> Of course *The S.P.* is not a work of art [he wrote in 1927, commenting on a review by Herbert Read]: Who ever pretended it was? I write better than the majority of retired army officers, I hope; but it is a long way from that statement to literature. . . . Isn't he slightly ridiculous in seeking to measure my day-to-day chronicle by the epic standard? I never called it an epic, or thought of it as an epic, nor did anyone else, to my knowledge. The thing follows an exact diary sequence, and is literally true, throughout.[29]

'Works of art have their own life, and so aren't best fitted to be railway timetables, or dictionaries, or histories,' he told E. M. Forster, who had offered certain formal criticisms. 'My thing was forced from me not as a poem, but as a complete narrative of what actually happened in the Arab Revolt.'[30] At other times he rejected such antitheses between history and art: '*You say "record of fact" or "work of art*",' he wrote to Shaw (about *The Mint*) in 1928: '. . . When I had writing ambitions they were to combine these two things. *The Seven Pillars* was an effort to make history an imaginative thing.'[31] In this mood he derided the notion that detached, objective history could be written by an actual participant. 'No man,' he declared, 'ever yet tried to write down the entire truth of any action in which he has been engaged. All narrative is parti pris.'[32] Neither Thucydides nor Clarendon was impartial, he noted on another occasion; and in the suppressed introductory chapter to the *Seven Pillars* he acknowledged the subjective, committed, partisan nature of his own narrative, as a record by a member of Feisal's army of 'what we felt, what we hoped, what we tried'.[33] It is an imaginative celebration, not an impersonal record, of the Arab Revolt, which seemed to him 'one of the most splendid [stories] ever given a man for writing'.[34] Lawrence's imagination had been fired by the great historical events of which he had been part. The Revolt constituted for him, in certain moods at any rate, a modern equivalent of the Crusades, which had pre-occupied him for many years and on which he had once hoped to write a monumental book. It had involved him personally in a quest greater and more terrible than those chronicled by Malory—a quest which he had carried to a triumphant conclusion in the taking of Damascus. And it had provided him, as an aspirant author, with 'a theme ready and epic to a direct eye and hand'.[35]

Lawrence's own eye and hand were not 'direct', however: he goes on to say that the epic mode was alien to him as to his generation. Yet the *Seven Pillars* has affinities—of scope and spirit, not of form—with both Homeric and Virgilian epic. Many of Lawrence's contemporaries had found a tragic discrepancy between war as they read of it in the *Iliad* and war as they encountered it in France, Flanders or Gallipoli;[36] but the discrepancy was much less noticeable in Arabia, where the social organisation and heroic ethos of the tribes linked the historical world of the Revolt to the imaginative one of Homer. 'The Arab,' as J. A. Notopoulos observes, 'had the very characteristics of Homer's warriors: individualism, family pride in the heroic code of honour, revenge, joy in arms, in booty . . .';[37] and the exotic setting, the blend of the primitive and civilised in Bedouin life, the acknowledged status of great warriors like Auda ben Tayi, the delight in war, the willing endurance of arduous conditions, the small scale of the actions fought, the scope for deeds of individual heroism—indeed the whole picturesque, adventurous quality of this desert war—made it the one campaign of 1914–18 which could be treated in an epic spirit without any sense of anachronism or incongruity. Lawrence once told Robert Graves that if Sassoon had served with him in Arabia instead of on the Western Front, he would have written war poetry 'in a completely different vein'.[38] And in the *Seven Pillars*, though acknowledging the volatile, cruel, quarrelsome and often venal nature of the Arabs, he points up the epic quality of his main figures; while Kennington's illustrations reinforce Lawrence's own verbal picture of their fierceness and nobility.

The *Seven Pillars* also deals, like the *Aeneid*, with the destiny of nations. To an historian of the First World War it may seem to chronicle only a minor aspect of a minor campaign—what Lawrence himself once called 'the sideshow of a sideshow'; but from another point of view it can be seen as the epic of emergent Arab nationalism (and, by implication, Asiatic, Third World nationalism)—a work of literature in the mainstream of twentieth-century history. Lawrence himself was well aware of the wider historical perspectives. Old-fashioned imperialists, he warned readers of the *Daily Express* in 1920, 'do not realise that Russia is also an Asiatic country, and that its revolution is an object-lesson to Asia of a successful rebellion of the half-educated and the poor';[39] while in his essay on 'The Changing East', published in *The Round Table* that same year, he insisted that the once unchanging East was changing very rapidly indeed under the impact of Western technology, and still more of Western political ideas—especially that of nationalism. This had replaced religion as the dominant influence on men's minds; it was the new force in Asia with which the West would have to come to terms; and the Arab Revolt, in which Moslem Arab had fought Moslem Turk, was the supreme example of its power. 'This was the final triumph, the highest expression there can ever be in Western Asia of the principle of nationality as the foundation of political action, opposed to the principle of a world-religion, a supra-national creed.'[40] Lawrence saw this—as Byron had seen it a century before in European independence movements—as a valid political ideal, with which he was proud to have identified himself. 'I meant', he wrote in 1919, 'to make a new nation, to restore a lost influence, to give twenty millions of Semites the foundation on which to build an inspired dream palace of their national thoughts';[41] and the *Seven Pillars* tells how this was done, or at least heroically attempted. Even when he realised that he had failed in his advocacy of the Arab cause at the Peace Conference, he could look back with bitter rhetorical nostalgia to the shared idealism, the ardours and endurances, of the Revolt itself:

> The morning freshness of the world-to-be intoxicated us. We were wrought up with ideas inexpressible and vaporous, but to be fought for. We lived many lives in those whirling campaigns, never sparing ourselves: yet when we achieved and the new world dawned, the old men came out again and took our victory to re-make in the likeness of the former world they knew.[42]

Yet that victory itself had been real and spectacular. Unlike the battles of attrition on the Western Front, in which the slaughter only seemed to modify the terms of stalemate, the Arabian campaign moved swiftly, decisively, dramatically to its climax. Hence the sub-title of the *Seven Pillars*: 'A Triumph'. Hence too the exhilaration of the narrative, which follows the northward and symbolically upward movement of the Revolt from the Hejaz to Akaba, and thence to Damascus, with checks and delays only adding to the final sense of triumphant achievement. To this movement all other events, including Allenby's crucial campaign in Palestine, are ruthlessly subordinated, so as to present 'a designed procession of Arab freedom from Mecca to Damascus'.[43] It is the great national theme so dear to neoclassic theorists of epic; and although the 'plot' was determined by the course of the historical campaign, Lawrence shaped it with conscious artistry which extended to the architecture of the book as well as to its ornament. (The terminology is his own.) Some of his personal experiences, for example, were excluded on the grounds that as they formed no part of the machinery of the Revolt, they were 'artistically unjustifiable'.[44] Furthermore, he wanted to achieve an emotional climax with the taking of Damascus: the preceding section (Book VIII) was therefore conceived of aesthetically 'as a "flat," to interpose between the comparative excitements of Book VII and the final advance . . .'—and he was prepared to adjust its content to secure the desired effect.[45] Although his narrative does deal primarily with historical, non-fictional events, they had for him a plasticity which allowed him to dispose them and select from them in accordance with his overall imaginative design, which was (in part at least) to show how 'the Arab epic tossed up its stormy road from birth through weakness, pain and doubt, to red victory'.[46]

What makes this 'epic' so remarkable, however, is the fact that Lawrence is himself the hero; and its affinities are as much with *The Prelude* as with the *Iliad* or the *Aeneid*. 'In these pages', he writes in one of his more disconcerting inconsistencies, 'the history is not of the Arab movement, but of me in it'[47]—though it would have been more accurate to say that it combined something of the history of both. He thought Conrad as an author 'as much a giant of the subjective as Kipling is of the objective': he now sought to combine the two modes in 'a sort of introspection epic';[48] and the reflections, the self-scrutiny, the anguished consciousness of the narrator-hero are essential to its greatness.

The *Seven Pillars* is indeed confessional and self-revelatory to an extent that caused him some embarrassment. It was an exaggeration to claim, as he once did, that the book was a full-length and unrestrained portrait of himself, his tastes, ideas and actions, or that it was a summary of what he had thought and done and made of himself in his first thirty years.[49] As autobiography the *Seven Pillars* is rigorously selective, dealing only with the phase of his life which had involved him in the Arab Revolt. There is nothing about his childhood, nothing about his school or university years, and nothing

about his family except for a single incidental reference to the fact that
two of his brothers had been killed in the war. There are only a few
brief allusions to his pre-war years in the Middle East, which he was to
rate as 'the best life [he] ever lived'.[50] There is a comparable reticence
about the two war years he spent in Cairo before embarking on the
Arabian adventure; and the book ends with his departure from
Damascus at the peak of his triumph in October 1918. There is
nothing about his later years—not even a mention of the part he
played in the settlement of 1921, although he came to see that as his
greatest achievement. The self portrayed in the *Seven Pillars*,
therefore, is exclusively a wartime self, seen only in relation to war
experience, though it is coloured by a post-war consciousness. Yet
within its deliberately chosen limits the autobiography is remarkably
uninhibited (evoking from Jean Beraud Villars a comparison with
Proust and Gide[51]). 'I'd like to publish the whole,' he wrote to Mrs
Shaw in January 1923, 'but that's as improbable as that I'd walk naked
down Piccadilly.'[52] 'I could not have deliberately confessed to so
much in public,'[53] he told Robert Graves, explaining why the book
should not be published unrestrictedly; and its limited circulation in
Lawrence's own lifetime is attributable partly to the sense of shame
which co-existed so strangely with his craving for publicity. When he
composed a number of magazine articles based on an early version of
the *Seven Pillars*, and allowed them to be published, for Graves's
financial benefit, in *The World's Work* for 1921, he stressed the fact
that 'all the personal (subjective) part is left out for dignity's sake'[54]—
though the effect is to make it more of a simple adventure story, with
a *Boy's Own Paper* kind of hero. When, subsequently, he produced a
popular abridgment of the *Seven Pillars*—*Revolt in the Desert*, which
was published in 1927 to meet the high costs of the subscribers'
edition of the *Seven Pillars*—Lawrence followed the same policy,
with similar results. He cut out 'all the high emotion', all the
introspection, all the reflections, and many of the horrors—only to
recognise that he had produced 'a dishonest little sweep of a book', a
mere parody of the *Seven Pillars*; and he commented wryly on 'the
difference between a real book (*The S. P.* being as truthful as I could
make it) and an edition for general consumption, put out just to make
money, and to stop the mouths of those who were crying for word
from me'.[55] Yet if *Revolt in the Desert* seemed dishonest in its
suppression of the truth, the *Seven Pillars* seemed indecent in its
revelation of it. The romantic tradition of spiritual autobiography
might have been invoked to justify his procedures; but he believed

that even the much-loved lyrics in *Minorities*, his personal anthology, were something of an indulgence ('chocolate éclairs of the spirit'[56]); and in any case he felt uneasily that in the *Seven Pillars* he was offending against a social rather than a literary code. 'The sort of man I have always mixed with,' he told Edward Garnett, 'doesn't so give himself away.'[57] He could not find a confessional mode that would be socially acceptable among men of action as well as men of letters; and his irresistible urge to self-expression, even indeed to self-exposure, was at odds with his own residual notions of self-respect based on restraint and self-control. Hence, surely, his repudiation of the *Seven Pillars* as 'a pessimistic unworthy book, full of the neurosis of the war', 'a rotten book, a dull book, hysterical, egotistical and long,' 'an orgy of exhibitionism'.[58] Yet though he might complain that the book 'stinks of personality', or worse, 'it stinks of me', he had also more perceptively observed that 'the personal revelations should be the key of the thing', since he was aiming above all at spiritual truth.[59] It was also to be a kind of moral balance-sheet: 'By putting all the troubles and dilemmas on paper,' he told Frederic Manning in 1930, 'I hoped to work out my path again, and satisfy myself how wrong, or how right, I had been.'[60] But he could find no simple answer to that question, since the rightness and wrongness of his actions were, he discovered, strangely and inextricably interwoven.

The book begins with an abrupt intimation of evil, and the opening chapter is one of profound, disturbing spiritual analysis. Virtually a prose poem, it is written—to the outrage of aesthetic puritans—in a much higher key than the narrative which follows:

> Some of the evil of my tale may have been inherent in our circumstances. For years we lived anyhow with one another in the naked desert, under the indifferent heaven. By day the hot sun fermented us; and we were dizzied by the beating wind. At night we were stained by dew, and shamed into pettiness by the innumerable silences of stars. We were a self-centred army without parade or gesture, devoted to freedom, the second of man's creeds, a purpose so ravenous that it devoured all our strength, a hope so transcendent that our earlier ambitions faded in its glare.[61]

This naked desert under its indifferent heaven constitutes a kind of moral vacuum where no metaphysical sanctions operate; and it functions like the jungle in *Heart of Darkness*, testing not only endurance but integrity, when the props of civilisation are removed.

The verbs 'fermented', 'dizzied', 'stained', 'shamed', 'devoured' and 'faded' all suggest a transformation, blemishing or impairment of the self; and the evil of the opening sentence is shown to be inherent not only in immediate circumstances, but in the basic paradox of a just war. The very nobility of their cause draws men to evil by freeing them from moral scruple:

> As time went by our need to fight for the ideal increased to an unquestioning possession, riding with spur and rein over our doubts. Willy-nilly it became a faith. We had sold ourselves into its slavery, manacled ourselves together in its chain-gang, bowed ourselves to serve its holiness with all our good and ill content. The mentality of ordinary human slaves is terrible—they have lost the world—and we had surrendered, not body alone, but soul to the overmastering greed of victory. By our own act we were drained of morality, of volition, of responsibility, like dead leaves in the wind.[62]

This metaphorical insistence justifies itself by the challenge it poses to Lawrence's own conception of the Arab Revolt as an armed pilgrimage, a crusade for freedom. The connotations of 'the ideal', 'faith', 'holiness' and 'victory' are drastically modified by the demonic implications of 'possession', the suggestion of Cossack-like brutality in their suppression of doubt, the debasement implied by 'slavery', the idolatry of 'bowed ourselves', the selfishness of 'overmastering greed'. And the image of dead leaves in the wind ('pestilence stricken multitudes'?) registers the spiritual price to be paid for prolonged commitment to battle, even in the noblest cause.

This collective evil with which the chapter opens is balanced by a threat of individual madness at its close—a madness which Lawrence himself approached, he tells us, through his dual role of Englishman and pseudo-Arab, or rather through a consequent dislocation of personality as he was alienated from his Western self without acquiring an alternative identity. Also, he frankly acknowledges experiences and psychological conditions which fall between these poles of evil and madness—'gusts of cruelty, perversions, lusts'—like the Arab cult of homosexuality, which he describes rather hectically in terms which suggest a mingling of attraction and revulsion; or like the ruthlessness involved in guerilla war and guerilla discipline in the naked desert under its indifferent heaven:

Blood was always on our hands: we were licenced to it. Wounding and killing seemed ephemeral pains, so very brief and sore was life with us. With the sorrow of living so great, the sorrow of punishment had to be pitiless. We lived for the day and died for it. When there was reason and desire to punish we wrote our lesson with gun and whip immediately in the sullen flesh of the offender, and the case was beyond appeal. The desert did not afford the refined slow penalties of courts and gaols. [63]

The abnormality of war ethics and psychology is well evoked. ('What now looks wanton or sadic seemed in the field inevitable, or just unimportant routine.') But there is an unmistakable touch of contempt for 'the refined slow penalties' of civilised justice, and an element of relish in his reference to their writing their lesson with gun or whip in the sullen flesh of the offender: it is the personification of the flesh as sullen and the revelatory use of 'in' rather than 'on' that introduce sadistic overtones of which Lawrence is well aware.

'In my notes,' he goes on, 'the cruel rather than the beautiful found place. We no doubt enjoyed more the rare moments of peace and forgetfulness; but I remember more the agony, the terrors, and the mistakes.' Yet his mood is not one of simple rejection, for the cruelties, the agonies, the pain and the exhaustion had themselves an obscure attraction for him. There was an ascetic, ultimately a masochistic element in Lawrence which drew him to the rigours of nomadic life, and to the inevitable intensification of these by the pressures of war. He was moved by deep compulsions 'to endure as far as the senses would endure, and to use each such advance as base for further adventure, deeper privation, sharper pain'[64]—a process which culminates in the *Seven Pillars* in the description of his traumatic experience of torture and homosexual rape when he was captured by the Turks at Deraa in November 1917. He records (in Chapter LXXX) his recollection of 'smiling idly' at the corporal in charge, at the very climax of his agony, 'for a delicious warmth, probably sexual, was swelling through me'.[65] And the discovery of such potentialities in his own nature dismayed him, inducing a mood of extreme self-loathing, and forcing him from then on 'to carry the burden, whose certainty the passing days confirmed: how in Deraa that night the citadel of [his] integrity had been irrecoverably lost'.[66]

There is a sense in which Lawrence as narrator-hero combines the roles of Marlow and Kurtz in *Heart of Darkness*—descending into depths of guilt and horror, yet retaining an ethical awareness which enables him to judge himself clear-sightedly and chart his own spiritual crises. The theme of sexual defilement recurs intermittently, but it is less central than some recent critics have suggested. There is a temptation to read back into the *Seven Pillars* knowledge of Lawrence's deviations in later life; but in the narrative itself he is much more concerned with other erosions, other sacrifices, of integrity, essentially connected with his wartime role. The narrative exemplifies the themes announced in the first chapter—not systematically or diagrammatically, but as occasion offers—showing, for example, how the war involved him not merely in passive suffering, but in the active infliction of pain, wounds and death, sometimes in circumstances of peculiar horror. Parnesius did not have to kill his mutineer; but on one desert journey, when a murder had been committed and the culprit condemned to death, Lawrence had to execute him with his own hands, to avoid the perpetuation of blood-feuds among the Arabs. The writing of lessons with gun or whip in the sullen flesh of the offender now becomes 'the horror which would make civilized man shun justice like a plague, if he had not the needy to serve him as hangmen for wages';[67] and his meticulous recording of every detail of the incident suggests an obsessive recollection, which he is now perhaps trying to exorcise:

> I made him enter a narrow gully of the spur, a dank twilight place overgrown with weeds. Its sandy bed had been pitted by trickles of water down the cliffs in the late rain. At the end it shrank to a crack a few inches wide. The walls were vertical. I stood in the entrance and gave him a few moments' delay which he spent crying on the ground. Then I made him rise and shot him through the chest. He fell down on the weeds shrieking, with the blood coming out in spurts over his clothes, and jerked about till he rolled nearly to where I was. I fired again, but was shaking so that I only broke his wrist. He went on calling out, less loudly, now lying on his back with his feet towards me, and I leant forward and shot him for the last time in the thick of his neck under the jaw. His body shivered a little, and I called the Ageyl; who buried him in the gully where he was. Afterwards the wakeful night dragged over me, till, hours before dawn, I had the men up and made them load, in my longing to be set free of Wadi Kitan. They had to lift me into the saddle.[68]

Although his helplessness was due to dysentery and fever, there is a hint of nervous collapse here. His sensitivity is not paraded; but the symbolism of the setting—that 'dank twilight place overgrown with weeds'—implies a judgment on the action; while his shaking hand, his wakeful night, his longing to escape from Wadi Kitan, are sufficient indications of his spiritual turmoil. ('A highly sensitive and imaginative man,' as Shaw remarks, 'cannot do such things as if he were doing no more than putting on his boots.'[69]) On Lawrence's own showing, however, the case for the execution was unanswerable, and he accepts its necessity in the *Seven Pillars* as he says he did in 1917, even while registering the psychological and moral cost. There is a comparable incident much later in the book, when he has to shoot a wounded member of his bodyguard—his favourite, Farraj—to prevent his being captured and burnt to death by the Turks. Whether these episodes are literally true, or whether (as Desmond Stewart suggests) they are merely emblematic of psychological or spiritual truth—of blood-guilt, for example—it is of the essence of Lawrence's case as he himself presents it that he repeatedly commits himself to actions which in some sense violate his conscience, but which he sees as necessary, and which he does not repudiate even in retrospect.

This is relevant to his treatment of deaths in battle. 'Blood was always on our hands: we were licenced to it', he declares: 'Wounding and killing seemed ephemeral pains . . .'; and though peace-time suggested different perspectives, he never seeks to repudiate or minimise his dual responsibility as commander and combatant. He usually describes events like their frequent ambushes of trains with vivid detail but professional detachment, depersonalising and de-humanising the enemy as soldiers in action necessarily do:

> As I watched, our machine-guns chattered out over my head, and the long rows of Turks on the carriage roofs rolled over, and were swept off the top like bales of cotton before the furious shower of bullets which stormed along the roofs and splashed clouds of yellow chips from the planking. The dominant position of the guns had been an advantage to us so far.[70]

Recurrently, however, he acknowledges a deeper level of response. In their annihilation of a Turkish battalion at Aba el Lissan the Arabs had only two men killed, but the strategic situation was so crucial that Lawrence, although economical of his men's lives, 'would have willingly lost much more than two'. 'On occasions like this,' he comments with the necessary ruthlessness of a commander, 'Death

justified himself and was cheap.'[71] He strikes a different note,
however, when he contemplates the bodies of the Turks killed in the
battle and then stripped of their uniforms:

> The dead men looked wonderfully beautiful. The night was
> shining gently down, softening them into new ivory. Turks were
> white-skinned on their clothed parts, much whiter than the Arabs;
> and these soldiers had been very young. Close round them lapped
> the dark wormwood, now heavy with dew, in which the ends of
> the moonbeams sparkled like sea-spray. The corpses seemed flung
> so pitifully on the ground, huddled anyhow in low heaps. Surely if
> straightened they would be comfortable at last. So I put them all in
> order, one by one, very wearied myself, and longing to be of these
> quiet ones, not of the restless, noisy, aching mob up the valley,
> quarrelling over the plunder, boasting of their speed and strength
> to endure God knew how many toils and pains of this sort; with
> death, whether we won or lost, waiting to end the history.[72]

Here his suppressed sensitivity reasserts itself in an extreme form. His
feelings are understandable as a reaction from the excitement and
exhilaration of the battle, but the sensibility displayed is rather
morbid. There is a trace of necrophilia in his preoccupation with the
beauty of the naked corpses, which are described as if they were
unblemished by their fatal wounds. His pity for them lapses, through
its very intensity, into sentimental futility ('Surely if straightened
they would be comfortable at last'); and it converts itself very readily
to self-pity in his longing to be himself one of 'these quiet ones'. The
passage, however, need not be taken as normative in intention: it
simply documents very convincingly a state of emotional disturbance, of revulsion from the Arabs and their war, and of guilt—
however momentary—at his own responsibility for taking life.

It is linked thematically to the deliberately horrible description, in
the penultimate chapter, of the Turkish dead in the abandoned
barrack-hospital in Damascus:

> I stepped in, to meet a sickening stench: and, as my eyes grew open,
> a sickening sight. The stone floor was covered with dead bodies
> side by side, some in full uniform, some in underclothing, some
> stark naked. There might be thirty there, and they crept with rats,
> who had gnawed wet red galleries into them. A few were corpses
> nearly fresh, perhaps only a day or two old: others must have been

there for long. Of some the flesh, going putrid, was yellow and blue and black. Many were already swollen twice or thrice life-width, their fat heads laughing with black mouth across jaws harsh with stubble. Of others the softer parts were fallen in. A few had burst open and were liquescent with decay.[73]

Descriptions of rotting corpses were to become part of the stock-in-trade of 'war books', but few convey this sense of fascinated horror, which stems from Lawrence's peculiar sensibility, and his sense of guilt. He is confronted in this hospital with an administrative problem to be solved immediately if Arab claims to govern are to have any credibility in British eyes; but he is also confronted symbolically with the results of his own war activities. 'In the phantasmagoric hospital,' writes Jeffrey Meyers, 'Lawrence seemed faced with the corpse of every man he had ever killed. . . .'[74] We have fresh in our memories his account, only four chapters earlier, of the massacre of the Turks from Deraa, in revenge for atrocities they had committed on women and children in the village of Tafas. The pathos and horror of that scene, superbly rendered, had seemed then to justify extremes of ruthlessness: 'I said, "The best of you brings me the most Turkish dead," and we turned after the fading enemy, on our way shooting down those who had fallen out by the roadside, and came imploring our pity.'[75] Lawrence's mood throughout most of that episode was shown as one of savage satisfaction, but the slaughter bred awareness of its own excess: 'In a madness born of the horror of Tafas we killed and killed, even blowing in the heads of the fallen and of the animals; as though their death and running blood could slake our agony.'[76] And the gloom and chill of the evening after they had shot the guilty but helpless prisoners point to a change of mood. The fact that the sick, wounded and dying in the barrack-hospital now implore his pity (like those shot by the roadside), whispering in unison ' "*Aman, Aman*" (pity, pity, pardon)',[77] therefore constitutes an accusation, a rebuke he cannot answer. These recent memories, as well as physical and nervous exhaustion, underlie his subsequent hysteria, when he bursts out laughing on being rebuked by a British medical officer for the state of the hospital. It was not just the irony of being called a 'bloody brute' when he had done everything possible to put things right: it was also the perception that the accusation was, in a profound sense, justified:

The major had not entered the charnel house of yesterday, nor smelt it, nor seen us burying those bodies of ultimate degradation, whose memory had started me up in bed, sweating and trembling, a few hours since. He glared at me, muttering 'Bloody brute.' I hooted out again, and he smacked me over the face and stalked off, leaving me more ashamed than angry, for in my heart I felt he was right, and that anyone who pushed through to success a rebellion of the weak against their masters must come out of it so stained in estimation that afterward nothing in the world would make him feel clean. However [he adds thankfully], it was nearly over.[78]

He was stained much more deeply in his own estimation by a sense of his political duplicity:

Had I been an honourable adviser [he reflects at one point] I would have sent my men home, and not let them risk their lives for such stuff [as the British promises]. Yet the Arab inspiration was our main tool in winning the Eastern war. So I assured them that England kept her word in letter and spirit. In this comfort they performed their fine things: but, of course, instead of being proud of what we did together, I was continually and bitterly ashamed.[79]

This shame runs like a leit-motif throughout the *Seven Pillars*. 'Inevitably and justly we should reap bitterness, a sorry fruit of heroic endeavour.' 'The fraudulence of my business stung me. . . .' 'Because pain hurt me so, I would not lay weight always on my pains in our revolt: yet hardly one day in Arabia passed without a physical ache to increase the corroding sense of my accessory deceitfulness towards the Arabs, and the legitimate fatigue of responsible command.' 'I exploited their highest ideals and made their love of freedom one more tool to help England win.' 'It might have been heroic to have offered up my own life for a cause in which I could not believe: but it was a theft of souls to make others die in sincerity for my graven image. Because they accepted our message as truth, they were ready to be killed for it. . . .'[80]

Such anguished reflections, and more fine-drawn speculations which arise from them, intermingle with his descriptions of desert journeys, raids and battles. They merge also with his sense of private as well as public fraud. As a man of action, he confesses, he was always playing a part, to satisfy himself and to impress his followers. His military exploits were 'intensely conscious efforts, with [his] detached self always eyeing the performance from the wings in criticism'[81]—and the performance, to continue the theatrical analogy, was designed to win applause. Throughout his life Lawrence was given to an almost narcissistic contemplation of the self, and he loved to see his image reflected in the eyes of others. Hence his readiness to pose for photographs, paintings and sculptures; hence too his surreptitious attendence at Lowell Thomas's film lectures about 'Lawrence of Arabia'; and hence his covert but extensive collaboration with both Graves and Liddell Hart when they were writing their biographies of him. Hence too, it might be said, the egotism of the *Seven Pillars*, in which he always occupies the centre of the stage, assuming, as he said himself, a false primacy.[82] Yet this (like Wordsworth's) is an egotistical sublime, justified not so much by his role in the Revolt as by the absorbing interest of his self-analysis, with its exploration of the predicament of a morally sensitive man in the world of action. It explores too his own secret weaknesses. He diagnoses in himself the very tendencies for which he is often condemned, admitting, for example, to 'a craving to be famous' and 'a horror of being known to like being known',[83] so that his modesty could become at times a cloak for vanity. His contempt for his own passion for distinction made him refuse proffered honours, yet, he confesses, he delighted in 'the oblique overheard remarks of others,' which 'best taught [him his] created impression',[84] and he was ashamed of feeling this delight. He even acknowledges, with wry wit, potential vanity in his genuine self-sacrifice: 'There was nothing loftier than a cross, from which to contemplate the world. The pride and exhilaration of it were beyond conceit.'[85] These long passages of meditation, both political and personal, are often inconclusive, rendering as they do 'the self-argument of a man who couldn't then see straight'.[86] They can also become convoluted, and at times pretentious, just as his rhetoric is occasionally rather forced; but these are mere local blemishes, easily sustained by a work of such psychological insight and narrative power; and there emerges, as there does from Byron's *oeuvre*, the sense of what Goethe called a puissant personality, the sense of a greatness which includes but transcends the literary, the sense of a man living a life of allegory on which his works are the comments.

The ambiguity of Lawrence's own motives is forgotten momentarily in the triumphant progress through Damascus. Ever since his boyhood reading of Swinburne's '*Super Flumina Babylonis*' he had longed 'to feel [himself] the node of a national movement'.[87] Now that Byronic dream had finally come true.

Every man, woman and child in this city of a quarter-million souls
seemed in the streets, waiting only the spark of our appearance to
ignite their spirits. Damascus went mad with joy. The men tossed
up their tarbushes to cheer, the women tore off their veils.
Householders threw flowers, hangings, carpets, into the road
before us: their wives leaned, screaming with laughter, through the
lattices and splashed us with bath-dippers of scent.

Poor dervishes made themselves our running footmen in front
and behind, howling and cutting themselves with frenzy; and over
the local cries and the shrilling of women came the measured roar
of men's voices chanting, 'Feisal, Nasir, Shukri, Urens,' in waves
which began here, rolled along the squares, through the market
down long streets to East gate, round the wall, back up the Meidan,
and grew to a wall of shouts around us by the citadel.[88]

After describing their frantic but successful efforts to establish an
orderly administration, or the semblance of one, before the British
entered formally the next day, Lawrence goes on to establish, in two
carefully cadenced paragraphs, the mood of thankfulness which
succeeded that first wild elation:

Later I was sitting alone in my room, working and thinking out as
firm a way as the turbulent memories of the day allowed, when the
Muedhdhins began to send their call of last prayer through the
moist night over the illuminations of the feasting city. One, with a
ringing voice of special sweetness, cried into my window from a
near mosque. I found myself involuntarily distinguishing his
words: 'God alone is great: I testify there are no gods, but God: and
Mohammed his Prophet. Come to prayer: come to security. God
alone is great: there is no god—but God.'

At the close he dropped his voice two tones, almost to speaking
level, and softly added: 'And He is very good to us this day, O
people of Damascus.' The clamour hushed, as everyone seemed to
obey the call to prayer on this their first night of perfect freedom.[89]

Revolt in the Desert ends on this note of thanksgiving, which seems to
set the final seal on their achievement; but the *Seven Pillars* text
continues: 'While my fancy, in the overwhelming pause, showed me
my loneliness and lack of reason in their movement: since only for
me, of all the hearers, was the event sorrowful and the phrase
meaningless.' This sense of isolation and futility stemmed partly from

his being an alien in race and creed, partly from his awareness of political duplicity among the Allies, which was soon to make the triumph meaningless as far as the people of Damascus were concerned. And there was also an emotional reaction to the final success which made him see only 'the emptiness of it';[90] just as after the battle at Aba el Lissàn he had noted a 'physical shame of success, a reaction of victory, when it became clear that nothing was worth doing, and that nothing worthy had been done'.[91]

Yet this does not constitute a nihilistic withdrawal from commitment; nor is it his final statement. There are two further chapters in the *Seven Pillars*, both packed with purposeful activity. There is the smashing of Abd el Kadir's abortive rebellion—politically necessary, and satisfying as revenge for his past treachery; and there is the cleansing of the barrack-hospital. Quietism, introspection and despair yield immediately to action in both cases; and this sequence is characteristic of Lawrence throughout the *Seven Pillars*. Time and again, self-analysis and self-reproach prevail, only to be put aside whenever he is faced with the immediate or the long-term needs of the campaign. When he shot the murderer in Wadi Kitan, for example, he had been *en route* for Abdulla's camp, which he reached in a state of near-collapse; but it was while convalescing there that he evolved his strategy for the whole insurrection. His revulsion from war and pity for the dead at Aba el Lissan were followed immediately by the swift advance on Akaba. After his shattering experience at Deraa he continued, outwardly unchanged, and was soon experimenting with insulated cable and explosives as a prelude to his next encounter with the Turks. The despair and exhaustion which led him, in February 1918, to beg to be relieved of his responsibilities, were at once suppressed when he was asked to cover Allenby's right flank in the next phase of the campaign: 'There was no escape for me. I must take up again my mantle of fraud in the East. With my certain contempt for half-measures I took it up quickly and wrapped myself in it completely. It might be fraud or it might be farce: no-one should say that I could not play it.'[92] The heart-searching and self-doubt which reached a crescendo on his thirtieth birthday (Chapter CIII) were interrupted by 'a disturbance from the Toweiha tents': 'Shouting men ran towards me. I pulled myself together to appease a fight between the Arabs and the Camel Corps, but instead it was an appeal for help against a Shammar raid two hours since, away by the Snainirat.'[93] Having dealt with which, he supervises the loading of six thousand pounds of gun-cotton on pack-camels, for their next set of attacks and demolitions. What Lawrence himself calls 'the wobbling of [his] will, and endless, vapid complainings'[94] are fully recorded; so too are his moods of doubt, despair, self-hatred, moral hesitation, and political outrage; and the cumulative effect is one of corroding guilt, increasing nervous strain, and psychological fatigue. But in every case these moods are, not transcended, but suppressed by efforts of the will: he deliberately brushes them aside as he moves to the next necessary action. It is only when victory has been won and brought to full fruition, with Feisal's authority established and acknowledged formally by Allenby, that Lawrence finally lays down the burden of responsibility. ('I feel,' he wrote a few days later, 'like a man who has suddenly dropped a heavy load—one's back hurts when one tries to walk straight.'[95]) This was the consummation he had longed for, since it had been 'a hard task for [him] to straddle feeling and action';[96] yet the last chapter of the *Seven Pillars* ends on a note of elegiac regret. The cryptic verse-dedication of the book, 'To S. A.', had expressed a morbid and defeatist sorrow; the epilogue now discloses 'the exhaustion of [his] main springs of action',[97] the collapse of his will.

Yet far from being a brittle intellectual who cracked beneath the strain, Lawrence had postponed that collapse time and time again until his task was completed and his quest fulfilled—but on his own showing he had done so at great cost. Lord Moran analyses courage as 'a moral quality; . . . a cold choice between two alternatives, the fixed resolve not to quit; an act of renunciation which must be made not once but many times by the power of the will';[98] though he recognises that no man has an unlimited supply of courage or of will, and that both can therefore be used up. The diagnosis is relevant to Lawrence's case. Throughout the *Seven Pillars* we see the hero's will triumphant over every obstacle, in every crisis, including those which arise from his own self-consciousness and scruples; but he seems never to have recovered psychologically from the violence thus done to his own nature. The Lawrence of his R. A. F. and Tank Corps years is a husk of a man—a burnt-out case—however great his intellect and charm: '. . . there is something broken in the works . . .: my will, I think', he wrote to Lady Astor a few days before his death.[99] That flash of self-analysis is fully as revealing as investigations of his secret masochism—and more pertinent to a proper understanding of the *Seven Pillars*.

'The hero is distinguished,' E. R. Curtius writes, 'by a super-abundance of intellectual will and by its concentration against the instincts. It is this which constitutes his greatness of character.'[100] It is this which also defines the nature of Lawrence's self-sacrifice—a conscious, chosen, willed self-sacrifice which is essentially tragic, not pathetic or perverse. *The Seven Pillars* shows him expending his reserves of will-power by his sustained commitment to heroic action, in a prolonged, reiterated effort which brings him to both victory and self-destruction. The book ends with his abandonment of all heroic action, a poignant, long farewell to all his greatness, but it leaves us with no sense of failure—that comes rather from the contemplation of his later life; and the final assertion, proudly though obliquely made, is of the magnitude of his achievement:

> *I had dreamed, at the City School in Oxford, of hustling into form, while I lived, the new Asia which time was inexorably bringing upon us. Mecca was to lead to Damascus: Damascus to Anatolia, and afterwards to Bagdad; and then there was Yemen. Fantasies, these will seem, to such as are able to call my beginning an ordinary effort.*[101]

4 The Common Man as Hero: Literature of the Western Front

'Incidents flash through the memory: the battles of the first four months: the awful winters in waterlogged trenches, cold and miserable: the terrible trench-assaults and shell fire of the next three years: loss of friends, exhaustion and wounds: the stupendous victories of the last few months: our enemies all beaten to their knees.

Thank God! The end of a frightful four years, thirty-four months of them at the front with the infantry, whose company officers, rank and file, together with other front-line units, have suffered bravely, patiently and unselfishly, hardships and perils beyond even the imagination of those, including soldiers, who have not shared them.' *General Jack's Diary, 1914–1918*, ed. John Terraine (London, 1964), p. 297.

'The grossly mismanaged First World War, into which I plunged as soon as I left school, gave us infantrymen so convenient a measuring-stick for discomfort, grief, pain, fear and horror, that nothing since has greatly daunted us. But it also brought new meanings of courage, patience, loyalty and greatness of spirit; incommunicable, we found, to later times.' Robert Graves, in Frank Richards, *Old Soldiers Never Die* (London, 1964), p. 1.

'Man, ruddy-cheeked under your squat chin-strapped iron helmet, sturdy under your leather jerkin, clapping your hands together as you dropped your burden of burning-cold steel, grinning and flinging old-home repartee at your pal passing by, you endured that winter of winters, as it seems to me, in the best way of manliness. I forget your name. I remember your superscriptions, "O.A.S." and "B.E.F.", your perpetual copying-ink pencil's "in the pink," "as it leaves me"; you played House, read Mr. Bottomley, sang "If I wore a tulip", and your rifle was as clean as new from an armoury. It is time to hint to a new age what your value, what your love was; your Ypres is gone, and you are gone; we were lucky to see you "in the pink" against white-ribbed and socket-eyed despair.' Edmund Blunden, *Undertones of War* (London, 1928), pp. 177–8.

The First World War 'cut deep', as one historian has said, 'into the consciousness of modern man';[1] and the traumas it induced are both recorded and perpetuated by imaginative literature. That literature, however, has often been presented too selectively and too simplistically as expressing first of all a naïve enthusiasm for war and then, after the shock of battle experience, an overwhelming sense of disillusion, anger and pity, culminating in pacifism and protest. Every schoolboy knows that this paradigm of British war experience can be extrapolated from the poems of Rupert Brooke, Siegfried Sassoon and Wilfred Owen read in appropriate sequence, and it is readily assumed to have been valid for all authors and combatants; but like most schoolboy certainties this is based on inadequate evidence and preconceived ideas. The clear diagrams drawn by some of the poets themselves and elaborated by a multitude of critics have tended to blind even more sophisticated readers to the fact that much of the finest literature of the war transcends the simplicities of protest to acknowledge a far greater complexity of response to disturbingly complex experience, and that much of it also reasserts an heroic ideal, stripped of romantic glamour certainly, but redefined convincingly in terms of grim courage and endurance in the face of almost unbearable suffering and horror.

*   *   *

The impact of this war on the English literary imagination was much greater than that of wars of any previous era. The reasons are primarily sociological: it was the first time in British history that so many authors or potential authors had had first-hand experience of battle, or indeed of military service. 'Tolstoy,' as Orwell wrote in 1942, 'lived in a great military empire in which it seemed natural for almost any young man of family to spend a few years in the army, whereas the British Empire was and still is demilitarised to a degree which continental observers find almost incredible.'[2] That situation changed abruptly, however, in 1914. The mass armies needed for modern industrialised warfare between nation-states had long been provided on the Continent by systems of conscription and compulsory military training, which built up large reserves to supplement the regular forces in the event of war. In Britain the mass armies were now improvised from volunteers based firstly on the Territorial Army, which formed infantry divisions and cavalry brigades of its own, with full supporting arms; secondly on the Special Reserve, which provided drafts for existing Regular Army units; and thirdly, on Kitchener's great New Army raised after the outbreak of war. The whole basis and scale of recruitment were thus transformed: nearly three million men, fired by patriotic zeal and a desire to prove themselves in battle, volunteered in the first two years of war; while conscription, which had been political anathema in pre-war Britain, was introduced in 1916.[3] Many men of literary sensitivity and talent, therefore, who would never normally have thought of soldiering, were now plunged with comparatively little preparation, psychological or military, into the experience of modern war.

The special nature of the First World War is a second factor influencing literary responses. Many of its features came as a surprise to the participants, professionals and amateurs alike. Britain's last major conflict with European powers had ended in 1815; the scale of human suffering and slaughter had long since faded from communal memory; and in the second half of the nineteenth century rapid technological developments in weapons and communications had revolutionised the possibilities of warfare.[4] Not only the general public, but also military planners throughout Europe, had failed to grasp the full implications of this revolution, which revealed themselves only in action. Vastly increased fire-power, together with the deployment of mass armies, soon put an end to the war of movement which both sides had envisaged on the Western Front, substituting the stalemate of trench warfare in which the whole battle-area was dominated by artillery, and No Man's Land by the machine-gun. The strategic impasse was due primarily not to the ineptitude of generals, but to the fact that military technology now favoured the defence at the expense of the attack. Notoriously, however, many commanders were slow to recognise this basic fact; and the very heavy casualties incurred in repeated attempts to break the deadlock are attributable partly to the large numbers of men engaged and the increased killing-power of modern weapons, but also to the failure of commanders to realise the nature of the problem or to devise effective solutions. Technological development had temporarily outstripped strategic and tactical thinking. The ultimate solution lay, no doubt, in still further technological advances—this time in the field of tank warfare, the potentialities of which were briefly demonstrated at Cambrai in November 1917; but in the meantime there was a notable lack of tactical ingenuity of the kind displayed by Rawlinson in his night-attack on the Somme on 14 July 1916, or by Plumer in his set-piece attack, preceded by the firing of nineteen huge mines, on Messines Ridge on 7 June 1917, or by Ludendorff in his use of infiltration tactics and gas-shell bombardments in March 1918. Inevitably, many lives were lost in the great battles and constant fighting which wore down the German armies as a necessary prelude to victory; but many too were uselessly thrown away, and this left an indelible impression on the front-line troops.

The very familiarity of this theme, however, tends to blur an important distinction between protests at inefficiency in the conduct of war and protests against war as such. The writings of military theorists like Liddell Hart and J. F. C. Fuller belong clearly to the former category, and the poems of Wilfred Owen to the latter; but many authors, because of their ambivalent attitude to war experience, are less easily assigned to one group or the other. Sassoon's elegiac address 'To Any Dead Officer' was certainly written as an anti-war poem, just after he had drafted his public protest against the continuance, not the conduct, of the war. Yet it is of the essence of that poem that the representative hero-victim was 'knocked over in a hopeless dud-attack': the anger and sense of waste derive not simply from the officer's being killed in battle, but from his being killed in such a futile, badly planned one. The implication here (as in 'The General') is that it could have been planned better, in which case we should have felt differently about it; hence the grimly ironic pathos of Sassoon's conclusion—'I'm blind with tears, / Staring into the dark. Cheero! / I wish they'd killed you in a decent show'—in which 'they' are the generals and staffs on his own side, not the enemy.[5]

The Western Front, on which decent shows were few and far between, was the principal matrix from which war literature emerged. Conditions there—exhausting, nerve-racking, nightmarish, loathsome, as well as dangerous—were experienced by a high proportion of combatants, since this was always the most important theatre of war. Quite apart from the French obsession with regaining their territories which Germany had over-run in 1914, and apart from Britain's own commitment to the liberation of Belgium, there was little scope in this war for a strategy of indirect approach, however eagerly politicians sought it as an alternative to the costly

and apparently fruitless struggle in the West. 'Side-shows' like
Gallipoli, Mesopotamia, Palestine, Italy and Salonika, not to mention
colonial campaigns in East, West and South-West Africa, might well
have other justifications (and considerable resources were diverted to
them); but they could have little effect on the main issue. This was the
unanswerable argument of the 'Westerners' who dominated Allied
strategy; especially in view of Russia's weaknesses, which gradually
became apparent, this was the one area where the German armies
could be effectively engaged and ultimately defeated; and it was
therefore to her sector of the Western Front, extending from Flanders
to Picardy, that Britain directed her main military effort. It was in this
comparatively restricted area that the greatest armies in her history
grappled with the Germans for four years; and the peculiar horrors of
trench warfare were intensified by this geographical constant, as the
horrors of tragedy can be intensified by strict observance of the unity
of place.

> The Palestine Campaign was merely the romantic fringe of the war
> [wrote Herbert Read resentfully in 1927, reviewing the *Seven
> Pillars*]. In France and Belgium men of infinitely finer quality than
> these Arabs were enduring day after day, without the inspiration of
> the open horizon and all that that conveys of adventure and
> surprise, the dull and dispiriting agony of trench warfare. No one
> will be fool enough to make out of that horror an epic story . . .;
> but this Arabian adventure was no more than a dance of flies in the
> air beside the magnitude of that terrific earthy conflict. [6]

This was a warfare at the furthest possible remove from the
conflicts of heroic individuals in epic and romance—a warfare
depersonalised, dehumanised, to an unprecedented degree—a war
often of men against material:

> The fighting was so impersonal as a rule [writes Richard
> Aldington] that it seemed rather a conflict with dreadful hostile
> forces of Nature than with other men. You did not see the men
> who fired the ceaseless hail of shells on you, nor the machine-
> gunners who swept away twenty men to death in one zip of their
> murderous bullets, nor the hands which projected trench-mortars
> that shook the earth with awful detonations, nor even the invisible
> sniper who picked you off mysteriously with the sudden imper-
> sonal 'ping' of his bullet. Even in the perpetual trench raids you

only caught a glimpse of a few differently-shaped steel helmets a couple of traverses away; and either their bombs got you, or yours got them. Actual hand-to-hand fighting occurred, but it was comparatively rare. It was a war of missiles, murderous and soul-shaking explosives, not a war of hand-weapons. The sentry gazed at dawn over a desolate flat landscape, seamed with irregular trenches and infinitely pitted and scarred with shell-holes, thorny with wire, littered with debris. Five to ten thousand enemies were within range of his vision, and not one would be visible.[7]

This form of war not only depersonalised the enemy—it often seemed to reduce humanity itself to insignificance. 'It is not merely', wrote H. V. Routh, 'that the numbers engaged were too vast to allow any single person, whatever his rank, to play a conspicuous part. It was rather that the science of destruction has developed to such a degree of ingenuity that human beings are left with nothing but a sense of annihilation.'[8] This is very much the emphasis in the action sequences of Barbusse's *Under Fire* (read with enthusiasm by Sassoon and Owen in 1917) and Remarque's *All Quiet on the Western Front*; but it is only half the truth—and the readiness of these novelists to rest content with half the truth is what relegates them to the category of propagandists. The necessary corrective is supplied not by enthusiasts for war like Grenfell or in his more sinister way Ernst Jünger, but by someone like Sassoon who can perceive simultaneously the dreadfulness of war and man's ability to withstand it:

> I . . . was entering once again [he writes in *Memoirs of an Infantry Officer*] the veritable gloom and disaster of the thing called Armageddon. And I saw it then, as I see it now—a dreadful place, a place of horror and desolation which no imagination could have invented. Also it was a place where a man of strong spirit might know himself utterly powerless against death and destruction, and yet stand up and defy gross darkness and stupifying shell-fire, discovering in himself the invincible resistance of an animal or an insect, and an endurance which he might, in after days, forget or disbelieve.[9]

For all its apparent impersonality, moreover, trench warfare, while alienating front-line troops from all who had not shared their ordeal, actually intensified their awareness of their own companions. This is why Sassoon can assure us that in making his protest in 1917 he was inspired by 'a comprehensive memory of war experience *in its intense and essential humanity*'. ('It seemed that my companions of the Somme and Arras battles were around me; helmeted faces returned and receded in vision; joking voices were overheard in fragments of dug-out and billet talk. These were the dead, to whom life had been desirable. . . .'[10]) Above all, this was a form of warfare which evoked bitter moral condemnation, but which also generated moral values of its own, the chief of which were comradeship and courage.

Although armies were such vast impersonal organisations, men found themselves in practice banded together in small units—'For an infantry subaltern,' notes Sassoon, 'the huge unhappy mechanism of the Western Front always narrowed down to the company he was in'—and these developed an intense group loyalty, fostered partly by regimental pride (which Graves and his fellow-instructors at the Bull Ring saw as 'the greatest moral force that kept a battalion going as an effective fighting unit'), partly by that 'delightful camaraderie' which Herbert Read thought 'peculiar to a fighting army', but above all by men's mutual dependence in adversity.[11] The dreadfulness of their shared experience forged a comradeship between them 'richer, stronger in war,' testifies Charles Carrington, 'than we have ever known since'[12] — a comradeship which was celebrated by Graves in his 'Two Fusiliers', by Blunden in 'The Watchers', and by Owen in 'Apologia Pro Poemate Meo';

> I have made fellowships—
>   Untold of happy lovers in old song.
> For love is not the binding of fair lips
>   With the soft silk of eyes that look and long
>
> By Joy, whose ribbon slips,—
>   But wound with war's hard wire whose stakes are strong;
>   Bound with the bandage of the arm that drips;
>   Knit in the webbing of the rifle-thong.[13]

Such fellowships are indeed the subject of the last words Owen ever wrote, in his last letter home, rejoicing, four days before his death, in the camaraderie and acceptance he found in the smoky dug-out near St. Souplet. ('It is a great life,' he declared, in spite of 'the ghastly glimmering of the guns outside, & the hollow crashing of the shells. . . . Of this I am certain you could not be visited by a band of friends half so fine as surround me here.'[14]) Those who had known such comradeship looked back on it in later years with deep and possibly rather suspect nostalgia: 'It is all so long ago now,' Blunden was to write in 1933; 'and yet when I think of the 11th Royal Sussex on a winter evening, under all its ordeals or in any of its recreations, "Bare winter suddenly is changed to spring." '15 At the front, however, when things were at their worst, it had been undeniably a real, operative force, helping to sustain men in their ordeal:

> We had seven days in the trenches [Herbert Read wrote to a friend in June 1917] and rather terrible days they were. But you can have no desire for me to 'paint the horrors'. I could do so but let the one word 'fetid' express the very essence of our experiences. It would be nightmare to any individual. But we create among ourselves a wonderful comradeship which I think would overcome any horror or hardship. It is this comradeship which alone makes the Army tolerable to me. To create a bond between yourself and a body of men and a bond that will hold at the critical moment, that is work worthy of any man and when done an achievement to be proud of.16

Here the concept modulates to that of leadership; but comradeship in either sense was an achievement, involving not the indiscriminate acceptance of one's fellows, but a mutual respect, trust and affection which had to be earned, and earned in the eyes of inexorable judges.

> Because [explains C. E. Montague] trench life is very domestic, highly atomic. Its atom, or unit, like that of slum life, is the jealously close, exclusive, contriving life of a family housed in an urban cellar. . . . Our total host might be two millions strong, or ten millions; whatever its size a man's world was that of his section—at most, his platoon; all that mattered much to him was the one little boatload of castaways with whom he was marooned on a desert island and making shift to keep off the weather and any sudden attack of wild beasts. . . . Constantly jammed up against one another, every man in each of these isolated knots of adventurers came to be seen by the rest for what he was worth, with the drastic clearness of open-eyed husbands and wives of long standing. They had domesticated the Day of Judgment. . . . Officers, watched almost as closely, were sorted out by the minds of the men into themes for contemptuous silence, objects of the

love that doeth and beareth all things, and cases of Not Proven Yet.[17]

The process is documented by Frank Richards in *Old Soldiers Never Die*, with its laconic comments on individual members of his battalion:

> His name was Mr. Fletcher, and all the men in B [Company] swore that he was not only the bravest man in France, but had more brains than all the Battalion officers put together. . . . We were very cut up over [Captain Thomas's] death: he was a soldier to his finger-tips and a very brave and humane man. . . . During the time the bank clerk had been with the Battalion he had seen much and endured much and became a pukka old soldier in action. . . . [The former divinity student's] bad language won universal approval and he also became highly proficient in drinking a bottle of ving blong, and proved himself a very brave and good soldier as well. He was killed in December on Passchendaele Ridge. . . . We had a man in our platoon who was one of the most windy men I ever saw in France, and when working on the parapet at night the report of a rifle was enough to make him jump back in the trench shivering with fright: it was pitiable to see him when the enemy were shelling our line. . . . I thought the Doctor would have been awarded the Victoria Cross. He had honestly earned it. . . . I have always held that he was the coolest man under fire that ever stepped foot in France.[18]

Richards's criteria are simple—'We always judged a new officer by the way he conducted himself in a trench, and if he had guts we always respected him'[19]—but many writers on a more sophisticated level shared his respect for courage and his preoccupation with the strengths and weaknesses revealed in men by war. An admiration for the military virtues is an outstanding feature of works as various as *Old Soldiers Never Die*, *Disenchantment*, the *Spanish Farm* trilogy (especially its second volume), *Parade's End*, *In Retreat*, *Undertones of War*, *Goodbye to All That*, *A Subaltern's War*, *Journey's End*, *Death of a Hero*, *Her Privates We*, and *In Parenthesis*. Indeed the fortitude and stoical endurance, as well as the sufferings, of soldiers at the front constitute one of the main, though much neglected, themes of war literature in English—as they constituted one of the main moral and psychological phenomena of the war itself.

They are also manifested in the soldiers' own songs, which are significant both as gauges of morale and as contributions to the literature or sub-literature of war. The bitterness and gaiety which Yeats predicated of the heroic mood, and which he sought nostalgically in the Anglo-Irish aristocracy, are realised in these contemporary folk-songs. With their cynical humour, their wry pathos, their 'fusion of self-mockery with self-pity', and their fundamental stoicism, they constitute, as C. M. Bowra notes, a genuinely proletarian art-form which expresses 'the response of men to an intolerable situation which they see in all its odiousness but by which they refuse to be completely defeated'.[20] Their main limitation lies in their expressing only the response, without any attempt at conveying the situation itself, knowledge of which is naturally assumed (just as it was by contributors to *The Wipers Times*, which displays comparably cheerful defence-mechanisms and a comparable 'resolution and humanity in the face of violent death'[21]). The best war poetry was written mainly for civilian readers, to confront them with the realities of modern war; the soldiers' songs were sung by men already in the midst of these realities, which did not therefore need to be evoked. Hence we have now to supply the context which gives the songs their full meaning, unless it is supplied for us as it was by the B.B.C. television series on the Great War in the early 1960s, or more tendentiously by Joan Littlewood and the Theatre Workshop in *Oh, What a Lovely War*.

The songs themselves, those 'angry marching rhymes / Of blind regret and haggard mirth',[22] have an indomitable quality which compels admiration; yet they are firmly rooted in emotional and military reality. The fighting-man's angry pride and resentment of civilian slackers are defiantly voiced in 'I Wore a Tunic'; but more typical is the serio-comic treatment of the vicissitudes of a soldier's life in 'Never Mind': 'If the sergeant steals your rum, Never mind!'—'If old Jerry shells the trench, Never mind!'—'If you get stuck on the wire, Never mind!'—with this final stanza acknowledging the worst possible eventuality, and the refrain, though heavily ironic, masking genuinely stoical acceptance. Typical also is the modulation from humour to pathos in 'The Old Barbed Wire', where the stock jokes at the expense of sergeants, quartermasters, sergeant-majors and commanding officers are followed by an elegiac stanza lamenting the passing of 'the old battalion', and suggesting the singers' own rueful familiarity with the barbed wire of the title:

If you want the old battalion,
I know where they are, I know where they are,
If you want the old battalion,
I know where they are,
They're hanging on the old barbed wire.
I've seen them, I've seen them,
Hanging on the old barbed wire,
I've seen them,
Hanging on the old barbed wire.

The special quality of such a song lies in its blend of vigour and grim pathos, with its swinging, vital marching-tune and its recognition of the singers' own probable fate. But this is only one mode among many. There is the more cheerful stoicism of 'Pack up your troubles': 'Of our battalion of about 800 strong,' Liddell Hart recalls, 'fewer than 70 men, with 4 officers, came back [from their first few days on the Somme]. On reaching the road, this remnant formed into columns of fours and moved along singing, "Pack up your troubles in your old kit-bag"—just as the full battalion had done six days earlier when setting out for "the great adventure".'[23] There are also the songs of half-humorous, half-serious complaint ('When this lousy war is over, / No more soldiering for me'; 'Nobody knows how tired we are / And nobody seems to care'; 'We're here because / We're here because / We're here because / We're here'); and there are those which, disclaiming stoicism altogether, offer frank and cynical professions of cowardice. One of the most popular in this vein was 'I Want to Go Home', with its yearning, rollicking, shameless avowals:

I want to go home,
I want to go home,
I don't want to go in the trenches no more,
Where whizz-bangs and shrapnel they whistle and roar.
Take me over the sea
Where the Alleman can't get at me.
Oh my,
I don't want to die,
I want to go home.

It must be realised, however, that this was sung habitually by men who endured and went on enduring almost unimaginable horrors; and as Eric Partridge and John Brophy indicate, it is far from being defeatist since 'it certainly expresses the soldier's war-weariness, but . . . also conquers it with ridicule'.[24] Indeed, many such songs have to be understood in terms of their psychological function in the situations in which they flourished:

> When the romantic conception of war proved false, out of date, useless [Brophy comments], the soldier was helped in his dour, relentless task if he could make a mock of all heroics and sing, with apparent shamelessness, *I Don't Want to Die, I Don't Want to be a Soldier*, or *Far Far From Ypres I long to Be*. For these songs satirized more than war: they poked fun at the soldier's own desire for peace and rest, and so prevented it getting the better of him. They were strong bulwarks against *défaitisme*.[25]

Such songs were in fact safety-valves for feelings allowed no outlet in action; and they were also the in-group jokes of fighting-men who deliberately played down their own unquestionable if reluctant heroism. 'No other army has ever gone to war proclaiming its own incompetence and reluctance to fight,' comments A. J. P. Taylor, 'and no army has fought better.'[26]

This raises a wider question about the relation of war literature to war experience. Morale in the British Army varied a great deal from time to time, from individual to individual, and from one campaign and unit to another, but its general soundness, to which there are innumerable—though sometimes biassed—testimonies, is also vouched for by events. The Russian armies voted with their feet, abandoning the war in 1917; the Italians were a doubtful quantity after the rout at Caporetto; the French mutinied after Nivelle's offensive, refusing to return to the attack, and had to be nursed along for the remainder of that year; but the British armies fought doggedly on, taking an increasing share in the battles of attrition in 1916–17, bearing the brunt of the German spring offensive of 1918, and playing a major part in the final victories of the summer and autumn of that year. It was a triumph of staying power and corporate will, which has often been contrasted with the pessimistic, despairing mood of much war poetry and of some prose treatments of the war in retrospect. Indeed this discrepancy has led some commentators to dismiss the literature as unrepresentative of general attitudes among the troops—to argue as Correlli Barnett does that it expresses only the 'highly subjective and untypical response of a sheltered minority',[27] and to suggest like Douglas Jerrold that the picture of war which it presents is 'fundamentally . . . statistically false even when it is incidentally true'.[28] In 1930 Cyril Falls complained at length of what he saw as the distortions of historical and psychological truth in many war books of that period, and his annotations in *War Books: A Critical Guide*[29] are concerned more with authenticity than literary value. No doubt it is salutary to be reminded that neither quality necessarily guarantees the other; and even if one thinks the indictment overstated, it is certainly true that there are grave dangers in attempting to base a psychological history of the war on purely literary evidence, especially on a limited sample:

> From beginning to end of the First World War [writes John Terraine] some eight-and-a-half million citizens of the British Empire entered the Services; over five million of these, at one time or another, served on the Western Front. If even a substantial number, let alone a majority of these men, had been permanently in the condition of nerves so clearly expressed by, say, the poems of Wilfred Owen or Sassoon, it is quite clear that the daily round *could not* have gone on. The inescapable, wonderful fact is that it did— and from this we might learn that the moods and frames of mind of the war-poets who harrow us are not untrue, but they are true only of particular moods and particular frames of mind experienced at certain times, and in these cases expressed by men of rare sensitivity and articulateness.[30]

This points not unfairly to the selective, fragmentary nature of the experiences mediated to us by most war poetry of the period, though Terraine's dismissive reference to a 'condition of nerves' undervalues the insights offered by both Owen and Sassoon. The short lyric or narrative poem had a rather limited potential: it could render vividly a scene, situation or event and register the poet's reaction to it, it could quintessentialise an emotion or perception, and in doing so it often achieved effects of great intensity; but it could not by its very nature deal with the totality of war experience.[31] (This is presumably why some of the best anthologies, like *Up the Line to Death* and *Men Who March Away*, group their material thematically in an attempt to offer a larger meaning, a more complete interpretation, than the individual poems—or indeed the individual poets—provide.) Yet any limitations inherent in the *genre* itself are less important than the limitations which many poets seem to have imposed on themselves. More extensive works could hardly be undertaken in the conditions of training, active service, leave or convalescence in which soldier-poets inevitably had to write; but it was open to them to express the full range of their responses to war over a series of short poems, as Graves sought to do in *Fairies and Fusiliers*. That some of the most famous do not do so—that they incline rather to the homogeneity of *Counter-Attack* or Owen's war poetry, is due paradoxically to their preoccupation with the truth. This was a key concept for poets writing as they were for a society blinded by lies and cant about the nature of war. 'All a poet can do today is warn,' wrote Owen. 'That is why the true Poets must be truthful.' Sassoon developed, he himself recalls, 'a ferocious and defiant resolve to tell the truth about the War in every possible way'. And Read saw himself as having crawled out of the mess of 1914—18

> with two medals and a gift of blood-money.
> No visible wounds to lick—only a resolve
> to tell the truth without rhetoric
> the truth about war and about men
> involved in the indignities of war.[32]

This truth about the physical, psychological and moral realities of war was conceived of polemically as a corrective to the falsities of traditional war poetry, journalistic rhetoric, official propaganda and civilian ignorance; but this very polemical intention, while sharpening the focus of their poetic vision, also narrowed its scope by restricting their conception of the truth that must be told.

The point is best made with reference to the reactions not of the less articulate majority but of the poets themselves.

Owen's case is of peculiar interest, because of the greatness of his poetry and his almost archetypal status. The poems in which he distils the pity of war are permanent additions to the language, powerful modifiers of our sensibility, classic expressions of the emotions humanly appropriate to certain aspects of war: their truth is as undeniable as their beauty—yet it is undeniably partial even in terms of his personal experience. Yeats excluded the war poets from his *Oxford Book of English Verse* on the grounds that 'passive suffering is not a theme for poetry': a more pertinent criticism would have been that to present soldiers merely as passive sufferers involves an element of falsification, and that Owen's characteristic portrayal of soldiers as victims often masks his awareness of their other role of executioners. Those who died like cattle were prepared to kill like butchers when

occasion offered, and his acknowledgment of this adds an important
dimension to a poem like 'Spring Offensive', which culminates in the
attackers' 'superhuman inhumanities, / Long-famous glories, immemorial shames'—the oxymoronic phrases registering sensitively and
precisely the moral paradox of war with its inevitable linking of
courage and cruelty. The climax of both 'Strange Meeting' and 'The
Show' comes with his recognition of his own participation in such
guilt—he was indeed 'a conscientious objector with a very seared
conscience';[33] while 'Apologia Pro Poemate Meo' goes even further,
acknowledging with confessional honesty his own temporary commitment to the special ethics and psychology of battle:

> Merry it was to laugh there—
>   Where death becomes absurd and life absurder.
>   For power was on us as we slashed bones bare
>   Not to feel sickness or remorse of murder.
>
> I, too, have dropped off fear—
>   Behind the barrage, dead as my platoon,
>   And sailed my spirit surging light and clear
>   Past the entanglement where hopes lay strewn;
>
> And witnessed exultation—
>   Faces that used to curse me, scowl for scowl,
>   Shine up and lift with passion of oblation,
>   Seraphic for an hour; though they were foul. . . .
>
> I have perceived much beauty
>   In the hoarse oaths that kept our courage straight;
>   Heard music in the silentness of duty;
>   Found peace where shell-storms spouted reddest spate.[34]

It is a poem which seems to point forward to a deeper self-
examination, and to a literature which would attempt to tell not just
the truth and nothing but the truth, but also something like the whole
truth about men at war. That Owen did not take this course is due
mainly to his overwhelming sense of moral outrage and the need for
protest. His own draft Contents list was quite explicit about the
function of his poems as an attack on evils like indifference at home,
heroic lies, the willingness of the old to sacrifice the young, the
vastness of losses, 'the inhumanity of war', 'the foolishness of war',

'the insupportability of war', and 'the horrible beastliness of war'.[35] His crusading zeal, therefore, imposed its own kind of selection, so that the complexity of attitude revealed in his life is largely excluded from his poetry.

One of Christ's essential commands might be 'Passivity at any price! Suffer dishonour and disgrace; but never resort to arms. Be bullied, be outraged, be killed; but do not kill.'[36] Yet Owen's commitment to the men at the front constituted in the end an ethical imperative more powerful than Christ's. After his fourteen months of security in Britain—months which enabled him to digest his former war experiences and transmute them into art—he returned to France 'to help these boys', as he said himself, '—directly by leading them as well as an officer can; indirectly, by watching their sufferings that I may speak of them as well as a pleader can.'[37] He had done the first, he told his mother early in October 1918, and it had involved a return to killing in the battle in which he won his Military Cross—a battle which 'passed the limits of [his] Abhorrence', and in which, he wrote, he 'lost all [his] earthly faculties, and fought like an angel'. In describing how he captured a German machine gun and scores of prisoners he minimised the violence involved: 'I only shot one man with my revolver (at about 30 yards!); The rest I took with a smile';[38] but the official citation for his M.C. tells a rather different story, and the glimpse it gives us of Owen 'personally manipulat[ing] a captured enemy machine gun in an isolated position and inflict[ing] considerable losses on the enemy'[39] suggests a somewhat different attitude to war. ('You would not know me for the poet of sorrows',[40] he had written ironically but prophetically to his mother in September.) Hating 'washy pacifists' as much as 'whiskied prussianists', he had felt a year before that he 'must first get some reputation of gallantry before [he] could successfully and usefully declare [his] principles';[41] but he needed to secure that reputation not just to influence the public, but to restore his own confidence in himself. His former spell of duty in the trenches had been very short indeed; his nerves had quickly gone to pieces, so that he had been invalided home with 'shell shock'; and according to Graves 'it had preyed on his mind that he had been accused of cowardice by his commanding officer'.[42] Certainly he had been found, in that state, unfit to command troops; and it seems clear that he was now delighted to have proved himself in battle, redeeming (like Lord Jim) what might be seen as a previous failure. Hence his insistence that his nerves were in perfect order after the October battle; hence too his

subsequent euphoria, and his joy at being so completely accepted in
the fellowship of the battalion.

This conflict between his military and poetic selves is typical of the
British war poets. The fact that most of them were brave, efficient
officers is no mere biographical irrelevance: it is of the very essence of
their case. Their initial sensitivity, their sharp awareness of the horrors
around them, and in some cases their doubts about justifications for
the war's continuance, all moved them to protest. Their hatred of war
is articulated in poems which document more fully and sensitively
than ever before its agonies, futilities, and horror; yet they themselves
remained committed to the activity which they condemned. None of
them was prepared, like Hemingway's protagonist, to bid an
ignominious farewell to arms. Nor was this simply a matter of their
being inextricably caught up in the military machine, in which as
Frank Richards reminds us to be 'absent from parading to go in front-
line trenches' was a crime punishable by death:[43] it was more
fundamentally a matter of their own acceptance, to a very large
extent, of many of the values which war generated.

Charles Sorley, for example, with his sceptical intelligence,
political sophistication, and love of Germany, was unmoved by
popular hysteria in 1914, and he quickly came to feel that the war
made people 'think too much of the visible virtues—bravery,
endurance and the obvious forms of self-sacrifice'.[44] He deliberately
avoided such 'glorification of the second-best': his two sonnets on
Death were written, it seems, partly as a corrective to Rupert
Brooke's, which he condemned for their self-regarding, sentimental
attitude;[45] and his poem 'A hundred thousand million mites we go'
gave a chilling picture of man's insignificance in the face of 'blind
Vicissitude'. His more serious political comments on the war—
sometimes he is rather flippant—show a remarkable maturity, and his
sonnet 'To Germany' expresses an unfashionable view of the whole
conflict as a tragic blunder for which both sides were to blame and for
which both were suffering. He avoids all stock responses to the
situations he encounters, offering a cool analysis of comradeship, for
example, in terms of friendships of circumstance, 'extraordinarily
close, really', but quite distinct from friendships of choice.[46] He hated
the monotony and stagnation of army life in England, and looked
forward to going out to France, 'not in the brave British drummer-
boy spirit, of course, but as a relief from this boredom'; though when
he got there his first impression of trench warfare was of 'a large
amount of organized disorderliness, killing the spirit'.[47] Soon,

however, he began 'to scent romance in night-patrolling'[48] which he took to with an enthusiasm reminiscent of both Grenfell and Sassoon. We catch a glimpse of him, through the eyes of a fellow-officer, reading *Faust* in the trenches, happy and careless the morning after a rather bloody incident in No Man's Land; and we also have his own disturbingly frank analysis of his sensations:

> Out in front at night in that no-man's land and long graveyard there is a freedom and a spur. Rustling of the grasses and grave tap-tapping of distant workers: the tension and silence of encounter, when one struggles in the dark for moral victory over the enemy patrol: the wail of the exploded bomb and the animal cries of wounded men. Then death and the horrible thankfulness when one sees that the next man is dead: 'We won't have to *carry* him in under fire, thank God; dragging will do': hauling in of the great resistless body in the dark, the smashed head rattling: the relief, the relief that the thing has ceased to groan: that the bullet or bomb that made the man an animal has now made the animal a corpse. One is hardened by now: purged of all false pity: perhaps more selfish than before. The spiritual and the animal get so much more sharply divided in hours of encounter, taking possession of the body by swift turns.[49]

He seems to be engaged in a process of self-discovery, only certain stages of which are recorded in his poetry, but which involves a movement towards an unsentimentalised heroic ethos already glimpsed in 'All the Hills and Vales Along', where his awareness of the doom the men were marching to gave an ironical perspective on their singing, but did not prevent his endorsing their joyful confrontation of destiny:

> On, marching men, on
> To the gates of death with song.
> Sow your gladness for earth's reaping,
> So you may be glad, though sleeping.
> Strew your gladness on earth's bed,
> So be merry, so be dead.

It is true that the ironies of this poem are ambiguous; true also that since writing it he had come to take a starker view of death, though one that involved acceptance rather than revulsion; but his own final commitment is clear. On 5 October 1915, on the eve of battle (what he himself called 'the eve of our crowning hour'), he wrote to a friend about his aspirations and fears:

> To be able to prove oneself no coward to oneself, will be great, if it comes off: but suppose one finds oneself fail in the test? I dread my own censorious self in the coming conflict—I also have great physical dread of pain. Still, a good edge is given to the sword here. And one learns to be a servant. The soul is disciplined. . . . Pray that I ride my frisky nerves with a cool and steady hand when the time arrives. [50]

A week later he was killed leading his company at Loos; and his final sonnet—'When you see millions of the mouthless dead / Across your dreams in pale battalions go'—was found among his kit sent home from France. Its bleak stoicism is his last word on death, but if we are to understand him properly it has to be read with the poem 'There is no fitter end than this', written a few weeks before in memory and praise of one of his contemporaries at Marlborough, who had just been awarded a posthumous V.C.

Herbert Read's 'War Diary', consisting of letters written mainly from the Front, displays a quick play of intelligence on art, literature, philosophy and politics. His attitude to the war itself fluctuates from a delight in adventure to a sense of its futility, and from revulsion from its horrors to pride in his men.

> We have had a terrible time [he wrote in October 1917]—the worst I have ever experienced (and I'm getting quite an old soldier now). Life has never seemed quite so cheap nor nature so mutilated. . . . Of course, everyday events are apt to become rather monotonous . . . but if the daily horror might accumulate we should have such a fund of revulsion as would make the world cry 'enough!'. So sometimes I wonder if it is a sacred duty after all 'to paint the horrors'. . . . My military progress continues—strange to say. I am now commanding a company. . . . I have got a fine lot of lads though they are fastly decreasing in numbers. 'Always merry and bright'—it's my aim to keep them so. And they are a gallant crew: we have more decorations in our company than in any other in the battalion. I got four Military Medals today out of seven for the battalion. And damn proud of it we all are. [51]

These contradictions are typical of many men's reactions to the war; and Read's feelings about the army itself were similarly complex: 'I like its manliness,' he wrote in May 1918, 'the courage it demands, the fellowship it gives. These are infinitely precious things. But I hate the machine—the thing as a whole and its duty (to kill), its very existence.'[52] The protagonist of his poem 'Kneeshaw Goes to War' is caught up by this machine:

> Kneeshaw felt himself
> A cog in some great evil engine,
> Unwilling, but revolv'd tempestuously
> By unseen springs.
> He plunged with listless mind
> Into the black horror.[53]

But a few days after correcting the proofs of this poem for a little magazine, Read himself had plunged, not with listless mind but with excitement and professional zeal, into the black horror of the German offensive of March 1918:

> We were rushed up to the line [he wrote on 1 April] in the early hours of morning and from then and for six days and nights we were fighting as I never dreamt I should fight—without sleep—often without food and all the time besieged by hordes of the Boche. The Colonel was wounded during the second day and I had to take command of the battalion. We were surrounded in our original position and had to fight our way through. We took up position after position, always to be surrounded. On the whole the men were splendid and there were many fine cases of heroism. But our casualties were very heavy and we who have come through may thank our lucky stars eternally.[54]

(These were the experiences which he was later to describe with considered artistry in *In Retreat*.) He was already compiling a volume of 'realistic' war poems—*Naked Warriors*—as 'a protest against all the glory camouflage that is written about the war';[55] and there is a strange dichotomy between the responses he records there—in a poem like 'The Happy Warrior', for example—and his comment that 'the men were splendid and there were many fine cases of heroism'. Another poem in the same collection, 'Liedholz', about the prisoner he captured on a raid in August 1917, keeps fairly closely to events as he describes them in his War Diary—the scuffle in No Man's Land, the return to British trenches, his taking Liedholz to Brigade on a beautiful morning with larks singing, their conversing in broken French and finding common interests in Beethoven and Nietzsche, the irony of their having done their best to kill each other a few hours before. But the poem says nothing of the efficiency with which Read conducted the raid, or the bravado with which he embarked on it: 'I've been chosen for a death or glory job soon to come off. I am very glad—glad in the first place because it gives me the first chance I've had of doing something—glad in the second place because it means that others recognize that I'm of the clan that don't care a damn for anything.'[56] The poem itself is none the worse for these exclusions, but it presents a version of the incident simplified in the interests of both art and protest; and it is significant that Read subsequently attempted a more inclusive treatment in 'The Raid'—a short, realistic prose narrative which offers a characteristic analysis of courage and cowardice, making clear his own commitment to the former. Of all his wartime poems 'My Company' is the only one which seems to do full justice to the complexity of his responses, and to acknowledge that in such circumstances 'it is perfectly possible, even normal', as he wrote in 1962, 'to lead a life of contradictions'.[57]

Sassoon's case is obviously comparable, but more extreme since his wartime art is so emphatically one of angry protest. 'Our inconsistencies,' he wrote years afterwards in *Sherston's Progress*, 'are often what make us most interesting, and it is possible that, in my zeal to construct these memoirs carefully, I have eliminated many of my own self-contradictions.'[58] But the charge is much more applicable to his poetry. His realistic vignettes of trench life, his satirical epigrams, and his poems of bitter protest all served 'to unmask the ugly face of Mars',[59] to disturb complacency, and to discredit the cant of journalists, war-correspondents, politicians and civilians generally. They are landmarks in the literature of war, and their unquestionable strength derives from his own involvement with the characters and situations he describes. Yet the suppressions are significant. The poems are recognisably the work of the Sassoon who protested publicly in the summer of 1917 at the prolongation of the war and of the sufferings of the troops; but one finds little trace in them of the Sassoon who patrolled blood-thirstily in No Man's Land to avenge the death of friends—the Sassoon his comrades nicknamed 'Mad Jack' for his reckless bravery in battle—the Sassoon who took German trenches single-handed on the Somme, shouting a 'view halloa' as the defenders stole away—the Sassoon who lightheartedly undertook a bombing counter-attack at Arras, and who, returning willingly to France in 1918 *after* his protest, went patrolling to the German trenches as exuberantly as Julian Grenfell ever did in 1914–15. His second-in-command in that last summer of the war was a former undergraduate—the 'Velmore' of *Sherston's Progress*—who had already read and admired Sassoon's war poetry, but who now found it hard to reconcile with his behaviour in the line:

> I found it a curious paradox [he writes] that the author of *Counter Attack*, which had just been published, that volume full of bitter indignation at the hideous cruelty of modern warfare, should also be a first-rate soldier and a most aggressive company commander. He was determined that A Company should demonstrate its superiority to the enemy as soon as possible, and he spent a large part of his nocturnal watches crawling through the deep corn in no-man's-land with a couple of bombs in his pocket and a knobkerrie in his hand.[60]

Sassoon alternated, as Graves said, between the roles of 'happy warrior' and 'bitter pacifist';[61] and in this he was typical of the soldier-poets. Their dilemma, basic, unresolvable, was that they subscribed to two conflicting ethics—one based on courage and comradeship and the other on compassion—so that the claims of duty coexisted for them with those of protest. The former predominated in their lives, the latter in their poetry, which can thus be seen not as an equivalent to the 'safety-valve' of soldiers' songs—that would be to ignore its moral intensity—but as a highly selective, almost indeed a censored version of their responses to war experience. Their artistic sight is often dependent (in Stevenson's phrase) on judicious blindness.

*   *   *

These limitations are transcended, however, in the best of the many works of fiction and autobiography which view the war in retrospect.

After the Armistice the need for protest lost some of its urgency, since public opinion was no longer sustaining the war and prolonging its agonies; but poets and others still felt compelled to bear witness and to take part in what Henry Williamson calls 'the mental war . . . against the righteous and bellicose attitudes' of those who had supported the war itself while knowing nothing of its reality.[62] The next few years saw the publication of many works of varying degrees of bitterness written during the war or in its immediate aftermath. There is complete continuity with the poetic impulses and programmes of the war years; and Sassoon strikes a characteristic note when he confesses, in his foreword to the posthumous edition of Wilfred Owen's poems, that 'his conclusions about War are so entirely in accordance with my own that I cannot attempt to judge his work with any critical detachment'.[63] The poems themselves still stand as memorials to the suffering of a generation and as warnings for the future; but as time went on the poets and other imaginative writers who survived the war seem to have felt increasingly the need to return to their experiences, to recollect them now in comparative tranquillity or to exorcise them by a therapy of total recall, to treat them in any case more comprehensively and on a larger scale (as Sassoon himself had yearned to do even in 1918).[64] Edmund Blunden, for example, who had gone on after the war 'attempting "the image and horror of it" . . . in poetry', reflected in 1924 that in spite of the harvest he had already gathered 'it was impossible not to look again, and to descry the ground, how thickly and innumerably yet it was strewn with the facts or notions of war experience. I must go over the ground again', he concluded—recognising that he might well have to keep on going over it until his death.[65] The reinterpretations offered by the main British writers who shared this compulsion are more complex than those formulated previously: indeed common to nearly all of them is a fundamental dualism acknowledged now instead of being suppressed—a recognition on the one hand of the horror, waste and futility, the essential evil, of war, and on the other hand an admiration for the courage and greatness of spirit men showed in confronting it.

> . . . I was rewarded [Sassoon wrote of his wartime self in 1930] by an intense memory of men whose courage had shown me the power of the human spirit—that spirit which could withstand the utmost assault. Such men had inspired me to be at my best when things were very bad, and they outweighed all the failures. Against the background of the War and its brutal stupidity those men had stood glorified by the thing which sought to destroy them.[66]

This is very different from the attitude he had struck in 1918 when he chose as epigraph to *Counter-Attack* a passage from Barbusse which stressed the brutalising, debasing, corrupting effect that war inevitably had on all participants.

That view was by no means consistently maintained in *Under Fire*, but it pervades the most famous of war-books, *All Quiet on the Western Front*:

> We march up, moody or good-tempered soldiers—we reach the zone where the front begins and become on the instant human animals. . . . We want to live at any price; so we cannot burden ourselves with feelings which, though they might be ornamental enough in peace-time, would be out of place here. . . . All other expressions lie in a winter sleep, life is simply one continual watch against the menace of death;—it has transformed us into unthinking animals in order to give us the weapon of instinct—it has reinforced us with dullness, so that we do not go to pieces before the horror, which would overwhelm us if we had clear, conscious thought—it has awakened in us the sense of comradeship, so that we escape the abyss of solitude—it has lent us the indifference of wild creatures, so that in spite of all, we perceive the positive in every moment, and store it up against the onslaught of nothingness. Thus we live a closed, hard existence of the utmost superficiality, and rarely does an incident strike out a spark. . . . *our inner forces are not exerted toward regeneration, but toward degeneration.* . . .[67]

The narrative exemplifies and illustrates this theoretical position. It has often been observed that Remarque is singularly unconvincing when he comes to portray front-line experience as opposed to life behind the lines. It might also be said that his characters were debased and brutal before they ever went to war: the beating-up of a sadistic corporal by the young recruits is itself an unpleasantly sadistic episode. But the novel as a whole is skilfully designed—much more skilfully than the loosely episodic *Under Fire*—'to tell of a generation of men who, even though they may have escaped its shells, were destroyed by the war'—men who, if not killed or maimed, would return home 'weary, broken, burnt out, rootless, and without hope'.[68] The emphasis on degradation, demoralisation and futility, and the repudiation of any conception of the heroic, were immensely influential, establishing in effect a new norm of war literature: it is all the more noteworthy that Remarque's main thesis, and the structure of feeling he articulates, differ significantly from those of authors—even disillusioned, battle-weary authors—like Sassoon himself, C. E. Montague, Richard Aldington, R. C. Sherriff, Robert Graves,

Edmund Blunden, David Jones and Frederic Manning.

Sassoon's indictment of war coexists in the Sherston trilogy with
his memories of 'the typical Flintshire Fusilier at his best, and the vast
anonymity of courage and cheerfulness which he represented'.[69]
Montague pays elegiac tribute to the idealism, decency and courage
of the volunteer armies, even as he charts the *via dolorosa* which they
had to tread to death or disillusion; and Aldington in *Death of a Hero*,
one of the most virulently anti-war books in the language, goes to the
opposite extreme from Remarque (though he admired him) in
applauding the soldiers' preservation of their essential humanity:

> [Winterbourne] hated the war as much as ever, hated all the
> blather about it, profoundly distrusted the motives of the War
> partisans, and hated the Army. But he liked the soldiers, the War
> soldiers, not as soldiers but as men. He respected them. . . . He was
> with them. . . . With them, because they were men with fine
> qualities, because they had endured great hardships and dangers with
> simplicity, because they had parried those hardships and dangers
> not by hating the men who were supposed to be their enemies, but
> by developing a comradeship among themselves. They had every
> excuse for turning into brutes, and they hadn't done it. True, they
> were degenerating in certain ways, they were getting coarse and
> rough and a bit animal, but with amazing simplicity and
> unpretentiousness they had retained and developed a certain
> essential humanity and manhood. With them, then, to the end,
> because of their manhood and humanity. With them, too, because
> their manhood and humanity existed in spite of the War and not
> because of it. They had saved something from a gigantic wreck,
> and what they had saved was immensely important—manhood
> and comradeship, their essential integrity as men, their essential
> brotherhood as men.[70]

Nothing that follows undercuts this sense of solidarity with the front-
line troops or this appreciation of their qualities, which is remarkable
in one of the most stridently debunking novels of its period. The
protagonist, Winterbourne, is representative of a generation 'who
spent their childhood and adolescence struggling, like young Sam-
sons, in the toils of the Victorians; whose early manhood coincided
with the European war'.[71] The novel records and endorses that
generation's rebellion against the values of its predecessors. As in
Butler's *Way of All Flesh*, though with greater sexual explicitness, the

tribulations of the young are blamed largely on the failings of their elders (though the causal connections are sometimes far from clear, and the author-narrator seems as outraged by the promiscuity of the hero's mother and the sexual liberation of his wife and mistress as he is by the prudery of 'the Victorians'). It is a book of violent rejections, insisted on by the hectoring, repetitive, sometimes almost hysterical voice of the narrator. There is a deliberate intent to shock by the violation of taboos in language—though this was partly vitiated by the British publisher's refusal to co-operate—and still more by the rejection of received ideas and stock attitudes. Winterbourne's mother, for example, on receiving the telegram informing her of his death in action, falls not to grieving but to making love, and the narrator is at pains to stress the necrophiliac element in her erotic arousal. The novel offers a hotch-potch of the author's views on life, attacking so many varied targets that it tends to lose formal and intellectual coherence; but the dominant note is one of revulsion at emotional and intellectual dishonesty in England, which is presented as reaching its peak in the war years. 'One human brain cannot hold, one memory retain, one pen portray the limitless Cant, Delusion, and Delirium let loose on the world during those four years. . . . It was the supreme and tragic climax of Victorian Cant. . . .' Because, he argues, 'it was the régime of Cant *before* the War which made the Cant *during* the War so damnably possible and easy'.[72] The war was in reality a 'long, unendurable nightmare'; his hero's death is symbolic 'of the whole sickening bloody waste of it, the damnable stupid waste and torture of it'; and he repudiates as 'nauseous poppycock' the patriotic rhetoric which would find spiritual benefits flowing from the soldiers' suffering.[73] There is a very telling juxtaposition, at the end of the novel, of the description of Winterbourne's death ('He felt he was going mad, and sprang to his feet. The line of bullets smashed across his chest like a savage steel whip. The universe exploded darkly into oblivion'), and the bland Victory proclamation issued by Foch the day after the Armistice.[74] Yet the main animus is against peace-time England and the war-time England which remains oblivious of what soldiers are having to endure, while Aldington's brilliant evocation of front-line experience—by far the best part of the novel—suggests pervasively another set of values. The character-sketch of a Kiplingesque subaltern is predictably satirical in tone: 'Evans was the usual English public-school boy, amazingly ignorant, amazingly inhibited, and yet "decent" and good-humoured. . . . He accepted and obeyed every

English middle-class prejudice and taboo'—which are listed in a long, amusingly derisive catalogue. Yet the passage culminates on an unexpected note:

> Evans possessed that British rhinoceros equipment of mingled ignorance, self-confidence, and complacency which is triple-armed against all the shafts of the mind. And yet Winterbourne could not help liking the man. He was exasperatingly stupid, but he was honest, he was kindly, he was conscientious, he could obey orders and command obedience in others, he took pains to look after his men. He could be implicitly relied upon to lead a hopeless attack and to maintain a desperate defence to the very end. There were thousands and tens of thousands like him.[75]

This admiration for Evans's soldierly virtues is unqualified by irony—and the lack of soldierly virtues in the low-quality battalion in which Winterbourne is afterwards commissioned is one source of his ultimate exhaustion and despair. The haggard, weary remnant of the 'Frontshires', who had 'been nearly wiped out in a desperate defence', are honoured by a sentry who presents arms as they pass, but also by the narrator, who pays tribute to the dogged, fatalistic, heroic endurance of the front-line troops in general:

> [Winterbourne] found that the real soldiers, the front-line troops, had no more delusions about the War than he had. They hadn't his feeling of protest and agony over it all, they hadn't tried to think it out. They went on with the business, hating it, because they had been told it had to be done and believed what they had been told. They wanted the War to end, they wanted to get away from it, and they had no feeling of hatred for their enemies on the other side of No Man's Land. . . . They went on in their stubborn despair, with their sentimental songs and cynical talk and perpetual grousing; and it's my belief that if they'd been asked to do so, they'd still be carrying on now. They weren't crushed by defeat or elated by victory—their stubborn despair had taken them far beyond that point. They carried on. People sneer at the War slang. I, myself, have heard intellectual 'objectors' very witty at the expense of 'carry on'. So like carrion, you know. All right, let them sneer.[76]

What is so striking here is the fact that Aldington, a passionate opponent of the war, is so deeply committed to the front-line troops and certain of their values that he sounds almost Blimpish in his indignation when these are undervalued. Similarly, his short stories in *Roads to Glory* (1930) are mostly anti-war tracts in fictional form, emphasising death, mutilation, neurosis and the predicament of men returning home 'weary, broken, burnt out, rootless and without hope'; but there is also bitter contempt in 'A Bundle of Letters' for the shirker who tries to wangle a safe posting; there is admiration in 'Farewell to Memories' for the endurance shown in what Aldington himself sees as an evil, futile conflict ('Down the Road come the weary battalions, platoon after platoon, heroic in their mud and silence'[77]); and finally, the collection includes 'At All Costs'—one of the finest stories of the war. With remarkable artistic restraint, with no trace of the intrusive rhetoric which mars *Death of a Hero*, Aldington here portrays the acceptance of duty and of certain death by four officers whose company is facing the German Spring offensive of 1918, and who are ordered to hold their position 'at all costs'. Like *Journey's End*, it is a classic celebration of courage without hope.

A similar complexity of attitude, involving condemnation of the war and admiration for some at least of the qualities men showed in it, is to be found in Graves, whose *Goodbye to All That* resembles *Death of a Hero* in the scope of its rejections—of English conventions, class values, public school orthodoxies and the like. Graves would have agreed with Sassoon that 'all squalid, abject, and inglorious elements in war should be remembered'[78]—this was very much his own approach in *Goodbye to All That*, which even outdid the aggressive realism of *All Quiet on the Western Front*. He records, for example, the disgusting appearance of corpses in No Man's Land:

> After the first day or two the bodies swelled and stank. I vomited more than once while superintending the carrying. The ones that we could not get in from the German wire continued to swell until the wall of the stomach collapsed, either naturally or punctured by a bullet; a disgusting smell would float across. The colour of the dead faces changed from white to yellow-grey, to red, to purple, to green, to black, to slimy.[79]

He records in a dead-pan way the most horrific details of trench life:

> Cuinchy was one of the worst places for rats. They came up from the canal and fed on the many corpses and multiplied. When I was

here with the Welsh a new officer came to the company, and, as a token of his welcome, he was given a dug-out containing a spring-bed. When he turned in that night he heard a scuffling, shone his torch on the bed, and there were two rats on his blankets tussling for the possession of a severed hand. This was thought a great joke.[80]

He records also, as this anecdote suggests, a protective callousness which he and his companions tended to develop in the trenches. The killing of prisoners, executions for cowardice, self-inflicted wounds, all kinds of brutality of speech and action, are discussed in deliberately hard-bitten, matter-of-fact tones, though he does allow himself to register distaste for 'the uncleanness of sex-life in billets':

> Two officers of another company had just been telling me how they had slept, in the same room, one with the mother and one with the daughter. They had tossed for the mother because the daughter was a 'yellow-looking little thing like a lizard.' And the Red Lamp, the army brothel, was round the corner in the main street. I had seen a queue of a hundred and fifty men waiting outside the door, each to have his short turn with one or the other of the three women in the house. . . .[81]

It is worth recalling Sassoon's reservations about Graves's testimony: '[He] . . . seemed to want the War to be even uglier than it really was. His mind loathed and yet attached itself to rank smells and squalid details. Like his face (which had a twist to it, as though seen in a slightly distorting mirror) his mental war-pictures were a little uncouth and out of focus.'[82] Yet in spite of this temperamental bias, and in spite of obvious prejudices freely indulged, Graves documents the physical and, within limits, the psychological realities of trench warfare more fully, more convincingly and more vividly than any other autobiographer. He is particularly good on the chaotic experience of battle:

> One of the officers told me later what happened to himself. It had been agreed to advance by platoon rushes with supporting fire. When his platoon had run about twenty yards he signalled them to lie down and open covering fire. The din was tremendous. He saw the platoon on the left flopping down too, so he whistled the advance again. Nobody seemed to hear. He jumped up from his

shell-hole and waved and signalled 'Forward.' Nobody stirred. He shouted: 'You bloody cowards, are you leaving me to go on alone?' His platoon sergeant, groaning with a broken shoulder, gasped out: 'Not cowards, sir. Willing enough. But they're all f——ing dead.' A machine-gun traversing had caught them as they rose to the whistle.[83]

Yet for Graves the fact that they rose to the whistle—that they were *not* cowards—is of paramount importance, angry though he is at their lives being thrown away in such a hopeless attack. Although he sees the war as madness, although he has no belief in its political objectives or in the strategy which governed military operations, he displays throughout a tough professionalism, a commitment to the values of courage and military efficiency, and a pride in his regiment—in its traditions, its morale, its fighting qualities. He records, since he is no sentimentalist, the rudeness and unfairness he often encountered in it; but he takes every opportunity 'of showing that it had all the soldierly virtues in unequalled measure' so that his loyalty to it was never disappointed;[84] and he has nothing but contempt for other units or for individuals who fell short of its high standards of reliability in battle. His pride in being a Royal Welch Fusilier was for him the main sustaining factor, the main motivating force, the main justification for his actions (as he had already testified in his wartime poem 'To Lucasta on Going to the Wars for the Fourth Time'). And if an ethic had to be extrapolated from his war narrative and commentary in *Goodbye to All That*, it would be a bleakly heroic code which insists on courage in battle regardless of the cause or the prospect of success: 'We waited on the fire-step from four to nine o'clock, with fixed bayonets, for the order to go over. . . . The sergeant who was acting company sergeant-major said to me "It's murder, sir." "Of course it's murder, you bloody fool", I agreed. "But there's nothing else for it, is there?"'[85] Graves does not seek self-sacrifice, and if such ill-omened attacks are called off he is cynically thankful; but if they are ordered he accepts that they must be carried out at whatever cost, in what might be conceptualised as an assertion of heroic manhood in an otherwise meaningless universe.

Undertones of War, published the year before *Goodbye to All That*, is more elegiac and compassionate in tone, more sensitive in its description of war's outrages on man and nature, and more consciously an endeavour of art. Graves had originally tried to present his narrative in novel form, but had soon abandoned the

attempt, and when he returned to it after the war he felt ashamed at
having distorted his material with a plot.[86] Frank autobiography
seemed to carry its own guarantee of authenticity: in *Goodbye to All
That* he set out to tell things simply as they happened, without regard
to formal, literary or social conventions; he wrote in haste, completing the book within three months of starting; and although he
evolved a brilliantly anecdotal method of narration, he quite
deliberately let his story trail off in the final chapter, since to end with
his return from Egypt would have been, he thought, 'to round it off
too bookishly'.[87] Unfortunately, this acceptance of life rather than
art as the shaping principle makes for obvious structural weaknesses,
especially in the last quarter of the book (and these are not really
eradicated by the changes made in his 1957 recension). *Undertones of
War* is much more carefully composed as a record of active service
only, beginning with the author's departure for France in 1916 ('I was
not anxious to go') and ending with his return early in 1918. If the
conclusion seems a little arbitrary compared with the significant
dénouements of fiction, it is none the less superior to an anticlimactic
continuation of the kind which Graves offers, and which would have
been provided by Blunden's own subsequent, rather drab wartime
experiences, as recounted in the essay 'Aftertones' (1929). The bare
narrative of 'A Battalion History' (1933), which gives facts largely
uninformed by feeling, and the false, early start on autobiography in
De Bello Germanico, in which he felt that he had got the tone quite
wrong, point up the felicity, indeed the delicacy of the major work,
where the aesthetic distance afforded by the passage of time enables
him to record very sensitively his psychological as well as physical
experiences. *Undertones of War* was written as a consummation of his
attempts to define 'the image and horror' of the war in poetry, but it
was also an elegy to the men he had served with, and a celebration of
their qualities: it was intended 'to preserve some of a multitude of
impressions, *and admirations*', and it constituted, as he said himself
long afterwards, 'a sketch of a happy battalion—happy in spite of
terrible tasks and daily destruction'.[88] It was, however, more than
that. He was aware of the limited, because autobiographical, nature of
the experiences he was recalling, but they seemed to him representative of wider significance. 'Do I loiter too much among little
things?' he asks at one point, and justifies himself on the grounds that
'each circumstance of the British experience that is still with me has
ceased for me to be big or little, and now appeals to me more even
than the highest exaltation of pain or scene in the "Dynasts". . . .'[89]

Blunden is offering essentially a tragic vision of man's nobility in the face of senseless suffering. (The dramatic analogy is suggested by his own subsequent suggestion that the Western Front 'was almost a philosophy, but also an *abattoir*, and yet most obviously a theatre of war. It . . . looked perpetual; and those who neared its firing lines came into a huge and tragic scene.'[90]) The war is seen as monstrous, futile, meaningless in its destructive horror:

> Cambrin was beginning to terrify. Not far away from that shafthead, a young and cheerful lance-corporal of ours was making some tea as I passed one warm afternoon. Wishing him a good tea, I went along three firebays; one shell dropped without warning behind me; I saw its smoke faint out, and I thought all was as lucky as it should be. Soon a cry from that place recalled me; the shell had burst all wrong. Its butting impression was black and stinking in the parodos where three minutes ago the lance-corporal's mess-tin was bubbling over a little flame. For him, how could the gobbets of blackening flesh, the earth-wall sotted with blood, with flesh, the eye under the duckboard, the pulpy bone be the only answer? At this moment, while we looked with dreadful fixity at so isolated a horror, the lance-corporal's brother came round the traverse. . . . [91]

Such isolated horrors merge into a larger, almost continuous nightmare. Impressionistically but precisely, by pictures and evocations, by delicate description and telling anecdotes, he recreates 'the black dreariness of trench warfare';[92] Yet its darkness is lightened by repeated evidence of men's courage and humanity. Blunden's realism does not preclude the use of a traditional vocabulary of praise: he can applaud the storming of Beaumont Hamel by the Highland and Naval divisions, and that of St Pierre Divion by his own division, as 'a feat of arms vieing with any recorded';[93] and subtly but pervasively he asserts the gallantry of his fellow-officers and men. The Quartermaster, 'a man whose warmth of heart often cheers me in these later times, a plain, brave, affectionate man'; a new medical officer going round the front-line with his flask in the foul cold, and being 'admired for his courage and charity at once'; Sergeant Worley, who had been the author's 'fearless, tireless "second"' at Third Ypres; C.S.M. Lee, 'tall, blasphemous, and brave'; the Adjutant's 'grave gallantry and quiet conversation' as he lay badly wounded, waiting for stretcher-bearers; the arrival in the battalion of 'the shyest young officer imaginable', who 'later became known to everyone as the most resolute'; a Hampshire colonel, 'sardonic and unshaken' in the 'justly termed . . . Black Line, along the Steenbeck'; Bartlett, 'a genial and gallant man' in another battalion, telephoning ('I hear his self-control still') to report that his headquarters had been pierced by a great shell and over thirty killed or wounded; Colonel Harrison 'with his merry eye and life-giving soldierly gesture' ('His likeness cannot come again in this life, nor can man be more beloved')—[94] these are only a few of the incidental, unobtrusive, but cumulatively effective tributes to the heroism of his companions. ('Barbusse would have "got them wrong",' he notes significantly of one group of men before the Somme, 'save in this: they were all doomed.'[95]) Even in the battalion's grimmest ordeal at Third Ypres—the battle which he saw as 'a vile and inglorious waste of our spirit'—men could still rise to heroic stature:

> What the companies in the forward craters experienced now I never heard in detail. Their narrative would make mine seem petty and ridiculous. The hero was Lindsey Clarke . . . nowadays known for his imaginative sculptures, then for his hoarse voice, modesty and inexhaustible courage. He took charge of all fighting, apparently, and despite being blown off his feet by shells, and struck about the helmet with shrapnel, and otherwise physically harassed, he was ubiquitous and invincible. While Clarke was stalking round the line like a local Cromwell in his great boots, poor Burgess in a pillbox just behind was wringing his hands with excess of pity, and his headquarters was full of wounded men.[96]

'In its moral aspect,' theorises Carrington, 'war resembles other great tragedies: the greater the horror, the nobler the triumph of the man who is not morally ruined by it';[97] and to preserve both courage and humanity at Passchendaele was an achievement worth recording. Horror and heroism are similarly interwoven throughout Blunden's narrative: this is what gives it its special distinction. Yet his awareness of the one never leads him to discount the other, nor does he ever glorify or seek to justify the war itself. What he expresses so poignantly is the paradoxical greatness of spirit men revealed in it:

> War had been 'found out', overwhelmingly found out [he wrote in 1929 in an essay on the Somme]. War is an ancient imposter, but none of his masks and smiles and gallant trumpets can any longer

delude us; he leads the way through the cornfields to the cemetery of all that is best. The best is, indeed, his special prey. What men did in the battle of the Somme, day after day, and month after month, will never be excelled in honour, unselfishness, and love; except by those who come after and resolve that their experience shall never again fall to the lot of human beings.[98]

Blunden is the supreme practitioner of what Sassoon calls 'the art of reminiscence'; yet even at its finest the memoir is an impure and defective art-form. The inherent superiority of the novel lies in its not being necessarily confined to the single consciousness of an author-protagonist, and in its not being limited, as autobiographies are by their very nature, to the author's actual experiences—which could be 'tedious and repetitional', as Sassoon notes, or 'local, limited, incoherent', as Blunden feared (quite needlessly) his own might prove.[99] Sassoon himself exemplifies some of the hazards. He cast his autobiographical trilogy in semi-fictional form by adopting the persona of George Sherston, 'a simplified version of my "outdoor self"' who was 'denied the complex advantage of being a soldier poet'.[100] This strategem ensures thematic unity and an admirable concentration of effect in *Memoirs of a Fox-Hunting Man* (where accounts of his early literary endeavours would have been a distraction), and also in *Memoirs of an Infantry Officer*—though here the advantage is more doubtful since Sherston is so evidently Sassoon himself, and the reader is tantalisingly aware that there was an additional, poetic dimension to the author's protest which is not acknowledged in the *Memoirs*. In *Sherston's Progress*, however, the device seems valueless, and in spite of the implied promise of the title the narrative itself fails notably to present a progressive discovery of truth. The trilogy as a whole is remarkable for its combination of an uncensored narrative of war experience with a growing awareness of the moral issues Sassoon came to see as being involved. Graves offers *Goodbye to All That* as 'a story of what I was, not what I am',[101] though he never in practice dissociates himself from certain of his wartime attitudes; Blunden presents his war experiences in a rich blend of immediacy and retrospective emotion; Sassoon deliberately exploits the discrepancy between then and now, juxtaposing past and present states of consciousness. At significant points these coalesce— when his reflecting wartime self achieves insights, for example, which he still endorses; but often they remain discrete, so that he presents a multiple awareness, describing his past self very honestly at each stage of his development, but 'placing' that self in the light of his maturing wisdom. The irony thus generated has an obviously normative function, undercutting his own rash heroism on more than one occasion, as when, during the battle of Arras, he checks some Cameronians who were retreating because (they told him) the Germans were all around them and they had run out of bombs:

> Feeling myself to be, for the moment, an epitome of Flintshire infallibility, I assumed an air of jaunty unconcern; tossing my bomb carelessly from left hand to right and back again, I inquired, 'But where *are* the Germans?'—adding 'I can't see any of them.' This effrontery had its effect (though for some reason I find it difficult to describe this scene without disliking my own behaviour). The Cameronian officers looked round them and recovered their composure. Resolved to show them what intrepid reinforcements were, I assured Macnair that he needn't worry any more and we'd soon put things straight. . . .[102]

Such irony, however, can prove double-edged, as it does when applied—protectively no doubt—to his own protest against the war. By casting implications of youthful folly on what was a profoundly serious moral action (as well as on what were at the time profoundly serious risks in battle), he betrays a radical, still unresolved uncertainty, which is most apparent in *Sherston's Progress* in his failure to analyse convincingly his reasons for returning to the war. ('A tumult in his own "little world of man" . . . grew up,' comments Blunden, 'and even he, in those ever companionable . . . prose reminiscences of his, seems scarcely able to investigate it to the full.'[103]) Significantly, the conflict posed between the claims of soldiering and pacifism is not explored—as a novelist might have explored it—through the narrative itself. Although *Memoirs of an Infantry Officer* traces very convincingly his developing awareness of the nature of war and the reversal of his early attitudes towards it, *Sherston's Progress* does not seem designed to follow this theme through. Indeed in this third volume of the trilogy the potentialities of fiction or of semi-fiction are ignored: in spite of his repeated references to art, Sassoon remains committed to the inconsequence of actual experience, including his long hunting interlude in Ireland, his uneventful tour of duty in Palestine, and his enthusiastic return to battle on the Western Front. So that the narrative, while biographically truthful, and indeed revelatory of his own confusions, seems artistically and thematically disappointing. We sense the need, on the one hand, of a more unremitting attention to form, and on the other, of a deeper self-analysis, of the kind Guy Chapman offers when he confesses that he stayed with his battalion after Passchendaele, when he could have transferred to England, not only because of *esprit de corps* and a sense of comradeship, but also because he felt, perhaps, 'a subtler, even a vile, attraction'. He experienced 'shrivelling fear' in action, he admits:

> And yet, in spite of it, there grew a compelling fascination. I do not think I exaggerate: for in that fascination lies War's power. Once you have lain in her arms you can admit no other mistress. You may loathe, you may execrate, but you cannot deny her. No lover can offer you defter caresses, more exquisite tortures, such breaking delights. No wine gives fiercer intoxication, no drug more vivid exaltation. Every writer of imagination who has set down in honesty his experience has confessed it. Even those who hate her most are prisoners to her spell. They may rise from her embraces, pillaged, soiled, it may be ashamed; but they are still hers. 'J'avais beau me débarbouiller et me laver les mains en la quittant, son odeur restait en moi.'[104]

* * *

Honesty, inclusiveness, psychological and moral insight, and the accurate notation of experience are all desiderata in war literature, but they are not sufficient in themselves: they must be combined with the search for an appropriate form and the struggle to articulate through this the author's complex vision of the truth. Such a combination is achieved most notably by Frederic Manning in *The Middle Parts of Fortune*—a novel which must rank as one of the masterpieces of war literature in English, uniting art with authenticity, fictional sophistication with documentary and psychological realism, and imposing significant form on the large untidiness of life and death.

It was published in 1929 in a strictly limited edition, because of its frank rendering of the incidental obscenities of soldiers' speech; it became available to a wider public the next year, in the bowdlerised version called *Her Privates We*; but it has now (in 1977) been republished in its original unexpurgated form. It is a work which establishes the supremacy of the novel, the great *genre* of the preceding century, in presenting and interpreting what Manning describes as 'the peculiarly human activity' of war; and he brings to this task analytical as well as creative powers. He shares with his protagonist, Bourne, a capacity for philosophical and psychological reflection which gives the book an unexpected quality of intellectual challenge, and which helps to make it not only a record of experience in the battle of the Somme, but also a definitive statement of the grimly heroic code he had found operative among his own companions there.

The situation of the protagonist—a cultured intellectual serving as a private soldier, alienated from the members of his own class who are officers, and integrated socially with the Other Ranks—reflects Manning's own experiences as a private in the King's Shropshire Light Infantry. His friend and publisher Peter Davies tells us that though Manning was 'an intellectual of intellectuals—poet, classical scholar, and author of the exquisite *Scenes and Portraits*—delicate in health and fastidious almost to the point of foppishness, he felt it his duty to enlist in the ranks . . .'; and furthermore, that 'he identified himself so completely with the life and point of view of the ordinary soldier that, in publishing the superb record of his experiences among them, he preferred to put only his regimental number, and not his name, on the title-page'—where in fact it did not appear until the posthumous edition of *Her Privates We* in 1943.[105] The anonymity of 'Private 19022' was specially appropriate since he was concerned mainly with 'the anonymous ranks'.

> There were many hundred thousand men in France and Flanders [Blunden reminds us] . . . who had emerged from attack into attack, and then into the next attack, well aware that they must become one morning mere heaps in oozing shell-holes, or bundles on the barbed wire. And still most of these men, obedient, unassuming, mute as Spartans, were expected to smile:
> Are we down-hearted?
> NO————
> Think we shall win?
> No answer. . . .[106]

It is of such men that Manning writes; and the distinction of the novel derives partly from his sympathetic but unsentimental depiction of his fellow-soldiers.

Charles Sorley had complained in July 1915 about 'the growing tendency to think that every man drops overboard his individuality between Folkestone and Boulogne, and becomes on landing either "Tommy" with a character like a nice big fighting pet bear and an

incurable yearning and whining for mouth
cigarettes: or the Young Officer with a face like
of giggling in the face of death'.[107] The you
them—could speak for themselves so effectivel
accustomed to seeing the war through their ey
their ardours and endurances, their conflic
agonised sense of responsibility for the sufferings as well as
welfare of their men. But with few exceptions the men themselves
were less articulate. R. H. Tawney, who fought as a sergeant on the
Somme, described his experiences in an article published in August
1916, giving some moving glimpses of his companions in the ranks:
' "If it's all like this it's a cake-walk," said a little man beside me, the
kindest and bravest of friends, whom no weariness could discourage or
danger daunt, a brick-layer by trade, but one who could turn his hand
to anything, the man whom of all others I would choose to have
beside me at a pinch; but he's dead.'[108] Later that autumn Tawney
protested bitterly in 'Some Reflections of a Soldier' against the false
stereotype of 'Tommies' as 'merry assassins', invariably cheerful,
revelling in the excitement of war, finding sport in killing other men,
'rejoicing in the opportunity of a "scrap" in which we know that
more than half our friends will be maimed or killed'; whereas in
reality, he maintained, war is for most soldiers 'a load that they carry
with aching bones, hating it, and not unconscious of its monstrosity,
hoping dimly that, by shouldering it now, they will save others from
it in the future. . . .'[109] Sassoon and Owen were soon to come
forward as spokesmen for the inarticulate anonymous mass of those
who had 'no skill/To speak of their distress, no, nor the will'; but they
tended to see their men predominantly from an officer's point of
view, sometimes with rather limited understanding:

It's queer, I thought, how little one really knows about the men
[records Sassoon, with the honesty that makes his memoirs so
invaluable as a source-book]. In the Line one finds out which are
the duds, and one builds up a sort of comradeship with the tough
and willing ones. But back in billets the gap widens and one can't
do much to cheer them up. I could never understand how they
managed to keep as cheery as they did through such drudgery and
discomfort, with nothing to look forward to but going over the
top. . . .[110]

'The men are just as Bairnsfather has them—expressionless lumps',

wen's astonishingly crass remark on first joining his battalion in
ace.[111] And though the discovery of working-class virtues by
middle-class officers was one of the most significant social experiences
of the war, differences in rank and the paternalism of the relationship
made inevitably for gulfs in understanding and communication.

> Did I know you [asks Guy Chapman]? I censored your letters,
> casually, hurriedly avoiding your personal messages, your poig-
> nant hopes: 'when we've finished with Fritz', 'roll on, leaf'. Alas!
> some of you have finished with Fritz many years back, and your
> 'leaf' rolled over and over, tumbled by high explosive. Did any of
> us know you? Ever pierce your disguise of goose-turd green,
> penetrate your young skin and look through you to learn the secret
> which is the essential spirit, the talisman against the worst that fate
> can offer? No. That was yours. As you would have said: 'Gawd
> knows; but 'E won't split on a pal.' So you still remain a line of
> bowed heads, of humped shoulders, sitting wearily in the rain by a
> roadside; waiting, hoping, waiting—but unknown.[112]

The Middle Parts of Fortune is the most sustained and successful
attempt in English at portraying the war from the point of view of the
Other Ranks; and its insights are deepened, not invalidated, by the
way experience is rendered through the fine consciousness of Bourne
himself as well as through the more limited perceptions of his
companions and the deeper understanding of the narrator. Manning
avoids the outmoded clichés of wartime journalism—which was only
to be expected—but he also avoids the more fashionable and
persuasive clichés of anti-war propaganda. He does not seek to
portray the troops as anonymous cannon-fodder or archetypal
victims like Williamson's symbolically named 'John Bullock' in *The
Patriot's Progress*. Each man is sharply differentiated; and their
interaction with each other and with those of other ranks is a finely
observed study in both character and military sociology. ('Here
indeed,' notes Cyril Falls approvingly, 'are the authentic British
infantrymen.'[113]) The mode is, of course, realistic: these men are
creatures of appetite, habitual scroungers, often drunk, and foul-
mouthed to a degree. Yet though their lives involve elements of
grossness and brutality, they also display complex patterns of mutual
respect and tolerance, and comradeship which rises on occasion, as
Bourne tells the Padre, 'to an intensity of feeling which friendship
never touches.'[114] As individuals they are capable of delicacy as well

as depth of feeling, both of which are evident when Pritchard speaks
of Swale's death in the first attack:

'. . . both 'is legs 'ad bin blown off, pore bugger; an' 'e were dyin'
so quick you could see it. But 'e tried to stand up on 'is feet." 'elp
me up", 'e sez, "'elp me up."— "You lie still, chum," I sez to 'im,
"you'll be all right presently." An' 'e jes gives me one look, like 'e
were puzzled, an' 'e died.'

Bourne felt all his muscles tighten. Tears were running down
Pritchard's inflexible face, like rain-drops down a window-pane;
but there was not a quaver in his voice, only that high unnatural
note which a boy's has when it is breaking; and then for the first
time Bourne noticed that Swale, Pritchard's bed-chum, was not
there; he had not missed him before. He could only stare at
Pritchard, while his own sight blurred in sympathy.

'Well, anyway' said Martlow, desperately comforting; ''e
couldn't 'ave felt much, could 'e, if 'e said that?'

'I don't know what 'e felt,' said Pritchard, with slowly filling
bitterness, 'I know what I felt.'

'Bourne, you can take that bloody bucket back to where you
pinched it from,' said Corporal Tozer, as he came into the tent,
wiping the soap out of his ears with a wet and dirty towel, and
Bourne slipped out as inconspicuously as a cat. Still rubbing his
neck and ears Corporal Tozer caught sight of Pritchard's face,
and noticed the constraint of the others. Then he remembered
Swale.

'Get those blankets folded and put the tent to rights,' he said
quietly. 'You'd better open it up all round and let some air in; it
stinks a bit in here.'

He picked up his tunic, put it on, and buttoned it slowly.

'Swale was a townie of yours, wasn't he, Pritchard?' he said
suddenly. 'A bloody plucky chap, an' only a kid too. I'm damned
sorry about him.'

'That's all right, corporal,' answered Pritchard evenly. 'Bein'
sorry ain't goin' to do us 'ns no manner o' good. We've all the
sorrow we can bear of our own, wi'out troublin' ourselves wi' that
o' other folk. We 'elp each other all we can, an' when we can't 'elp
the other man no more, we must jes 'elp ourselves. But I tell thee,
corporal, if I thought life was never goin' to be no different, I'd as
lief be bloody well dead myself.'

He folded up his blanket neatly, as though he were folding up something he had finished with and would never use again. Then he looked up.

'I took 'is paybook an' some letters out o' 'is tunic pocket, but I left 'is identity-disc for them as finds 'im. If our chaps hang on to what we got, there'll be some buryin' parties out. There's 'is pack, next mine. I suppose I'd better 'and them letters in at th' orderly-room. There were a couple o' smutty French photographs, which I tore up. 'e were a decent enough lad, but boys are curious about such things; don't mean no 'arm, but think 'em funny. 'Tis all in human nature. An' I'll write a letter to 'is mother. Swales is decent folk, farmin' a bit o' land, an' I'm only a labourin' man, but they always treated me fair when I worked for 'em.'

'I suppose Captain Malet will write to her,' said Corporal Tozer.

'Cap'n'll write, surely,' said Pritchard. ''e's a gentleman is Cap'n Malet an' not one to neglect any little duties. We all knew Cap'n Malet before the war started, an' before 'e were a cap'n. But I'll write Mrs Swale a letter myself. Cap'n Malet, 'e mus' write 'undreds o' them letters, all the same way; 'cause there ain't no difference really, 'cept tha know'st the mother, same as I do.'[115]

The episode shows how the military community has evolved its own decencies of sympathy and grief—we are far removed from the callousness of *All Quiet on the Western Front*, where the young men are waiting for their friend's death to secure his coveted airman's boots. The pity of war is fully present here, and it is to recur throughout the novel, especially with the deaths of Martlow and of Bourne himself. Yet it is not the only or indeed the dominating theme. In the world these characters inhabit death is common, though not seen as commonplace, and the need to face its continual menace or to escape awareness of it temporarily is the basic condition of their lives. In its original format *Her Privates We* had an emblematic cover-illustration, showing a grim-faced infantryman in steel-helmet, cape and battle-order, followed closely by a skeleton laying its bony fingers on his shoulder. Clearly the man is doomed (like Bourne and his companions), but his dogged, powerful, resolute appearance dominates the picture as he trudges on apparently regardless of Death's summons. This epitomises the predicament and the response of soldiers in the novel: 'The problem which confronted them all equally, though some were unable or unwilling to define it, did not concern death so much as the affirmation of their own will in the face of death'; and this affirmation has to be made over and over again by continual and sometimes agonising efforts:

> Most of them had made their decision [about the war] once and for all, and were willing to abide by the consequences, without reviewing it. It was useless to contrast the first challenging enthusiasm which had swept them into the army, with the long and bitter agony they endured afterwards. It was the unknown which they had challenged; and when the searching flames took hold of their very flesh, the test was whether or not they should flinch under them. The men knew it. We can stick it, they said; and they had to retrieve their own failures, to subdue their own doubts, to master their own pitiful human weaknesses, only too conscious for the most part, even when they broke into complaints, that the struggle with their own nature was always inconclusive.[116]

This on-going struggle with their own nature in the determination to 'stick it' is the central experience of the novel (which was, not surprisingly, one of T. E. Lawrence's favourite war books); and it constitutes a genuinely heroic theme, which the whole narrative is designed to explore and emphasise.

The action is confined with classical economy to three phases of one battalion's experiences on the Somme. It opens with the aftermath of a successful attack, which is recreated in the memory and from the point of view of the protagonist. This is followed by a period of rest, recuperation and retraining while the battalion is brought up to strength again—a period which reveals the characters of the men, their relationships with each other, and their attitudes to the war. Then comes their return to the line and another attack—unsuccessful this time—followed by a spell of trench-duty during which Bourne takes part in a night raid and is killed on his way back through No Man's Land. The period and scope of the action are restricted: so too is the world portrayed. We are shown nothing of life outside the battle and rest areas and nothing of the soldiers' private lives except what is revealed by their conversations or letters and parcels from home. (Significantly, we do not even know the hero's Christian name.) Theirs is an enclosed, self-sufficient military world, which most of them entered voluntarily, but from which there can be no escape except by death or wounds, or temporarily in certain circumstances by promotion. The deliberate restriction of range enables Manning to explore that world in depth; and though its abnormality is rooted in the special conditions of the Western Front, the Shakespearian chapter-headings suggest that it has universal as well as historical significance, since the situations portrayed and men's response to them are in their essence not peculiar to the war of 1914–18, but recurrent in human experience.

The first phase of the narrative establishes the physical, and still more the psychological experience of battle. The attack at the beginning was not the battalion's first action but the culmination of five weeks' fighting on the Somme, and in its aftermath the survivors are shown in a state of nervous as well as physical exhaustion:

> 'Come on [says a young officer]. . . . you and I are two of the lucky ones, Bourne; we've come through without a scratch; and if our luck holds we'll keep moving out of one bloody misery into another, until we break, see, until we break.' Bourne felt a kind of suffocation in his throat: there was nothing weak or complaining in Mr Clinton's voice, it was full of angry soreness. . . . 'Don't talk so bloody wet,' Bourne said to him through the darkness. 'You'll never break.'[117]

The officer 'gave no sign of having heard the sympathetic but indecorous rebuke'; but the phrase echoes in Bourne's mind as he falls asleep that night after reliving the attack in memory—the crossing of No Man's Land under heavy shellfire, the desperate hand-to-hand fighting in the German trenches, the glimpse of two men of another regiment breaking back, momentarily demoralised, until Sergeant-Major Glasspool checked their flight:

> 'Where the bloody hell do you reckon you're going?'
> He rapped out the question with the staccato of a machine-gun; facing their hysterical disorder, he was the living embodiment of a threat.
> 'We were ordered back,' one said, shamefaced and fearful.
> 'Yes. You take your fuckin' orders from Fritz,' Glasspool, white-lipped and with heaving chest, shot sneeringly at them. They came to heel quietly enough, but all the rage and hatred in their hearts found an object in him, now. He forgot them as soon as he found them in hand.
> 'You're all right, chum,' whispered Bourne, to the one who had spoken, 'Get among your own mob again as soon as there's a chance.'

The man only looked at him stonily. . . .[118]

Finally Bourne is overwhelmed by thoughts of death and mutilation, and by memories of the unburied corpses in Trones Wood—'Briton and Hun impartially confounded, festering, fly-blown corruption, the pasture of rats, blackening in the heat, swollen with distended bellies, or shrivelling away within their mouldering rags. . . . Out of one bloody misery into another, until we break. One must not break.' And with this thought, 'One must not break', he sinks into oblivion.

In the second phase—of recovery and further preparation—these experiences are overlaid by the pleasures of food, drink, rest and sensuality, and by routine activities out of the line; but they cannot be forgotten. Indeed the knowledge that they are bound to recur is always present. ('They've only let us come 'ere for a couple of days to 'ave a bon time before they send us up into the shit again,' predicts Corporal Greenstreet when they find themselves in reasonable comfort at Bruay.) The men have already shown their courage ('I didn't think heroism was such a common thing' says Bourne), but they are sceptical about 'chivalrous commonplaces' about patriotism, sacrifice, duty and honour—indeed 'in moments of bitterness it seemed to them that duty and honour were merely the pretexts on which they were being deprived of their most elementary rights'.[119] They dislike intensely the 'romantic swagger' of their temporary C.O. from another regiment; but like Frank Richards they respect good fighting officers and stern just disciplinarians who look after their men. Their notions of the cause for which they are fighting are clouded or contradictory; and though most of them acknowledge that the Germans must be stopped somehow, they find themselves trapped in a situation where they have to evolve and live by their own code of values, with little regard to religious, political or patriotic considerations:

These apparently rude and brutal natures comforted, encouraged, and reconciled each other to fate, with a tenderness and tact which was more moving than anything in life. They had nothing; not even their own bodies, which had become mere implements of warfare. They turned from the wreckage and misery of life to an empty heaven, and from an empty heaven to the silence of their own hearts. They had been brought to the last extremity of hope, and yet they put their hands on each others' shoulders and said with a passionate conviction that it would be all right, though they had faith in nothing, but in themselves and in each other.[120]

This vision of the men sustaining—or perhaps creating—human values in a meaningless world, a metaphysical vacuum, is substantiated by the novel as a whole; and their code, significantly, is based on the familiar virtues of comradeship and courage. This is why, despising 'slackers and conchies' at home, they also look with loathing and contempt on the deserter Miller, who had disappeared before their very first attack and is now under arrest. He figures throughout the novel, in his cunning, degeneracy and cowardice, as the antithesis of the code they live and die by.

> They were bitter and summary in their judgment on him. The fact that he had deserted his commanding-officer, which would be the phrase used to describe his offence on the charge-sheet, was as nothing compared to the fact that he had deserted them. They were to go through it while he saved his skin. It was about as bad as it could be, and if one were to ask any man who had been through that spell of fighting what ought to be done in the case of Miller, there could only have been one answer. Shoot the bugger. But [reflects Bourne, with sure insight] if that same man were detailed as one of the firing-party, his feelings would be modified considerably.[121]

Their verdict still stands, however, when Miller's death-sentence is commuted to penal servitude and he returns to duty: ' "They ought to 'ave shot that bugger," said Minton, indifferently. " 'e's either a bloody spy or a bloody coward, an' 'e's no good to us either way." ' There is something repulsive about Miller's appearance, something indecent about his very presence; and his symbolic role becomes even clearer when he deserts again on the eve of their next attack, so that he never faces, like them, the test of action. His self-regarding cowardice is juxtaposed with their anguished endurance and commitment to each other, with the qualities epitomised in the grotesque, lugubrious figure of Weeper Smart: 'Bourne found himself contrasting Miller with Weeper Smart, for no one could have had a greater horror and dread of war than Weeper had. It was a continuous misery to him, and yet he endured it. Living with him, one felt instinctively that in any emergency he would not let one down, that he had in him, curiously enough, an heroic strain.'[122]

Their heroism, like Weeper's, lies not in freedom from fear, but in their knowing within themselves and struggling to overcome the fear that Miller yields to. In David Jones's *In Parenthesis* the heroic dimension sometimes seems to be imposed on the troops by his over-insistent analogies with martial legends of the past: in Manning's novel it is firmly established by his presentation of the characters in speech and action, by his analysis of their emotions, and above all by his insight into 'the moral and spiritual conflict, almost superhuman in its agony, within [them]' at times of crisis.

Their previous experiences mean that when they march back to the line in preparation for their next show, many of them know what awaits them; yet their initial mood is one of cheerful defiance:

The men sang, sang to keep up cheerful hearts:

> ''ere we are, 'ere we are, 'ere we are, again,
> Pat and Mac, and Tommy and Jack, and Joe!
> Never mind the weather! Now then, all together!
> Are wé dówn 'eártéd? NO! ('ave a banana!)
> 'ere we are, 'ere we are . . .'

It might have gone on indefinitely, but the men suddenly switched on to *Cock Robin*, into which some voices would interject 'another poor mother 'as lost 'er son,' as though to affront the sinister fate against which they were determined to march with swagger. As they marched through one little village, at about ten o'clock, doors suddenly opened and light fell through the doorways, and voices asked them where they were going. 'Somme! Somme!' they shouted, as though it were a challenge. 'Ah, no bon!' came the kindly pitying voices in reply; and even after the doors closed again, and they had left that village behind, the kindly voices seemed to drift across the darkness, like the voices of ghosts: 'Somme! Ah, no bon!'[123]

The note of warning doom is unmistakable; yet that first day's march ends in hilarity, as they sing 'one of their regimental marching-songs, chronicling in parody their own deeds' to the tune of the Marseillaise:

> 'At La Clytte, at La Clytte,
> Where the Westshires got well beat,
> And the bullets blew our buttons all away,

And we ran, yes, we ran,
From that fuckin' Alleman;
And now we are happy all the day!'

That first euphoria, however, could not be long sustained. 'Between
the acting of a fearful thing/And the first motion, all the interim is /
Like a phantasma or a hideous dream', is the epigraph to one of the
chapters; and in this section of the novel Manning charts all the
modulations in their feelings, as a group and as individuals,
throughout the long prelude to their attack—from the first briefing
(disrupted by a lugubrious aside of Weeper Smart's), the postpone-
ments and changes of plan, the rehearsals and final preparations, up to
the peak of tension before zero-hour:

> Bourne's fit of shakiness increased, until he set his teeth to
> prevent them chattering in his head; and after a deep, gasping
> breath, almost like a sob, he seemed to recover to some
> extent. . . . He heard men breathing irregularly beside him, as he
> breathed himself; he heard them licking their lips, trying to
> moisten their mouths; he heard them swallow, as though over-
> coming a difficulty in swallowing; and the sense that others
> suffered equally or more than himself, quietened him. Some men
> moaned, or even sobbed a little, but unconsciously, and as though
> they struggled to throw off an intolerable burden of oppression.
> His eyes met Shem's, and they both turned away at once from the
> dread and question which confronted them. More furtively he
> glanced in Martlow's direction; and saw him standing with bent
> head. Some instinctive wave of pity and affection swelled in him,
> until it broke into another shuddering sigh, and the boy looked up,
> showing the whites of his eyes under the brim of his helmet. They
> were perplexed, and his underlip shook a little. Behind him Bourne
> heard a voice almost pleading: 'Stick it out, chum.'
> 'A don't care a fuck,' came the reply, with a bitter harshness
> rejecting sympathy.
> 'Are you all right, kid?' Bourne managed to ask in a fairly steady
> voice; and Martlow only gave a brief affirmative nod. Bourne
> shifted his weight on to his other foot, and felt the relaxed knee
> trembling. It was the cold. If only they had something to do, it
> might be better. It had been a help simply to place a ladder in
> position. Suspense seemed to turn one's mind to ice, and bind even
> time in its frozen stillness; but at an order it broke. It broke, and one

became alert, relieved. They breathed heavily in one another's faces. They looked at each other more quietly, forcing themselves to face the question.

'We've stuck it before,' said Shem.[124]

The parallels, not too schematic, between this attack and the previous one emphasise the repetitious nature of their ordeal. Here again, in the confusion, there are men—some wounded but some whole and sound—who break back in disorder:

> One of the fugitives charged down on Jakes, and that short but stocky fighter smashed the butt of his rifle to the man's jaw, and sent him sprawling. Bourne had a vision of Sergeant-Major Glasspool.
>
> 'You take your fuckin' orders from Fritz!' he shouted as a triumphant frenzy thrust him forward.[125]

After the exultation and horror of the charge, after Shem has been wounded and Martlow killed, after Bourne himself has killed in his berserk fury for revenge, after they have cleared the German trench and then been forced to fall back to their own lines, it is Bourne's turn to write to Martlow's mother as Pritchard had written to Swale's ('Another poor mother 'as lost 'er son'); and the pathos is intensified by 'the extraordinary reserve and courage' of her reply. The sense of recurrence and of doom is very strong as character after character is killed or wounded, in a sequence which culminates in Bourne's own death. 'Fortune? O, most true, she is a strumpet', runs the chapter-heading, and ironically, Bourne is hit just when he thinks himself safe. His body is carried in by Weeper Smart, who turns back for him in a vain attempt at rescue ('"A'll not leave thee," said Weeper in an infuriate rage'); but at the end of the novel the corpse is left propped against the side of the trench, like the German corpse Bourne had passed by unregardingly in the opening chapter. Our sense of the malignity of fate is intensified by the knowledge that he had been recommended for a commission and was due to return to England for training—by the knowledge also that his death was due partly to the latent hostility of his new company commander. Yet Bourne had himself insisted on staying with the battalion for the second attack; and although unfair pressure was put on him to volunteer for the fatal patrol, the decision—quite deliberately taken—was his own. He is not a simple victim therefore, but a moral agent, as indeed are all the other characters, although their continual exercise of moral choice can operate only in restricted fields. Reflecting, after the first attack, on the willed acceptance of the risk of death, Bourne had concluded that 'the true inwardness of tragedy lies in the fact that its failure is only apparent, and as in the case of the martyr also, the moral conscience of man has made its own deliberate choice, and asserted the freedom of its being.'[126] At the end of his own life Bourne has made precisely such an existential act of choice, an assertion of the will which defines the self and asserts its values, so that our anger and pity coexist with admiration and acceptance. And Bourne, though exceptional in many ways, is representative in this respect.

'It was hard luck,' said Sergeant-Major Tozer with a quiet fatalism. . . . [He] moved away, with a quiet acceptance of the fact. It was finished. He was sorry about Bourne, he thought, more sorry than he could say. He was a queer chap, he said to himself, as he felt for the dug-out steps. There was a bit of a mystery about him; but then, when you come to think of it, there's a bit of a mystery about all of us.[127]

And with the trite reflection he turns his attention to the other men, whose mysteries remain undisclosed—whose endurance is still under test, and for whom the internal struggle still goes on: 'Then they all bowed over their own thoughts again, listening to the shells bumping heavily outside, as Fritz began to send a lot of stuff over in retaliation for the raid. They sat there silently: each man keeping his own secret.'

5 The Christian as Hero: Waugh's *Sword of Honour*

'"I take it," said Captain Waugh, "that the whole purpose of this examination is to find out whether I have sufficient strength of character to stand the anxiety and shock of battle?"

"Yes," said the psychiatrist, "in a general, unscientific way that does describe it."

"Then why do you make no reference whatever to the most important of all the agents that form a man's character?"

"You mean?"

"Religion," said Captain Waugh.' Eric Linklater, *The Art of Adventure* (London, 1947), p. 49.

'INTERVIEWER: Would you say that there was any direct moral to the army trilogy?

WAUGH: Yes, I imply that there is a moral purpose, a chance of salvation, in every human life. Do you know the old Protestant hymn which goes: "Once to every man and nation/Comes the moment to decide"? Guy is offered this chance by making himself responsible for the upbringing of Trimmer's child. . . . He is essentially an unselfish character.' *Writers at Work. The 'Paris Review' Interviews*, 3rd series, introd. Alfred Kazin (London, 1968), p. 112.

'[The] soldier also, as well as the saint, might write his tractate *de contemptu mundi*, and differ from him only in the angle and spirit from which he surveyed the same bleak reality.' Frederic Manning, *The Middle Parts of Fortune* (London, 1929), p. 137.

The *Sword of Honour* trilogy—probably the greatest work of fiction to emerge from the Second World War—results from Waugh's having deliberately immersed himself in the destructive element, seeking military experience instead of avoiding it like the real-life equivalents of Parsnip and Pimpernell or the group of progressive novelists in firemen's uniform who squirt a significantly feeble jet of water into the blazing shell of Turtle's at the opening of *Officers and Gentlemen*.

Waugh sought active service partly for its potential value to him as a novelist: 'Nothing would be more likely than work in a government office to finish me as a writer,' he wrote in August 1939; 'nothing more likely to stimulate me than a complete change of habit. There is a symbolic difference between fighting as a soldier and serving as a civilian, even if the civilian is more valuable.'[1] There were also deeper emotional compulsions. In *Lions and Shadows* Isherwood describes the delayed effect of the First World War on many of the younger generation:

> We young writers of the middle twenties were all suffering, more or less subconsciously, from a feeling of shame that we hadn't been old enough to take part in the European war. . . . Like most of my generation, I was obsessed by a complex of terrors and longings connected with the idea 'War.' 'War,' in this purely neurotic sense, meant The Test. The test of your courage, your maturity, of your sexual prowess. 'Are you really a Man?' Subconsciously, I believe, I longed to be subjected to this test; but I also dreaded failure. I dreaded failure so much—indeed, I was so certain that I *should* fail—that, consciously, I denied my longing to be tested altogether.[2]

Orwell offers a comparable analysis, beginning with the pacifist reaction to the War among public schoolboys:

> To be as slack as you dared on OTC parades, and to take no interest in the war, was considered a mark of enlightenment. The young officers who had come back, hardened by their terrible experience and disgusted by the attitude of the younger generation to whom this experience meant just nothing, used to lecture us for our softness. Of course they could produce no argument that we were capable of understanding. . . . We merely sniggered at them. . . . For years after the war, to have any knowledge of or interest in military matters . . . was suspect in 'enlightened' circles. 1914–18 was written off as a meaningless slaughter, and even the men who had been slaughtered were held to be in some way to blame. . . . But the dead men had their revenge after all. As the

war fell back into the past, my particular generation, those who had been 'just too young', became conscious of the vastness of the experience they had missed. You felt yourself a little less than a man, because you had missed it. [3]

Hence, he suggests, part at least of the fascination the Spanish Civil War had for people of about his age.

Waugh seems to have gone through a comparable sequence of emotions. As a small boy he had played patriotic war-games with 'the Pistol Troop', defending Britain against imaginary German invasions. ('We were rather priggishly high-minded,' he recalls. ' "Honour" was a word often on our lips. Dishonesty, impurity or cruelty would have been inconceivable to us. . . .') Later, in the summer holidays of 1915, he acted as a messenger in the War Office: 'My ambition was to serve Lord Kitchener. I often passed his door, but was never summoned to his presence. . . . I believed I was genuinely in the King's service; the whole experience was a delight.' [4] By 1919, however, his whole attitude had changed. In his diary entry for 11 November he called the King's proposal for a two-minute silence to commemorate the fallen 'a disgusting idea of artificial nonsense and sentimentality'; [5] and in his last few years at Lancing he was one of the ringleaders in deriding and discrediting the O.T.C.:

. . . Always we drilled with ostentatious incompetence, dropping rifles, turning right instead of left, making the movement of forming fours odd and even numbers together, and so forth. On field days we either hid from action or advanced immediately at the 'enemy' so that we were 'killed' at the first moment of battle.

When, route-marching, we were exhorted to sing, we ignored the ballads sanctified by the infantry of the World War and loped along out of step droning the American ditty:

'I didn't raise my boy to be a soldier.
I brought him up to be my pride and joy.
Who dares to put a rifle on his shoulder,
To shoot another mother's darling boy?' [6]

After he went up to Oxford in 1922, his feud with his tutor, C. R. M. F. Cruttwell, epitomises the antagonism between the war generation and their juniors. Cruttwell, the Dean and subsequently Principal of Hertford, was, Waugh acknowledged later, 'a wreck of the war in which he had served gallantly' (and of which he wrote one of the

standard histories), but for years their antagonism was total.[7] Yet
Waugh seems to have felt the need to match the courage shown by
Cruttwell's generation. His own travels in Abyssinia, the Arctic and
South America were primarily in search of material for journalism,
travel-books or fiction, but he was also proving his capacity for
enduring hardships and discomfort, and occasionally danger. 'We
have most of us marched and made camp since then,' he reflected in
1945, 'gone hungry and thirsty, lived where pistols are flourished and
fired. At that time it seemed an ordeal, an initiation to manhood.'[8]
The war itself came as a challenge to him as a man and as an artist. He
threw himself enthusiastically into soldiering, took part in a Commando raid on Bardia, and gave ample proof of his cool courage
under fire in the campaign in Crete. (General Laycock, his commander there, said afterwards that 'Evelyn and Randolph Churchill
were two of the bravest officers he had ever known.') Lord
Birkenhead, who served with Waugh in Yugoslavia in 1944–5,
writes of his 'extraordinary love affair with the army'[9]—a metaphor
which Waugh himself employs and elaborates in both *Brideshead
Revisited* and *Sword of Honour*. Charles Ryder and Guy Crouchback
are of course both fictional creations, but both of them reflect aspects
of their creator—not least in the romantic dream which underlies
their military enthusiasm. Both come to disillusion, but the poig-
nancy of this derives from the intensity of the emotions they had
invested in the illusion—which could itself be genuinely inspi-
rational. To be wholly without illusions from the outset is, it seems, to
exist on a more superficial, not a deeper level of awareness, which
suggests the need for a more careful scrutiny of the 'illusions'
themselves. Ryder's comments on Hooper, for example, work
entirely to the latter's disadvantage:

> Hooper had no illusions about the Army. . . . He had come to it
> reluctantly, under compulsion, after he had made every feeble
> effort in his power to obtain deferment. He accepted it, he said,
> 'like the measles.' Hooper was no romantic. He had not as a child
> ridden with Rupert's horse or sat among the camp fires at Xanthus-
> side; at the age when my eyes were dry to all save poetry,—that
> stoic, red-skin interlude which our schools introduce between the
> fast flowing tears of the child and the man—Hooper had wept
> often, but never for Henry's speech on St. Crispin's day, nor for
> the epitaph at Thermopylae. The history they taught him had had
> few battles in it but, instead, a profusion of detail about humane

legislation and recent industrial change. Gallipoli, Balaclava, Quebec, Lepanto, Bannockburn, Roncevales, and Marathon—these, and the Battle in the West where Arthur fell, and a hundred such names whose trumpet-notes, even now in my sere and lawless state, called to me irresistibly across the intervening years with all the clarity and strength of boyhood, sounded in vain to Hooper.[10]

Waugh's enforced inaction in 1942–3, due to his own unpopularity and inability to 'manage men', which made him virtually unemployable, bred bitterness and disappointment. Yet the experiences he had garnered were to be invaluable for him as an artist—as indeed he clearly recognised even at the time.

I dislike the Army [he wrote petulantly in August 1943]. I want to get to work again. I do not want any more experiences in life. I have quite enough bottled and carefully laid in the cellar, some still ripening, most ready for drinking, a little beginning to lose its body. I wrote to Frank [Pakenham] very early in the war to say that its chief use would be to cure artists of the illusion that they were men of action. It has worked its cure with me. I have succeeded, too, in dissociating myself very largely with the rest of the world. I am not impatient of its manifest follies and don't want to influence opinions or events, or expose humbug or anything of that kind. I don't want to be of service to anyone or anything. I simply want to do my work as an artist.[11]

This was not a permanent mood. He welcomed the chance of active service in Yugoslavia; in 1945 he was eager to influence opinion and events so as to be of service to the millions of Catholics in Croatia who were falling under Communist rule; and impatience with manifest follies and humbug was to be the motive force of much of his later writing. But the primacy of his art was certainly to be a constant.

As an artist, he is the most accomplished of all those considered in this study, but he is also the most controversial and provocative. 'You see it is equally possible to give the right form to the wrong thing, and the wrong form to the right thing,' says Lactantius in *Helena*;[12] and though the rhetorician's commonplace is anathema to critics who assume (as I do) near-identity of style and meaning, of aesthetic form and moral content, we may be tempted to invoke a comparable formula as we find ourselves relishing Waugh's consummate artistry while repudiating many of his values. ('His *bons mots* deserve to be repeated exactly,' writes A. E. Dyson in a finely perceptive essay: 'Take away the verbal precision, and you crash down too violently on the meaning.'[13])

That verbal precision, however, is itself a virtue for the novelist as well as the mere craftsman. Lactantius, uncertain what to express, none the less 'delighted in writing, in the joinery and embellishment of his sentences, in the consciousness of high rare virtue when every word had been used in its purest and most precise sense, in the kitten games of syntax and rhetoric'.[14] In Waugh such stylistic virtuosity contributes not just to its own peculiar pleasure, but to the exact registration and the subtle if at times eccentric valuation of experience. When interviewed about his work in 1962 he complained that the questions put to him were dealing too much with the creation of character and not enough with the technique of writing: 'I regard writing not as investigation of character, but as an exercise in the use of language, and with this I am obsessed.'[15] It was an obsession that lay at the very heart of his achievement as a novelist: in the war trilogy, which is his masterpiece, his concern for the niceties of linguistic usage underlies the excellence of dialogue, narrative, and authorial commentary. The very organisation of his sentences, with their conscious elegance of syntax, cadences and punctuation, gives an effect of effortless superiority, of cool urbanity, of detached intelligence in supreme control of its material; and this technical expertise can be employed more daringly, more paradoxically, to convey sympathetic insight, as in the flashback to Virginia's past—to 'her seduction by a friend of her father's, who had looked her up, looked her over, taken her out, taken her in, from her finishing-school in Paris. . . .'[16] The substance of a sensitive 'woman's novel' is condensed by Waugh into a single sentence. For the first time we are given a deeper understanding of the 'bright fashionable girl' Guy married; and the verbal clowning which seems at first sight to preclude a serious response shows the author withholding pity and indignation only to imply their necessity, and diagnosing a cynicism which is not his own but that of the family friend and the social group he represents. The perfect blending of form and substance, which Conrad advocated in his Preface to *The Nigger of the Narcissus*, has become a commonplace in discussions of plot, theme and structure, but his plea for 'an unremitting never-discouraged care for the shape and ring of sentences' is less obviously applicable to contemporary fiction: Waugh is one of the very few modern novelists whose phraseology and syntax are themselves a source of delight, illumination and discovery.

The disposing intelligence which thus manifests itself in sentence structure and verbal wit also controls the organisation of the trilogy as a whole. At first its close-knit unity was not apparent. When *Men at Arms* was first published in 1952 its comic force was immediately recognised, and its authenticity as a picture of Army life. Moreover, the formality of Waugh's procedure, the conscious felicity of style, the progression from retrospective prologue to main narrative, the mannered, almost precious, subdivision of that narrative into three sections—'Apthorpe Gloriosus', 'Apthorpe Furibundus', 'Apthorpe Immolatus'—all testified to the author's awareness of his novel as a work of art. Yet structurally it failed to satisfy. Apart from occasional loose ends in the plot, excessive attention seemed to be given to Apthorpe, while the hero's own progress from idealism to minor disillusion hardly seemed sufficient, thematically, to sustain the whole narrative structure. The dedication, 'To Christopher Sykes: Companion in arms', tended to associate the author with his subject-matter, and this process was carried further in 1955 by the dedication of *Officers and Gentlemen* to Major-General Sir Robert Laycock: Waugh's allusion to 'those exhilarating days when he led and I lamely followed' came near to identifying himself with the limping hero, whose military fortunes so closely paralleled his own. Hence in spite of his assurance in the dedication that this story is 'pure fiction: that is to say of experience totally transformed', it seemed at this stage as if the transformation might be less than total—that this series might develop into an uneasy combination of fiction and autobiography, like some of the First World War hybrids. Waugh's assertion, moreover, in the first edition of *Officers and Gentlemen*, that he had thought at first that the story would run into three volumes but now found that two would do the trick,[17] suggested that the whole thing was being extemporised rather than designed.

Such suspicions, however, did less than justice to Waugh as an artist. His military service, which he later ranked with travel as a major stimulus to his imagination,[18] had already provided him with themes in *Put Out More Flags* and *Brideshead Revisited*. In returning to it now he was exercising the privilege which his *alter ego* Pinfold envied painters—that of returning 'to the same theme time and time again, clarifying and enriching until they have done all they can with it'.[19] The trilogy is his attempt to do all he could with his own war experiences and observations; and far from consisting of unshaped reminiscence, it embodies a grand design, the proportions and significance of which were not fully apparent until *Unconditional Surrender* was published in 1961. The earlier 'less than candid assurance (dictated by commercial interest) that each [volume] was to be regarded as a separate, independent work' has since been repudiated by Waugh himself: he insists in his final recension of the trilogy that it was intended from the outset to be read as a single story.[20] When so read it gains not merely from the completion of an otherwise defective narrative, but from the reader's perception of structural relationships hitherto unapprehended, and of thematic developments startling in their implications.

The trilogy is a form specially appropriate for such progressive revelation. The old three-volume novel, as Kathleen Tillotson has shown, was convenient for publishers, circulating libraries, and readers, but also for authors, presenting them as it did with a structural framework for their narratives. The trilogy is a radically different form, yet it too has artistic and commercial advantages. It provides three novels of normal length at suitable intervals, instead of a single monster which could price itself out of the market. It spreads Income Tax burdens. It keeps the author's name before the public (and whets readers' appetites so that the sales of individual novels reinforce each other), while relieving him of the strain of excessively prolonged gestation. But above all it suggests a way of patterning experience, of imposing clearly perceptible order on a large body of material. This may be overdone, as it is by Grassic Gibbon in the rigid structuring of *A Scots Quair*, or neglected, as in Ford Madox Ford's ambitious Tietjens series; but in Waugh's hands the full potential of the form is realised. Each novel records a distinct phase in the hero's emotional, spiritual, and military progress; each deals with a separate aspect and theatre of war; each forms, as Malcolm Bradbury observes, 'a distinctive experience'. Yet they are closely linked by the continuity of the narrative, the recurrence of major themes, the reappearance of old characters in new roles, and by a formal parallelism: 'All three books,' comments Bradbury, 'begin in light spirit with a series of events in training, set in England, with Guy's mood a hopeful one, and all conclude with events in action abroad, where Guy witnesses and is involved in a betrayal, as a result of which he suffers in reputation, hope and faith.'[21] Each ends, one might add, with a return to England, and each contributes to the elaborate patterning of events, of recurring and contrasting *motifs*, which characterises the trilogy as a whole. The resulting sense of unity in diversity is so satisfying, aesthetically and thematically, that one is tempted to speculate on the unique felicity of tripartite division in any complex work of art.

Certainly, admirers of the trilogy in its original form will not readily be reconciled to Waugh's one-volume recension, published in 1965. We may discount a mere nostalgia for the actual physical form in which the books were first read: for the *aficionado* even the original dust-jackets had their charm, as did the dedications which rooted the narrative in biographical reality, or the 'Synopsis of Preceding Volumes' provided by the author himself in *Unconditional Surrender*, but excised from the one-volume version. More serious are the cuts in the text itself. These were simply intended, Waugh tells us, to remove 'repetitions and discrepancies' and 'passages which, on re-reading, appeared tedious';[22] they may also have facilitated presentation of the novel in this new handsome format; yet they are a grievous loss. Only an author prodigal of wit could have sacrificed so ruthlessly the comic extravaganza on a film of the '45, or the description of a game of Housey-housey organised by Ritchie-Hook, or the episode of the Loamshire officers suspected of being fifth-columnists; the disappearance of all references to Captain Truslove obscures the relation between Guy's boyhood reading and his romantic attitude to war; and the resentful reader misses many other passages which were relished on first reading and remembered long afterwards. (Only occasionally do we applaud Waugh's second thoughts. Colonel Tickeridge's dismissive comment on Guy at the end of *Men at Arms* belied his essential kindliness; the additional effect of bleak disillusion was achieved illegitimately, we may feel, at the expense of consistent characterisation; and the removal of this short passage therefore seems an improvement on the original.) Nor are the changes merely local in effect. The formal structure of the novel is obscured too by the now continuous narration; the three main phases of the action are less obviously distinguished; Guy's returns to England, for example, seem less significant as chapter endings than they did when marking the close of separate volumes. Yet when all such protests have been made, it remains true that these are only minor changes: fundamentally, the main rhythm of the novel is unaltered and its significance unaffected by Waugh's revision. Discriminating readers may well refuse to accept this as the definitive text, but they will not be embarrassed in their interpretation by any changes of attitude, technique or theme between the original trilogy and its 'final' recension.

As a moralist Waugh has always been elusive or provocative. Critics who see literary greatness as dependent on moral insight tend to be ill at ease with comedies like his, which are only intermittently satiric. His refusal to comment on the outrageous content of his early novels can be seen as an extreme reaction against the intrusive narrators of Victorian fiction, and against the predictable moral norms which they invoked. His own cool abnegation of values made cynicism the passport to a world of comic irresponsibility, which must be justified in psychological rather than moral terms—in terms, we may say, of the therapeutic effect of an art-controlled emotional release, a comic catharsis. Nevertheless, Waugh's fiction also flirted with religion and morality: Father Rothschild in *Vile Bodies* makes some typical gestures towards Eternal Truth amid the flux of decadence, which Waugh seems to find both shocking and delightful. This ambivalence towards the world that he portrays is reflected in the ambiguity of *Vile Bodies* or even *A Handful of Dust* (which can be read cynically or satirically according to taste), and in his occasional self-deception about the nature of his own art. He sought to defend the eating of Prudence in *Black Mischief* as an episode showing 'the sudden tragedy when barbarism at last emerges from the shadows and usurps the stage',[23] but this claim hardly counteracts the impression made by the pervasively flippant narration and amoral hero. Here as elsewhere the potential moral pattern is unrealised as the virtues are undermined and the vices mitigated by Waugh's sense of the absurd. We may certainly distinguish between a dead-pan narrative style which seems to be and is in practice cynical, and one which assumes the mask of cynicism to imply normative values which remain unstated. But often the distinction is a fine one, difficult to confirm without more pointers than Waugh's early narrative convention allows, while his own irony tends continually to erode the moral universe towards which he aspires from his native realm of comic anarchy.

In *Brideshead Revisited* we find the opposite extreme of dogmatic commitment and artistic overstatement, for the Catholic-aristocratic values which Waugh now asserts are untested (though not wholly untouched) by his once habitual irony. The fulsomeness with which they are presented is intensified by the narrator-hero's rich corrupt nostalgia, but the problem is not merely one of literary tact. Exquisitely as the vanished past is recalled—and Donat O'Donnell's allusion to Proust is far from inappropriate—we must feel uneasy about this Catholicism which 'is hardly separable from . . . personal romanticism and . . . class loyalty', [24] this religion which figures as a glamorous adjunct to true aristocracy. Nevertheless, there was artistic courage of a kind in Waugh's writing, frankly and without defensive irony, a lament for the doomed English upper class, making public his own private myth of the aristocracy as 'the unique custodians of traditional values in a world increasingly threatened by the bar-barians'. [25] The potent magic of his style induces an unwilling suspension of our disbelief for the moment: his elegiac romantic vision is persuasive and imaginatively compelling within the confines of the work itself. It shrivels only when confronted with reality. Hooper is an amusingly repellent character, but manifestly not representative of Youth in the way Waugh would have us believe. Brideshead itself is beautifully rendered—as is the dinner at Paillard's—but neither can sustain the symbolic value imposed on them by the narrator-hero. Complex truth, it would seem, cannot be told in the simplified terms of either myth or caricature, though these are among Waugh's favourite fictional devices.

For his trilogy he evolves a narrative method which includes both but transcends them, combining his old detached ironic manner with the passionate conviction of his later works, and fusing his comic with his tragic vision in an attempt to do full justice to the facts of war.

These are presented as 'seen and experienced by a single, un-characteristic Englishman', [26] who is uncharacteristic in ways that meet with Waugh's particular approval. There are obvious differ-ences between author and observer-hero—differences in social origins, marital circumstances, and spiritual history—yet in many ways the two are very close. Guy may not be heroic, but he is neither a cipher like Paul Pennyfeather nor a *picaro* like Basil Seal. His undistinguished but honourable service parallels Waugh's own. His values, social, religious and political, seem identical with his creator's; and Waugh is well aware of how unrepresentative these are—how unacceptable to the majority of readers.

News [of the Russian-German alliance] that shook the politicians and young poets of a dozen capital cities brought deep peace to one English heart. . . . [Guy] lived too close to Fascism in Italy to share the opposing enthusiasms of his countrymen. He saw it neither as a calamity nor as a rebirth; as a rough improvisation merely. He disliked the men who were edging themselves into power around him, but English denunciations sounded fatuous and dishonest. . . . The German Nazis he knew to be mad and bad.

Their participation dishonoured the cause of Spain, but the troubles of Bohemia, the year before, left him quite indifferent. When Prague fell, he knew that war was inevitable. He expected his country to go to war in a panic, for the wrong reasons or for no reason at all, with the wrong allies, in pitiful weakness. But now, splendidly, everything had become clear. The enemy at last was plain in view, huge and hateful, all disguise cast off. It was the Modern Age in arms. Whatever the outcome there was a place for him in that battle. [27]

The tolerance of Mussolini, the approval of Franco, the indifference to Munich, the loathing of Russia as much as Germany—these are deliberate affronts to liberal and left-wing orthodoxy. The idea of war as a Crusade in the cause of reaction outrages progressive and pacifist opinion simultaneously. Waugh intends his new value judgments to be as provocative as his old cynicism; and there is no suggestion here of any political divergence between hero and narrator. A traditionalist and cuckold like Tony Last, Guy too lives in a world of betrayal; but Broome provides a firmer base than Hetton for the reassertion of aristocratic values, while Catholicism offers more profound religious insights than Tony's ridiculous (though not wholly ridiculous) C. of E. The spiritual value of these two inherited traditions is embodied in Guy's father, whose deep piety and family pride flower—unexpectedly perhaps—in the charity which was so notably lacking in *Brideshead Revisited*. (It is hard to imagine Charles Ryder saying 'Here's how' to Major Tickeridge, or showing kindness and courtesy to Miss Vavasour of the Marine Hotel; and charity was indeed the virtue Waugh himself found it most difficult to attain.) The affectionate comedy that plays over Mr Crouchback does nothing to discredit his goodness, which is a point of moral reference throughout the trilogy; his function being, as Waugh told F. J. Stopp, 'to keep audible a steady undertone of the decencies and true purpose of life behind the chaos of events and fantastic characters', though he was also to figure as 'a typical victim . . . in the war against the Modern Age'. [28] To this complex of values must be added those of military tradition. After eight years in a spiritual wasteland since the failure of his marriage, eight years of loneliness and shame, Guy (like the hero of *Maud*) is again one with his kind when his country embarks on a just war. Even in his religion he had felt no sense of brotherhood: now he re-establishes communion with his fellow-men in the comradeship of arms—first with the middle-class, unfashionable Halberdiers, then with the upper-class friends of X Commando, the anachronistic 'flower of the nation'.

Such commitments are defensible, though controversial; but the interest of the trilogy lies less in Waugh's initial assertion than in his testing of the hero's values. By the end of *Officers and Gentlemen* Guy can see that he began the war in a state of euphoric illusion; by the end of *Unconditional Surrender* his disenchantment is complete. The Crusade on which he set out proudly and happily becomes a pilgrimage of painful discovery, of humble expiation.

The author's foreknowledge of this is not shared, however, with the reader. There are only a few hints, anticipations, which will be developed in the later sombre movements of the trilogy. It is significant that Sir Roger, at whose tomb Guy prays in the prologue, was a Crusader who never saw the Holy Land but died in a local scuffle 'with a great journey still all before him and a great vow unfulfilled': clearly Waugh foresaw from the outset his own hero's ultimate frustration. Nevertheless, the story of *Men at Arms* is told almost entirely from Guy's point of view, which the narrator seems to share, so that as we read we are fully involved in the process, immersed in the experiences which the hero undergoes.

At this early stage, buoyed up by his romantic idealism, he takes war and soldiering light-heartedly: that is why the comic figure of Apthorpe bulks so large, whereas later episodes are dominated by ambiguous or sinister characters like Ludovic or Frank de Souza. Waugh relishes all the Army's idiosyncrasies of speech and behaviour, its taboos and shibboleths, its stereotyped or wildly eccentric personalities, its tragi-comedies of pettiness and muddle; but in spite of the comic mode which he adopts, Waugh's purpose transcends the satirical: this is not an exposure but an authentic record and joyous celebration of British regimental life (based on his own experiences in the Royal Marines). For those who have known such life, this novel provides the delight—aesthetically suspect but undeniably intense— of recognition; to the uninitiated it gives pleasure by revealing a new, uniquely entertaining social world; for both it quintessentialises an in-group experience known to many, but rarely if ever so well communicated. Robert Graves, for example, strikes a note of strident boastfulness in his account of the Royal Welch Fusiliers, which is hardly redeemed by the unconvincing irony that precedes and follows it—'And so here ends my very creditable (after eleven years) lyrical passage'.[29] Kipling provides excellent vignettes of life in mess and barrack-room, but his own awareness of being an outsider leads to frequent faults in tone: 'The talk rose higher and higher, and the Regimental Band played between the courses, as is the immemorial custom. . . .'[30] That last phrase overstresses what should have been left implicit, and when, a few lines later, Kipling describes the drinking of the Queen's health, his punning comparison between the sacraments of mess and mass inflates, rather offensively, the value of the military ritual. Such overemphasis is a recurrent defect in his portrayal of Army life, whereas Waugh brings to the same material a perfect blend of knowledge and detachment, of enthusiasm and stylistic tact, of love and irony. Guy rejoices in the Halberdiers because of their courage, efficiency, kindliness, and good fellowship, their traditions, their ceremonial, their sense of hierarchy. And Waugh rejoices with him, though retaining some awareness of the limitations of this mode of vision in an age of total war:

> At length when the cloth was drawn for dessert, the brass departed and the strings came down from the minstrels' gallery and stationed themselves in the window embrasure. Now there was silence over all the diners while the musicians softly bowed and plucked. It all seemed a long way from Tony's excursions in no-man's-land; farther still, immeasurably far, from the frontier of Christendom where the great battle had been fought and lost; from those secret forests where the trains were, even then, while the Halberdiers and their guests sat bemused by wine and harmony, rolling east and west with their doomed loads.[31]

This is one of the few points where the narrator registers a sense of the inadequacy of the hero's responses: how inadequate they are we do not learn in full till *Unconditional Surrender*, but even now, with the Halberdiers representing an ideal of chivalric order, we are warned of adjustments to be made (alas) all too soon:

> Those days . . . he realized much later, were his honeymoon, the full consummation of his love of the Royal Corps of Halberdiers. After them came domestic routine, much loyalty and affection, many good things shared, but intervening and overlaying them all the multitudinous, sad little discoveries of marriage, familiarity, annoyance, imperfections noted, discord.[32]

That discord is as fully rendered as the harmony. Waugh excels in his portrayal of the grit in the military machine—the stupidities, 'flaps', inefficiencies, rivalries, personal antagonisms—culminating in the injustice Guy suffers after Apthorpe's death and his estrangement from the Corps.

Yet it is important to note the limits of his disillusion. The Halberdiers may fall short of the perfection he had once attributed to them, but they remain a good regiment, efficient, disciplined and brave, and these are virtues Waugh was never to repudiate. Writing in 1951 to an historian of the sad campaign in Crete, he mentions 'the heartening appearance on the last day when discipline everywhere was low, of a small detachment of the Welch Regiment under a captain, marching in with their equipment in perfect order'.[33] In that nether world of Crete as Waugh so brilliantly portrays it—that Inferno of defeat, disorder, shame—the Halberdiers preserve their honour untarnished. Amid the chaos Colonel Tickeridge and his companion are 'cleanshaven. . . . all their equipment in place, just as they had appeared during battalion exercises at Penkirk'; 'everything was in order' in the Halberdiers' defensive position, where we glimpse them fighting a model holding action; and although after X Commando they seem rather lacking in sophistication, their limitations and strengths are intimately related. (' "They say it's *sauve qui peut* now," said Fido. "Don't know the expression," said Colonel Tickeridge.'[34])

Courage for Waugh remains one of the cardinal virtues, and cowardice an unforgivable sin—Fido Hound lying his way ruthlessly towards safety, Ivor Claire deserting his own men, the Yugoslav partisans failing to support Ritchie-Hook in his last battle. In this world of evil, treachery and cowardice, the Halberdiers' is the life of Do Wel, and it is a malignity of Fate that prevents Guy three times over from accompanying them into battle, so that he is left to face other, deeper crises in which their virtues are of no avail.

These crises involve agonising reappraisals of his own habitual assumptions and beliefs. For nearly two years the war's infinite complexity of pain and pleasure had been accompanied for Guy by an overbalance of enjoyment. For X Commando he had come to feel a deep affection not untouched by what Edmund Wilson calls the 'beglamored snobbery' of *Brideshead Revisited*.[35] His brother officers seemed the living embodiment of an obsolescent but noble aristocratic ideal: ' "The Flower of the Nation", Ian Kilbannock had ironically called them. He was not far wrong.' And for Guy their fineness was epitomised in Ivor Claire:

[He] remembered Claire as he first saw him in the Roman spring in the afternoon sunlight amid the embosoming cypresses of the Borghese Gardens, putting his horse faultlessly over the jumps, concentrated as a man in prayer. Ivor Claire, Guy thought, was the fine flower of them all. He was quintessential England, the man Hitler had not taken into account, Guy thought.[36]

Bernard Bergonzi aptly compares Guy's mood and idiom here with Charles Ryder's in some of the least inhibited passages of *Brideshead Revisited*, but the author stands now in a different relation to his hero, and the syntax of that final sentence shows the narrator hinting that Guy's certainties may be unfounded. (The omission of the last two words in Waugh's recension was a sad mistake.) Cherished prejudices on the relation between heroism and breeding are being jettisoned, however reluctantly. Sarum Smith, who was as socially detestable as Trimmer, behaves rather well in Crete ('He was not a particularly attractive man, but man he was'); while Ivor's cowardice shatters an illusion dear to Waugh as well as to his hero—the belief in a peculiarly aristocratic virtue.[37] This individual failure is soon swamped, however, in the general dishonour of Britain's alliance with Russia. Now, for Guy, the clear moral issues of the war have been confused, its just cause contaminated. He had thought of it as a Crusade: 'Now that hallucination was dissolved, like the whales and turtles on the voyage from Crete, and he was back after less than two years' pilgrimage in a Holy Land of illusion in the old ambiguous world, where priests were spies and gallant friends proved traitors and his country was led blundering into dishonour.'[38]

Dishonour is indeed more widely prevalent than Guy yet realises. The narrator's standards throughout *Officers and Gentlemen* have again been close to the hero's, but the story has been told less exclusively from his point of view. We have been shown many episodes of which Guy is unaware. We know, as he does not, the full extent of Major Hound's disgrace. We have seen Virginia sink to taking Trimmer as a temporary lover. We know how Ivor's betrayal of the values of his caste is paralleled by Ian Kilbannock's: the journalist-peer's cynicism, amusing at first, is revealed as hateful and corrupting when he becomes the main agent of Virginia's final degradation, forcing her against her will into a prolonged liaison with Trimmer. The latter's contemptible commando 'raid' stands in obvious contrast to Guy's patrol at Dakar or the agony of Crete (though his scramble for the boat is an ironic forecast of Ivor Claire's).

And his build-up as a national hero is symptomatic—we suppose—of the replacement of truth and honour by propaganda as the Modern Age girds on its arms.

It is through this darker world that Guy moves in *Unconditional Surrender*. On completing *Officers and Gentlemen* Waugh 'knew that a third volume was needed' but 'did not then feel confident that [he] was able to provide it';[39] indeed more than five years were to pass before he began on *Unconditional Surrender*. His doubt and delay may be attributed in part to his distaste for the material he knew he had to handle in this volume—Crouchback's experiences in Yugoslavia, the final defacing of his own romantic images of war, the deeper probing into his hero's motives and ideals. The atmosphere is one of melancholy verging on despair. The knight's sword of the prologue to *Men at Arms* is replaced by the Sword of Stalingrad, symbolic tribute to what Guy sees as a cruel and evil ally. (The trains in the secret forests had rolled east as well as west with their doomed loads.) Theories of conspiracy, which provided material for farce in earlier volumes, assume sinister significance as Sir Ralph and his communist associates begin to influence the aims and conduct of the war. Treachery and betrayal of trust are now almost commonplaces of behaviour, and even men of honour like Brigadier Cape find themselves having to acquiesce in deeds of shame. The prevailing darkness is of course continually lightened by sardonic comedy, but the only real alternative to despair is offered by Guy's father: '*The Mystical Body doesn't strike attitudes and stand on its dignity* [he writes to Guy]. *It accepts suffering and injustice. It is ready to forgive at the first hint of compunction. . . . Quantitative judgments don't apply. If only one soul was saved that is full compensation for any amount of loss of "face".*'[40] These words, acquiring new solemnity from Mr Crouchback's death and funeral, go on reverberating in Guy's mind until he finds their application to his own life. In remarrying Virginia, down and out now and with child by Trimmer, he is reversing all conventional ideas of individual and family honour.

'Knights errant [he says in self-justification] used to go out looking for noble deeds. I don't think I've ever in my life done a single, positively unselfish action. I certainly haven't gone out of my way to find opportunities. Here was something most unwelcome, put into my hands; something which I believe the Americans describe as "beyond the call of duty"; not the normal behaviour of an officer and a gentleman; something they'll laugh about in Bellamy's.'[41]

His chivalric quest is directed no longer towards adventure, comradeship and victory: it is now a lonely mission of self-sacrifice. Not.
the easy sacrifice of his own life in battle, but the sacrifice of his
personal honour and the pure lineage of which his father was so
proud. To give his name to Trimmer's bastard is the most unwelcome
thing Guy could have dreamed of: he accepts it in the hope that the
soul of the unborn child may thus be saved, for to his new way of
thinking that would be 'full compensation for any amount of loss of
"face" '. This is the climax of the trilogy, the decision which is Guy's
salvation.

In 1955 Waugh had announced that in the next volume he hoped to
deal with 'Crouchback's realization that no good comes from public
causes; only private causes of the soul.'[42] And for Guy the possibility
of simple heroic action is now gone forever. The decline and death of
his old hero Ritchie-Hook are emblematic of Waugh's altered vision.
In Yugoslavia he finds himself helpless in face of the partisans' inertia,
tyranny, and ignorant suspicion, their preoccupation with taking
over the country rather than with fighting Germans. There are
obvious temptations here to retreat into mere comfortable indignation, but confronted with the sufferings of the Jewish refugees,
the archetypal victims of this war, Guy is forced to search his own
heart more deeply and acknowledge the guilt he shares with
Communist and Nazi:

> 'Is there any place that is free from evil [asks Mme Kanyi]? It is
> too simple to say that only the Nazis wanted war. These
> communists wanted it too. It was the only way in which they could
> come to power. Many of my people wanted it, to be revenged on
> the Germans, to hasten the creation of the national state. It seems to
> me there was a will to war, a death wish, everywhere. Even good
> men thought their private honour would be satisfied by war. They
> could assert their manhood by killing and being killed. They
> would accept hardships in recompense for having been selfish and
> lazy. Danger justified privilege. I knew Italians—not very many
> perhaps—who felt this. Were there none in England?'
> 'God forgive me,' said Guy, 'I was one of them.'

With this realisation he 'had come to the end of the crusade to which
he had devoted himself on the tomb of Sir Roger. His life as a
Halberdier was over. All the stamping of the barrack square and the
biffing of imaginary strongholds were finding their consummation in

one frustrated act of mercy.'[43] When that one act of mercy *is* frustrated—when all his efforts on behalf of the Jews result only in their becoming Displaced Persons in Italy instead of Yugoslavia, and when he finds that the Kanyis have been executed because of the very interest he had shown in them—then Guy's cup of bitterness is full to overflowing, and the main narrative comes to an end.

This schematic account distorts by stressing theme at the expense of local excellence: the trilogy, with its highly wrought art, clearly proposes to itself such delight from the whole as is compatible with a distinct gratification from each component part. Yet this gratification, however intense, must not be allowed to obscure the total pattern of meaning which the component parts serve to create. Steven Marcus, writing on *Men at Arms* and *Officers and Gentlemen* in 1956, suggested that 'the qualities that make [these novels] interesting and worthy are not organic to their structure or their moral implication'—that their charm lies rather in the 'buoyant and indestructible characters' and 'the rich accumulation of anecdotes about the eternal mismanagement of war'.[44] That view is hard to sustain with the finished work before us: Guy Crouchback's progress is so clearly and impressively the thematic core (though presented, certainly, in a dense context of admirably rendered circumstance). We do delight, of course, in the particulars that Marcus praises, but central to the pleasure the whole trilogy provides is our sense of being involved in a progressive exploration of experience. We cannot gauge the extent to which the final form of the sequence was predetermined, in the sense of being planned in detail before Waugh began to write, or the extent to which he made certain moral discoveries and artistic decisions in the course of composition. He said himself that 'it changed a lot in the writing', although some things like 'the sword in the Italian church and the sword of Stalingrad were . . . there from the beginning'.[45] Certainly we feel as we read that the author as well as the hero is achieving new self-knowledge, growing in moral insight, and we too are involved in the process: it is our own imaginative participation stage by stage in Guy's experience, including his illusions, that makes the conclusion so disturbingly effective. Paradoxically, however, this exploratory mode is combined with finished artistry. We find ourselves passing from light-hearted comedy to tragical mirth, from romantic idealism to disenchantment, from gay acceptance of life's variety to a deeper moral seriousness than we could ever have foreseen, yet these later developments are so closely connected, formally and thematically, with what has gone before that we have no sense of discontinuity, breaches in decorum, or changing conventions. The completed narrative satisfies both as aesthetic pattern and as moral vision. To these historical accuracy is at times subordinated. The Yugo-slavian episode, for example, fulfils perfectly its rhetorical function of mediating the hero's (and presumably the author's) disillusion with the war. Yet it is demonstrably unfair as an account of the partisans' war effort. Fitzroy Maclean, who headed the British Military Mission to Yugoslavia, confirms several of Waugh's impressions, but he and his observers were convinced that the partisans were fighting the Germans and fighting them effectively. Having served with them for a year and a half, he acknowledges their considerable virtues as well as their defects, and gives a much less pessimistic account of the whole conduct of that Adriatic war. (To focus only on one detail, we may note that the part played by two rocket-firing Beaufighters in the reduction of Valjevo was very different from the futile show of strength which Waugh describes in the air-strike on an isolated block-house.[46]) Maclean was, certainly, a member of Tito's entourage: things may have looked rather different at the local level, in particular areas at certain times; and no doubt we shall have to wait for specialised historical accounts of the whole war in Yugoslavia before trying to estimate the precise degree of Waugh's distortion. It may be less than we suppose: when he portrays the Spaniards of Hookforce as disorderly, rapacious, unreliable in battle, we might attribute this to xenophobic anti-Republican bias—if we had not come on inde-pendent references to the behaviour in Crete of the Spanish company of Layforce, the Commando Brigade in which Waugh served; and Lord Birkenhead's account of their experiences in Croatia tends to confirm at least some of Waugh's criticisms of the partisans.[47] Nevertheless, an element of distortion is undoubtedly involved in his presentation of this theatre of war: we are faced with a conflict between the novelist's right to mould reality to a truth at once more personal and more philosophical than history's, and his obligation to hold the mirror up to nature, showing things as they 'really' are. In literary terms Waugh's portrayal of 'the Jugs' is convincing though one-sided: in a hundred years it may be accepted as readily as Dickens's distortions are, as elements in a self-justifying, autonomous, artistic vision; but we are close enough to the events to feel uneasily that moral and psychological insights which compel respect are being mediated in terms of extreme political prejudice.

Prejudice, indeed, lies near the heart of Waugh's achievement—as of every satirist's. Through it he often confronts us with partial truths that we would rather not acknowledge. (Heterodoxy is always the other man's doxy, and accusations of prejudice are usually made when our own prejudices are offended.) Furthermore, the satirist's deliberate restriction of sympathy, his refusal to see both sides of a question, his unshakeable confidence in his own values, give a sharp distorted focus, a mode of perception which is the basis of Waugh's wit, as it is of Pope's. It amuses while revealing at least an aspect of the truth—about P.T. instructors, or Highland lairds, or Scottish Nationalists, or American war correspondents, or the uncharted horrors of life in the R.A.F. From such comic prejudice, indulged even to the point of fantasy, we derive an essentially amoral delight, which can, however, be combined with the satiric perception of error, with joy in the oddity and variety of human nature, or with bitter disillusion (for the reactionary novelist may find, like Mr Scott-King, 'a peculiar relish in contemplating the victories of bar-barism'[48]). A writer's prejudices, like his obsessions, are indeed a reservoir of power. Uncontrolled, they limit his achievement; carefully exploited, they enhance it; challenged and transcended, they can convert it into major art. Waugh's trilogy presents a uniquely successful fusion of prejudice indulged with prejudices overcome, as the vision that seemed by its very nature static shows itself continually capable of change and growth. That Guy's final position (or Waugh's) is not our own need not disturb us, for it is the intensity of the process as much as the conclusions reached that gives it its validity, wins our respect, and earns the hero his right to a wryly uncon-ventional happy ending.

'Things have turned out very conveniently for Guy,' Box-Bender says resentfully in the last sentence of the trilogy. But the Epilogue, with its changed point of view, has excluded us from the hero's consciousness, and Box-Bender is himself an imperceptive unreliable observer, so that we are left to judge for ourselves the degree of irony in that conclusion. The Epilogue shows the Modern Age triumphant. Traditional values are flouted or forgotten in the dreariness of post-war London, where Waugh's social distaste still operates, not ineffectively, as moral judgment. The world of politics is rejected now with Swiftian contempt: England is ruled, we gather, by knaves like Gilpin instead of fools like Elderberry and Box-Bender, but the difference hardly seems significant. Good men may prosper, but so, much more noticeably, do the wicked: the Castello Crouchback, memorial to Hermione's happy marriage with which the trilogy began, is soon to house the unholy loves of Ludovic and the Loot. From this sad world Tony has withdrawn to a monastery, Guy to the life of a country gentleman. Comparatively wealthy now, he has re-established himself at Broome—in the Lesser House, admittedly—and married the daughter of an old Catholic family like his own. She manages the home farm and bears his sons. (At least she does in *Unconditional Surrender*, though in the recension we hear that 'they haven't any children of their own'.) Guy rarely comes to London. When we glimpse him on this last occasion he is meeting his old Commando friends, the happy warriors, at a reunion in Bellamy's; and we note that Ivor Claire has reappeared with a D.S.O. and an incapacitating wound, both honourably acquired with the Chindits in Burma, whereas Trimmer has disappeared ignominiously from human ken, having jumped ship—it would seem—in South Africa on being posted to the Far East. So many fragments has Guy shored against his ruin that it might seem a simple case of virtue rewarded, and an unthinking reversion on the author's part to the ideals of *Officers and Gentlemen*—except that we know Guy's heir is Trimmer's son. He has never repudiated his act of compassion or its con-sequences, which were not ended by Virginia's death. This is his secret sacrifice, the price he has paid and continues to pay for spiritual peace. We cannot say with confidence that Guy is happy, but the modicum of worldly happiness he has is well-deserved. His distinction is less military than moral, and he would hardly have qualified for the traditional sword of honour; but as we contemplate his progress we perceive that in an age when honour and swords seem equally archaic, when the title of this trilogy is certain therefore to be read ironically, one sword at least was not dishonoured.

6 The Spy as Hero: Le Carré and the Cold War

'*King* Have you heard the argument? is there no offence in't?
Hamlet No, no, they do but jest, poison in jest, no offence i' the
world.'

'If plots of thrillers bear any resemblance to the methods of actual
intelligence operations it is purely coincidental. No one who is
professionally familiar with a security or espionage organization
should expect to find in books written by men who have never
been agents, representations of counterintelligence as it is actually
practiced. . . . Thrillers are not meant to be documentaries, or
even fictional accounts of the lives of real spies. They are not
concerned with the real or external world at all. Rather, they are
written for the sake of and about the interior life of man.' Ralph
Harper, *The World of the Thriller* (Cleveland, Ohio, 1969), p. 79.

'Those who read me know my conviction that the world, the
temporal world, rests on a few very simple ideas; so simple that
they must be as old as the hills. It rests notably . . . on the idea of
Fidelity.' Joseph Conrad, *Some Reminiscences* (London, 1912),
p. 20.

The novel of espionage or counterespionage has flourished, for
obvious reasons, in the period of Cold War and *détente*, achieving at
its best a high degree of technical sophistication; but its literary status
remains largely unacknowledged. The authors of spy thrillers are for
the most part entertainers, in Steven Marcus's sense of writers 'who
[do] not press upon us the full complexities of life, who [do] not
demand from us a total seriousness in making moral judgments, and
who [do] not necessarily bring to bear on experience a mature and
searching intelligence'.[1] Yet this description is less dismissive than it
sounds. The claims of such art merit serious consideration in literary-

psychological if not in literary-moralistic terms; and the spy thriller can also become, like romance, the medium for an obliquely rendered criticism of life. Le Carré, the supreme exponent of the *genre*, uses it to explore the varieties of experience exploited more or less successfully by his fellow-practitioners. Like them, he provides us with exciting, disturbing, therapeutic fantasies of action and intrigue; but in his best work he also engages with political, moral and psychological complexities, demonstrating the capacity of entertainment art to transcend its own self-imposed limitations.

The spy thriller stands in an ambiguous, shifting relation to historical reality, on which it draws selectively, with sometimes more, sometimes less regard for verisimilitude. It is basically a form of fiction which might properly be called escapist, were it not for the pejorative, simplistic implications that term has acquired; and it is best illuminated by those theorists who have acknowledged and explored non-ethical, irrational dimensions in their own experience of literature.

'The slightest novels,' Stevenson maintained in 1881, 'are a blessing to those in distress, not chloroform itself a greater';[2] and the implications of that view had been elaborated in a letter to Professor Meiklejohn, written from California in the previous year in what was for Stevenson a period of illness, penury and depression:

> When I suffer in mind [he confessed then], stories are my refuge; I take them like opium; and I consider one who writes them as a sort of doctor of the mind. And frankly, Meiklejohn, it is not Shakespeare we take to, when we are in a hot corner; nor certainly, George Eliot—no, nor even Balzac. It is Charles Reade, or old Dumas, or the Arabian Nights, or the best of Walter Scott; it is stories we want, not the high poetic function which represents the world. . . . We want incident, interest, action: to the devil with your philosophy. When we are well again, and have an easy mind, we shall peruse your important work; but what we want now is a drug.[3]

This is disconcertingly true to experience, but it is a truth on which the moralistic critic does not care to dwell, impatient as he tends to be with all forms of literary experience which elude his categories. Stevenson, however, goes boldly on to extend his argument to states of health as well as sickness. The love of incident, of fit and striking incident, is, he maintains, a natural human appetite from the schoolboy to the sage; it is the basis of our delight in epic; but in his own day it was best catered for by novels of adventure, of the kind he enjoyed so much and wrote so well—novels which appealed, as he puts it, 'to certain almost sensual and quite illogical tendencies in man'.[4] The limitations in his own experience did not, he thought, disqualify him as a story-teller in this vein: '. . . it will be found true,' he contended, '. . . in a majority of cases, that the artist writes with more gusto and effect of those things which he has only wished to do, than of those which he has done. Desire is a wonderful telescope, and Pisgah the best observatory.'[5] For him such fiction constituted an escape not only from his life of chronic ill-health and sickbeds to an imaginary life of action and adventure, but also from the humdrum, law-abiding ethic of real life to one of imaginary ruthlessness and slaughter.

> Seriously [he wrote to Cosmo Monkhouse in 1884], do you like to repose? Ye Gods, I hate it. . . . And when a man, seemingly sane, tells me he has 'fallen in love with stagnation,' I can only say to him, 'You will never be a Pirate!' This may not cause any regret to Mrs. Monkhouse; but in your own soul it will clang hollow—think of it! Never! After all boyhood's aspirations and youth's immoral day-dreams, you are condemned to sit down, grossly draw in your chair to the fat board, and be a beastly Burgess till you die. Can it be? Is there not some escape, some furlough from the Moral Law, some holiday jaunt contrivable into a Better Land? Shall we never shed blood? This prospect is too grey. . . . But in heaven, when we get there, we shall have a good time, and see some real carnage. For heaven is—must be—that great Kingdom of Antinomia, which Lamb saw dimly adumbrated in the *Country Wife*, where the worm which never dies (the conscience) peacefully expires, and the sinner lies down beside the Ten Commandments.[6]

Wish-fulfilment, in this view, is not an unacknowledged aberration on an author's part, but an essential constituent of his creation, and an essential constituent also of the reader's pleasure, since the great creative writer, according to Stevenson, 'shows us the realisation and the apotheosis of the day-dreams of common men. His stories may be nourished with the realities of life, but their true mark is to satisfy the nameless longings of the reader, and to obey the ideal laws of the day-dream.'[7] Such satisfaction, such obedience, are seen not as corrupting or disabling, but as beneficial, indeed medicinal, providing the relief of drugs or opium in time of affliction, while acting as tonics or restoratives in time of health.

The medical analogy is used by Fielding in his Preface to *Joseph Andrews*, in a justification of the irrational, non-satiric pleasure which burlesque affords. In the comic the author confines himself strictly to Nature and imitates life as it really is, bringing out the ridiculous errors which spring from affectation, in a satiric exposure of vanity and hypocrisy; whereas in burlesque—one thinks of modern equivalents like *Monty Python's Flying Circus*—the author displays things monstrous and unnatural, rousing our delight by the 'surprising Absurdity' of what he presents to us. Fielding argues that the comic provides 'a more rational and useful Pleasure', but that burlesque is not to be despised, since

> it contributes more to exquisite Mirth and Laughter than any other [kind of writing]; and these are probably more wholesome Physic for the Mind, and conduce better to purge away Spleen, Melancholy and ill Affections, than is generally imagined. Nay, I will appeal to common Observation, whether the same Companies are not found more full of Good-Humour and Benevolence, after they have been sweeten'd for two or three Hours with Entertainments of this kind, than when soured by a Tragedy or a grave Lecture. [8]

This emphasis on the psychologically therapeutic (as opposed to morally illuminating) function of some forms of literature leads on to Lamb's defence of Restoration Comedy, which Stevenson referred to in his playful description of an Antinomian Heaven. Lamb offers an analysis of his own delight in such comedy, in spite of its debased morality which he would find wholly unacceptable in real life:

> I confess for myself that (with no great delinquencies to answer for) I am glad for a season to take an airing beyond the diocese of the strict conscience,—not to live always in the precincts of the law-courts,—but now and then, for a dream-while or so, to imagine a world with no meddling restrictions— to get into recesses, whither the hunter cannot follow me—
>
>> —Secret shades
>> Of woody Ida's inmost grove,
>> While yet there was no fear of Jove—

I come back to my cage and my restraint the fresher and more healthy for it. I wear my shackles more contentedly for having respired the breath of an imaginary freedom. I do not know how it is with others, but I feel the better always for the perusal of one of Congreve's—nay, why should I not add even of Wycherley's—comedies. I am the gayer at least for it. . . .[9]

Man has, this argument implies, anarchic, Dionysiac impulses which in ordinary life are subject to the control of Apollonian conscience. This involves an element of repression, as these impulses are restrained or channelled into more acceptable activities, so that they are integrated into an approved conception of the good life. This conception is governed by religion and the moral law—hence Lamb's allusion to the diocese and law-courts in connection with strict conscience. There are moods however, when these latent impulses to anarchy are activated, and tend to open Dionysiac rebellion. In such moods the Apollonian restrictions normally accepted gladly as conditions of fully human life seem merely meddlesome: they are thought of now in terms of a cage or of restraining shackles; while the loving God who would have been appealed to as the ultimate sanction for codes of morality is metamorphosed into a hunter, to be escaped from if possible, or an Olympian tyrant from whose tyranny men shrink, yearning for an idyllic freedom imagined as existing before he exercised his baneful sway. Once conscious of this tension between Apollonian and Dionysiac within himself, a man may react like Lamb's contemporary William Blake, who rebelled against the mind-forged manacles which fettered man's delight, and against what he saw as a false god, the authoritarian Jehovah of the Old Testament with his negative morality of 'Thou shalt not'—the god whose priests in black gowns could be seen walking their rounds, binding with briars our joys and desires. Lamb's own reaction was, however, very different. He was not a moral revolutionary; and it may be that the dreadful episode in which his sister Mary murdered their mother in a fit of lunacy had given him a deeper insight than most men into the abyss of horror which can reveal itself in the human personality released from moral or from rational control. However this may be, he accepted an orthodox morality as self-evidently true, and clearly recognised that the characters of Congreve and Wycherley, translated into real life, would be 'profligates and strumpets', living on 'principles which, universally acted upon, must reduce this frame of things to a chaos'.[10] Yet he delights in entering imaginatively into their dramatic world—a world carefully circum-scribed by the boundaries of art—a world in which his orthodox morality does not apply, and in which therefore it can be abandoned without any evil consequence in life—a world from which he can return refreshed, exhilarated, gayer and healthier, happy to resume his normal standards, but happy also to have exercised thus harmlessly elements in his personality which would normally be under restraint.

The analysis corresponds very closely to Freud's account of literary experience in his essay 'Creative Writers and Day-Dreaming.' Stevenson had already suggested that 'fiction is to the grown man what play is to the child; it is there that he changes the atmosphere and tenor of his life'.[11] Freud now argues more elaborately that 'the creative writer does the same as a child at play. He creates a world of fantasy which he takes very seriously—that is, which he invests with large amounts of emotion—while separating it sharply from reality.' As people grow up, they cease to play, but derive a comparable pleasure from fantasies or day-dreams, the motive forces of which are unsatisfied wishes: 'every single fantasy is the fulfilment of a wish, a correction of unsatisfying reality'. Adults normally conceal their fantasies because they are ashamed of them, but the creative writer reveals his, and gives us pleasure by so doing. That pleasure seems to Freud to be of a complex nature: it derives in the first instance from the formal qualities of the work, but the provision of such aesthetic delight enables the artist to tap in us deeper sources of gratification:

> We give the name of an *incentive bonus*, or a *forepleasure*, to a yield of pleasure such as this, which is offered to us so as to make possible the release of still greater pleasure arising from deeper psychical sources. In my opinion, all the aesthetic pleasure which a creative writer affords us has the character of a forepleasure of this kind, and our actual enjoyment of an imaginative work proceeds from a liberation of tensions in our minds. It may even be that not a little of this effect is due to the writer's enabling us thenceforward to enjoy our own day-dreams without self-reproach or shame.[12]

Such theories are obviously inadequate as accounts of literature in general, and of the greatest literature in particular; but they do define and categorise certain modes of literary experience which are undeniably real and enjoyable, and which are therefore proper objects of our critical attention. Clearly the spy thriller falls into these categories, and specially relevant to the peculiar pleasure it provides is

Freud's assertion that 'the unreality of the writer's imaginative world . . . has very important consequences for the technique of his art; for many things which, if they were real, could give no enjoyment, can do so in the play of fantasy, and many excitements which, in themselves, are actually distressing, can become a source of pleasure for the hearers and spectators at the performance of a writer's work'.[13] A clear perception of the fictive nature of the world we are entering imaginatively is a necessary condition for our enjoyment of most thrillers. It is also the main guarantee that the experience involved will be cathartic rather than corrupting (though there is also the question of the permissible—or rather the psychologically as well as sociably acceptable—range of fantasy itself). The clearer the art status and entertainment function of the work, the less it carries necessary implications for real life, and the more conspicuous the notice reading 'No Road Through To Action'. The more the boundary between life and art is blurred, and the more the fictive world claims seriously to be an imitation of reality, the more its values may seem to propose themselves as ethically valid. Yet paradoxically, this very development which renders fantasy potentially more dangerous, may also invest it with a higher seriousness.

'The novel,' writes Gillian Beer, 'is more preoccupied with representing and interpreting a known world, the romance with making apparent the dreams of that world.'[14] The spy thriller, a contemporary version of romance, articulates dreams of adventure and to some extent of love—the traditional romance ingredients transposed into a modern idiom. Man's aggressive and erotic impulses are both brought into play, and so too are his dreams of heroism—of the individual as master of his fate, confronting evil and destroying it. But the thriller also draws on nightmares—not least those based on aspects of reality which we prefer to banish from our daily consciousness. The division of the world into antagonistic power blocs, the continuing possibility of nuclear war, the East's ideological hostility to Western society, Russia's overwhelming military strength (and her use of it in Hungary and Czechoslovakia), the barbarism of her forced labour camps and psychiatric prisons, the continual probing of our institutions and defences even in periods of *détente*, the existence of communist sympathisers and supporters in our own society—very different from the largely mythical Fifth Column of the Fascists—all of these are such familiar facts that we have learned to live with them and virtually ignore them, unless they are forced on our unwilling attention by international crises. This suppressed awareness is tapped and exploited by spy thrillers, in which menace and treachery are two of the most frequently recurring themes; but our anxieties, once roused, are then assuaged by the frustration of the villains' knavish tricks and the triumph of the hero. Nevertheless, the popularity of the *genre* suggests that this unease is endemic though suppressed in our society, and that the need for reassurance as well as the thirst for vicarious adventure is continually present. Trilling, moreover, speaks of 'the mithridatic function, by which tragedy is used as the homeopathic administration of pain to inure ourselves to the greater pain which life will force upon us';[15] and it may well be that our fantasy encounters with the secret brutalities of international conflict have a similar effect on us.

The ethics of the *genre* are far from constant. Espionage in *Kim* was still the Great Game which had been played by British officers throughout much of the nineteenth century to forestall Russian encroachments on India and to establish our hegemony in Central Asia.[16] Sometimes these agents came to thoroughly unpleasant ends, but the sporting metaphor they favoured speaks for itself; and the same spirit was often carried over into fiction. The traditional spy story of the early twentieth century was set in a world full of hazards but free from moral ambiguities—apart from the fundamental ambiguity, rarely perceived by the authors or the reading public, of a double standard applied to espionage and counterespionage activities, depending on whether these were carried on by 'us' or 'them'. In Buchan's Richard Hannay stories, the most popular and influential of their kind, the hero may admire a brave enemy (in the spirit of those who honour while they cut him down the foe who comes with fearless eyes), but he has a total confidence, shared by the author, in the rightness of his own cause and the wrongness of the enemy's. This goes beyond a simple patriotism. Buchan had an acute sense of the vulnerability of civilised life: 'You think,' exclaims the sinister Mr Lumsley in *The Power-House* (1913), 'that a wall as solid as the earth separates civilisation from barbarism. I tell you that the division is a thread, a sheet of glass.' This prophetic insight, later praised by Graham Greene, was accompanied by what has been described (a shade portentously) as Buchan's 'Gothic, almost apocalyptic vision of the dark, destructive forces contained in human beings and in society'.[17] It is against these, as well as against Germany the nation state, that Hannay is contending; yet he adheres determinedly, quixotically, to decent methods and fair play, whatever devil's work the other side may contemplate. The *locus classicus* occurs in *Mr*

Standfast (1919), when Hannay balks at shooting the arch-spy who is planning to destroy the British Army by releasing anthrax germs on its main lines of communication. The discovery of the plot fills him with horror: 'I was fairly well used to Boche filthiness, but this seemed too grim a piece of the utterly damnable. I wanted to have Ivery by the throat and force the stuff into his body, and watch him decay slowly into the horror he had contrived for honest men.' Yet when 'Ivery' appears a few minutes later, Hannay cannot bring himself to act with the appropriate ruthlessness:

> I had my hand on my pistol, as I motioned Mary farther back into the shadows. For a second I was about to shoot. I had a perfect mark and could have put a bullet through his brain with utter certitude. I think if I had been alone I might have fired. Perhaps not. Anyhow now I could not do it. It seemed like potting a sitting rabbit. . . .[18]

It is easy to make fun of such passages, though they stem from an honourable belief that if one must fight, one should fight as cleanly as possible—that if one must touch pitch, one should try to remain undefiled instead of plunging into it and wallowing. The same attitude, which underlies the Geneva Convention itself, survives today in popular fiction and reality, but in a much attenuated form. It has been eroded partly by the sinister appeal of violence in literature and life, but more by the perception that even 'clean' fighting necessarily involves considerable ruthlessness. This is even more true of clandestine operations, as the Second World War made manifest.

> To succeed in resistance [writes M. R. D. Foot], you needed extra strong, steely, flexible nerves, no inhibitions at all, and uncanny quickness of wit. As witness . . . 'Felix', a Jew of Alsatian-Polish origins who was assistant wireless operator to the young 'Alphonse', a British agent in southern France. He, 'Alphonse', and 'Emanuel' the wireless operator all got out of the same train at Toulouse; 'Felix', carrying the transmitter in its readily recognizable suitcase, went up to the barrier first. Two French policemen were conducting a cursory check on identity papers. Behind them, two uniformed SS men were sending everyone with a case or big package to the *consigne*, where more SS were making a methodical luggage search. 'Felix' took in the scene; ignored the French police; held his suitcase high; and called in authoritative German, 'Get me a car at once, I have a captured set.' He was driven away in a

German-requisitioned car; had it pulled up in a back street; killed
the driver, and reported to 'Alphonse' with the set for orders.[19]

The situation was pure Buchan; so was Felix's inspired bluff; but the
killing of the driver puts the episode in a different moral world.

The secret agents of Cold War fiction move through an even
harsher and more brutal world than this; and (unlike Ashenden, in
Maugham's pallidly realistic anecdotes of spy-work in the First
World War) they are themselves directly involved in its harshness and
brutality. The fact that James Bond, their crude prototype, was a
professional assassin, licensed officially to kill in cold blood, typifies
the moral ambiguity of their proceedings. They share Hannay's sense
of being on the side of good against some kind of evil: this is the
political and ethical assumption on which their activities and our
delight in them are based, though one of the conventions of the *genre*
as it has developed is to allow doubts to arise from time to time in
their minds and our own. (There is, for example, a recurrent contrast
between the heroic code they live by and the decadence or selfishness
of the Western society they are defending.) The main enemy for most
of them is not so much Communism as Russian tyranny—cruel,
oppressive and expansionist, as it revealed itself to be in the post-war
years, with its evil nature fully manifested by the methods it
employed. Yet their own methods are less scrupulous than Hannay's,
and their consciences less tender. They are professionals, not
gentleman amateurs, and though they do retain some scruples which
help to engage our sympathies, they realise that ruthless enemies have
sometimes to be fought by ruthless means. There is therefore a casual
tolerance of violence and dirty tricks, so long as they are used in a
good cause. 'Our kind of work,' declares the Master in *The Us or
Them War*, 'comes with a kind of built-in absolution. All-purpose
remission for every imaginable kind of sin on the grounds of higher
national interest';[20] and we relish, with a frisson of delighted horror,
the ruthlessness and double-dealing characteristic of the *genre*. Yet we
also go on thinking in terms of good guys versus bad, the inherent
contradiction being obscured by the plot-mechanism, which usually
allows us to have our moral cake and eat it.

Le Carré offers a more complex pleasure, by combining
psychological release with radical moral concern, as distinct from the
show of morality which serves in many thrillers as a spice to sin or
justification for violence. *The Spy Who Came in from the Cold* (1963)
insists upon the inhumanity of actions undertaken nominally on

humanity's behalf. Early in the novel, for example, we are brought up sharply by Control's restatement of the fundamental problem of ends and means:

> . . . 'The ethic of our work, as I understand it, is based on a single assumption. That is, we are never going to be aggressors. Do you think that's fair?'
>
> Leamas nodded. Anything to avoid talking.
>
> 'Thus we do disagreeable things, but we are *defensive*. That, I think, is still fair. We do disagreeable things so that ordinary people here and elsewhere can sleep safely in their beds at night. Is that too romantic? Of course, we occasionally do very wicked things'; he grinned like a schoolboy. 'And in weighing up the moralities, we rather go in for dishonest comparisons; after all, you can't compare the ideals of one side with the methods of the other, can you, now?'
>
> Leamas was lost. He'd heard the man talked a lot of drivel before getting the knife in, but he'd never heard anything like this before.
>
> 'I mean you've got to compare method with method, and ideal with ideal. I would say that since the war, our methods—ours and those of the opposition—have become much the same. I mean you can't be less ruthless than the opposition simply because your government's *policy* is benevolent, can you now?' He laughed quietly to himself: 'That would *never* do,' he said.[21]

Control's cynicism and self-satisfaction do not necessarily invalidate his argument, but its more disturbing implications are explored in the action which follows. *The Spy Who Came in from the Cold* combines the excellences of the thriller and the moral fable. It transcends the limitations of the former, but accepts (reluctantly perhaps) those of the latter. The ingenious plot, with its multiple deceptions and double double-crosses, dramatises a cold Machiavellian *real-politik* in which human sympathies have no place. It presents us with a metaphysically bleak world of action, in which for the Christian as much as for the Communist the end is seen as justifying the means, and individuals are deliberately sacrificed for the general good. There is a frightening void where one might have expected to find fundamental values: 'That is the price they pay,' says Leamas of his masters—'to despise God and Karl Marx in the same sentence.'[22]

The epigrammatic indictment is a telling one; yet it seems out of character for the uncomprehending Leamas of the earlier dialogue. The thematic intention is no doubt to show his growing awareness of the issues, but this is rendered, in the manner of a moral fable, too schematically to be psychologically convincing. On the other hand, the book eschews moral simplicity. *Our Man in Havana* stated in a mode of comic fantasy the claims of individual human beings against those of secret services, nation states, or international power blocs. *The Spy Who Came in from the Cold* presents the same claims as constituents of a tragic dilemma. The sinister power of Russia and her satellites, and their threat to 'ordinary people here and elsewhere' are self-evident within the novel. Kipling's Wall was an impressive barrier against Rome's enemies, for the protection of her citizens and subjects. The Wall against which Leamas and Liz are shot is a barrier to prevent East Germany's own citizens from escaping to the West, and it is described significantly as 'a dirty, ugly thing of breeze blocks and strands of barbed wire, lit with cheap yellow light, like the backdrop for a concentration camp'.[23] The need for secret services as one line of defence in such a world 'is real—not illusory as it was shown to be in Greene's Havana. Leamas, even in his revulsion from his calling, sees it as necessary 'for the safety of ordinary, crummy people like you and me', and the fact that it condemns them both to death does not dispose of his contention. Certainly the final note is one of protest. Leamas himself turns out to be a pawn in the game in which we thought he was a knight; and Liz, for all her half-baked Communism, is an innocent victim whose death evokes the image of a child in a small car smashed between great lorries. The pathos of the end is modified only by Leamas's own final act of affirmation. His climbing down the Wall to die with her instead of jumping to safety, his refusal to go on living on the terms he would be left with, is in its way a triumph of the spirit. Yet the dilemma the book poses remains unresolved. As in *Kim*, where the claims of contemplation are weighed against those of action—the world of the Lama against that of Mahbub Ali—our satisfaction comes not from being presented with a neat solution, but from seeing the incompatible alternatives so powerfully presented.[24]

We are left with the question whether it is possible to be a secret agent and a fully human being—or rather, since the agent in this formula is merely an exemplar, whether personal integrity can ever be preserved in the corrupting world of action. The true Le Carré hero, Smiley, is the test case. He had already figured as protagonist in *Call for the Dead* (1961) and *A Murder of Quality* (1962). Neither book aspired to be more than a good thriller, but they established him as a more fully apprehended character than Leamas—an unfashionable secret agent fully aware of the psychological and moral hazards of his calling.

> His emotions in performing this work [of selecting German agents before the war] were mixed, and irreconcilable. It intrigued him to evaluate from a detached position what he had learnt to describe as 'the agent potential' of a human being; to devise minuscule tests of character and behaviour which could inform him of the qualities of a candidate. This part of him was bloodless and inhuman—Smiley in this role was the international mercenary of his trade, amoral and without motive beyond that of personal gratification.
>
> Conversely it saddened him to witness in himself the gradual death of natural pleasure. Always withdrawn, he now found himself shrinking from the temptations of friendship and human loyalty; he guarded himself warily from spontaneous reaction. By the strength of his intellect, he forced himself to observe humanity with clinical objectivity, and because he was neither immortal nor infallible he hated and feared the falseness of his life.[25]

Against this, however, worked his love of England, his hatred of Nazism, which constituted for him a clear unambiguous enemy, and his capacity for sympathy and pity, which was to grow from his own suffering. He had been recruited at Oxford by his tutor Jebedee, now dead. ('He had boarded a train at Lille in 1941 with his radio operator, a young Belgian, and neither of them had been heard of again.') Smiley's own exploits were of that wartime past, viewed now with middle-aged, elegiac regret. In spite of, or perhaps because of, his sensitivity, he had done well. (' "The best," Adrian had said. "The strongest and the best." '[26]) But there is a frank acknowledgment of the nervous strain he had had to endure, and the toll it took of him:

> He had never guessed it was possible to be frightened for so long. He developed a nervous irritation in his left eye which remained with him fifteen years later; the strain etched lines on his fleshy cheeks and brow. He learnt what it was never to sleep, never to relax, to feel at any time of day or night the restless beating of his own heart, to know the extremes of solitude and self-pity, the sudden unreasoning desire for a woman, for drink, for exercise, for any drug to take away the tension of his life.[27]

This sketches in his past: his present is one of apparent mediocrity and failure, disproved only in action. Unimpressive in appearance, scholarly by temperament, middle-aged and middle-class, cuckolded by his aristocratic wife, a figure of some pathos though also of hidden strength, Smiley is portrayed in greater depth than either of these narratives really requires. He seems a character in search of a plot which will be adequate, as these are not, to his potential.

He reappears in *The Spy Who Came in from the Cold* in a minor but ambiguous role. (Each of Le Carré's works is self-contained and self-sufficient, but cumulatively they reinforce each other, as the same characters or themes recur in different contexts.) We gather that he was opposed to the whole operation, but once it is launched he takes an active part, providing the incriminating evidence to be seized on by the East German tribunal. Near the very end, however, we glimpse his concern for the two victims:

> [Leamas] heard a voice in English from the Western side of the wall:
> 'Jump, Alec! Jump man!'
> Now everyone was shouting, English, French and German, mixed; he heard Smiley's voice from quite close:
> 'The girl, where's the girl?'[28]

He figures comparably in *The Looking-Glass War* (1965), that study in futility, self-deception and betrayal. The mission which we follow with excited apprehension is misconceived and badly executed, but it is also deliberately aborted by Control to discredit finally the remnant of the rival service which had mounted it. Smiley, high now in the counsels of 'the Circus', indicates revulsion when he realises what Control has done, what he himself has been involved in, though it falls to him to close the operation down, leaving the agent to his fate. As well as dissecting the ruthlessness of inter-service rivalries, the novel exposes a corrupt nostalgia for wartime experience, and the desire this breeds in the young as well as in the middle-aged to relive or replay a supposedly heroic past; but from this spiritual temptation Smiley seems immune. In contrast with the febrile enthusiasm, the pathetic aspirations of Leclerc's organisation, he figures, in the glimpses which we have of him, as highly professional, enigmatic, yet humane.

In both these novels he is more a function than a character; in *Tinker Tailor Soldier Spy* (1974) he holds the centre of the stage. Le Carré here allows himself the amplitude and the complexity of treatment of the novel proper, though his conventions remain those of the spy thriller. These are in no way disabling. Greene had already proved their value in his entertainments and more serious fiction as images or paradigms of normal experience. And in Le Carré's *A Small Town in Germany* (1968), a considerable novel in its own right, the security investigation had revealed not the suspected flight of a defector, but a tangled web of professional and personal relationships, of loyalties and betrayals, in the British Embassy at Bonn. The investigating agent there became the novelist's device for uncovering the truths of character and ultimate belief concealed by the façade which constitutes daily reality. A similar device is now employed in Smiley's struggle to identify a traitor high in the security service itself. As he threads his way through the labyrinth of evidence, each character whom he encounters, each interview that he conducts, helps to throw light on the central problem of disloyalty, but also provides insights into a wide spectrum of personalities and values. It is through the process of investigation that the novel creates its own fully authenticated human world. The main structural motif of a quest, difficult and perilous in the extreme, culminating in a confrontation with the powers of evil—a quest undertaken by a solitary hero with (in this case) a few trusted followers—gives unity and tension to the narrative. (*The Naive and Sentimental Lover*, the one work in which Le Carré totally rejects the thriller framework, is curiously flabby by comparison.) We relish, as we do in works by Adam Hall, Len Deighton, William Haggard, all the technicalities of secret service work—the arcane tradecraft: realism of presentation is common form in the spy thriller, even when the content is plainly fantasy. The extent to which Le Carré's realism extends here to content could, however, be a matter for debate. Kim Philby complained of *The Spy Who Came in from the Cold* that 'the whole plot, from beginning to end, is basically implausible—at any rate to anyone who has any real knowledge of the business';[29] but few of us can claim such knowledge, and Philby's own career outdid spy fiction in its bizarre actuality, forcing us to reconsider our criteria of probability. Perhaps it will suffice that *Tinker Tailor Soldier Spy* carries enough conviction for us to suspend our lingering disbelief; and its significance, in any case, is not confined to the esoteric world of secret agents which provides its subject matter: it is to be read analogically as well as literally.

This novel is not primarily concerned with ends and means, though that theme was to be restated in *The Honourable Schoolboy*

(1977), in which Smiley broods on the paradox of being '*inhuman in defence of our humanity, . . . harsh in defence of compassion; . . . single-minded in defence of our disparity.*'[30] The concern here is intense but oddly intermittent, failing to inform the narrative as a whole: the over-researched plot of *The Honourable Schoolboy* is expanded and elaborated to a point where it begins to disappoint us structurally and thematically. Whereas *Tinker Tailor Soldier Spy* achieves a perfect fusion of spy plot and universal theme, as it explores the antithetical phenomena of treason and fidelity.

The world it presents us with is one of multiple betrayals—of treason, infidelity, disloyalty and broken faith. Bill Roach, the pathetically vulnerable schoolboy of the sub-plot, suffers from his parents' broken marriage. His case is juxtaposed with the absurd one of the headmaster's father, who has run away with a receptionist from the nearby hotel, gladly abandoning wife, son and school. That two former teachers have been guilty of breaches of trust and of the law, is a comic-satiric detail reinforcing the main theme. The unfaithfulness of Smiley's wife, especially her liaison with Bill Haydon, is a motif which recurs in conversation after conversation, as well as in Smiley's own tortured awareness. Sexual infidelity is paralleled by professional disloyalty. Networks are blown, operations aborted, and agents liquidated, by covert treachery. Irina, offering to defect to Britain with key information about the traitor, is herself betrayed and shipped back to Moscow (as the wretched Volkov was by Philby's own manipulations). Above all, Jim Prideaux, simple, kindly, patriotic, now part-crippled by his wound, was shot in the back, literally and metaphorically, on a mission which turned out to be a baited trap. Examples of treachery, of obligations broken and trust betrayed, proliferate like the metaphorical extensions of sin and disorder in Shakespearean tragedy. There is a sense of corruption at the very heart of things; and Smiley's search for the source of evil has affinities with Oedipus's quest for truth or Hamlet's for revenge.

The tension of the plot depends on all—or almost all—foreknowledge of the outcome being withheld. We work through the evidence with Smiley himself, and it is only in retrospect or on re-reading, when our knowledge is complete, that we realise how closely textured the whole narrative has been—how devoid of superfluities, and how potently functional in its elaborated detail. In the opening chapter, for example, the dialogue between Bill Roach and Jim seems so simply naturalistic that we do not on first reading give its trivialities a second thought:

'New boy, eh? Well *I'm* not a new boy,' Jim went on, in altogether a much more friendly tone. . . . 'I'm an old boy. Old as Rip Van Winkle if you want to know. Older. Got any friends?'

'No sir,' said Roach simply, in the listless tone which schoolboys always use for saying 'no', leaving all positive response to their interrogators. Jim however made no response at all, so that Roach felt an odd stirring of kinship suddenly, and of hope.

'My other name's Bill,' he said. 'I was christened Bill but Mr Thursgood calls me William.'

'Bill, eh. The unpaid Bill. Anyone ever call you that?

'No, sir.'

'Good name, anyway.'

'Yes, sir.'

'Known a lot of Bills. They've all been good 'uns.'[31]

We soon realise, however, that Jim *is* a Rip Van Winkle in still holding to a simple, old-fashioned patriotism. By the end we know that he has said 'no' repeatedly to interrogators worse than any Bill Roach has encountered. We also know by then that he was deliberately betrayed to captivity and torture, if not death, by his oldest, closest friend, Bill Haydon—one Bill who was not a good 'un. And the unpaid Bill of the opening is settled well and truly when Jim, following in Smiley's footsteps, comes on his betrayer and leaves him with his neck as neatly broken as that of the owl he had disposed of when it fluttered down the classroom chimney. 'Only a gamekeeper, declared Sudely, who had one, would know how to kill an owl so well'; and we recognise Jim's handiwork when we read, some three hundred pages later, that '[Haydon's] eyes were open and his head was propped unnaturally to one side, like the head of a bird when its neck has been expertly broken'.[32]

It would be hypocritical to deny that while we relish the plot parallels and verbal echoes (Freud's forepleasures), we feel deeper satisfaction at this even-handed justice, meted out by the man who has suffered most from Haydon's treachery. The revenge ethic seems appropriate in circumstances such as these; moral revulsion is not invoked as a response; but we are left to speculate on the degree of perturbation in Jim's spirit.

For the rest of that term, Jim Prideaux behaved in the eyes of Roach much as his mother had behaved when his father went away. He spent a lot of time on little things, like fixing up the lighting for the school play and mending the soccer nets with string, and in French he took enormous pains over small inaccuracies. But big things, like his walks and solitary golf, these he gave up altogether, and in the evenings stayed in and kept clear of the village. Worst of all was his staring, empty look when Roach caught him unawares, and the way he forgot things in class, even red marks for merit: Roach had to remind him to hand them in each week.[33]

Roach's perceptions are sound even though his understanding is inadequate—Jim had praised him, we remember, as a watcher—and his opening comparison is apter than he knows. The emotion Jim conceals, or reveals intermittently, while he is lying low after the murder, is presumably not guilt but grief, at having been betrayed by someone he had loved.

The nature of Bill Haydon's treason is defined indeed largely in terms of its personal implications. '[He] had betrayed,' Smiley reflects. 'As a lover, a colleague, a friend; as a patriot; as a member of that inestimable body which Ann loosely called the Set: in every capacity, Haydon had overtly pursued one aim and secretly achieved its opposite. Smiley knew very well that even now he did not grasp the scope of that appalling duplicity. . . .'[34] This scope, however, is precisely what the novel reveals to us. The excuses and explanations which are offered cannot reconcile us to the facts—Haydon's making love to Ann only to cloud Smiley's judgment; his sacrificing Jim—his old comrade-in-arms in more senses than one—only to discredit Control and safeguard his own secret; his systematic betrayal of all the colleagues and subordinates who had trusted and admired him. 'I hate the idea of causes,' E. M. Forster wrote in 1939, 'and if I had to choose between betraying my country and betraying my friend, I hope I should have the guts to betray my country.'[35] The forcible-feeble challenge assumes an ethic based exclusively on personal relationships, ignoring the truth George Eliot insists on, that 'there is no private life which has not been determined by a wider public life'.[36] Forster does not pause to consider whether the betrayal of his country (*anno domini* 1939) might involve the betrayal of not one but many friends, and the violation of personal relationships on a nightmare scale. Yet the opposite extreme of an ethic based exclusively on public life, with its impersonal abstractions like patriotism or communism, is equally illusory. Man, as the realistic novel continually reminds us, is uniquely individual but also, and essentially, a social animal, existing by his very nature in a complex of relationships with, and obligations to, his fellow-men and women; and any moral judgment on his actions must take due account of these.

Romance does frequently detach its heroes from this social context, so as to deal (as James puts it) with 'experience liberated . . . experience disengaged, disembroiled, disencumbered, exempt from the conditions that we usually know to attach to it'. It therefore lends itself to great symbolic actions—quests and conflicts, for example, which tend to the allegorical—but romance achieves its greatest intensity, James argues, 'when the sacrifice of community, of the "related" sides of situations, has not been too rash'.[37] Too rash it may well be in most spy thrillers, delighting as they do in solitary heroes untrammelled by normal social ties and obligations. (Even when they are members of an organisation, they often rebel against the bureaucrats who run it; they usually disregard it when it interferes with their activities; and they are in any case on their own when facing greatest danger: this, of course, is part of their imaginative appeal.) In *Tinker Tailor Soldier Spy* Le Carré re-establishes the human context, the sense of community and the 'related' sides of situations in his espionage plot. To understand Haydon's betrayal of his country is to see that it involves the betrayal of his class, his profession, his own past—but also of his colleagues, friends and intimates. Jim Prideaux's role is a symbolic one, although his story is moving and horrifying in its own right. The analysis is moral rather than ideological or sociological as it was in Le Carré's earlier comments on the Philby case.[38] Haydon is shown to have a basic cynicism, a calloused sensibility of the kind Philby unwittingly reveals in his own memoirs. Betrayal has become for him a habit, a life-style, which he extends even to old friends, or present intimates like the girl with the baby (his, presumably) in the squalid flat in Kentish Town, whom he pays off with a cheque for £1,000 as he prepares to leave for Moscow.

Smiley, on the other hand, is a man of feeling, with an overwhelming, almost an exaggerated sense of responsibility (glimpsed in his distress when Lacon's daughter tumbles from her pony). Instead of seeking personal revenge on Haydon, he argues for trading him to Russia in exchange for the agents behind the Iron Curtain whose identities have been betrayed. We last see him humbly bound for an attempted reconciliation with his wife. He shows a sensitive awareness of the personalities, the prejudices, the susceptibilities, of the people whom he has to deal with, and he is throughout a man of conscience. In all respects but courage and professional skill he is the antithesis of Haydon, who had been a more glamorous figure, but whose heroism had had no firm moral basis. Even at his romantic best, as a 'latter day Lawrence of Arabia', Haydon had embodied Conrad's 'spirit of adventure' rather than the 'spirit of service' of which Smiley is a representative.

> The mere love of adventure is no saving grace [Conrad wrote in *Notes on Life and Letters*]. It is no grace at all. It lays a man under no obligation of faithfulness to an idea and even to his own self. Roughly speaking, an adventurer may be expected to have courage, or at any rate may be said to need it. But . . . there is no sort of loyalty to bind him in honour to consistent conduct.[39]

This was indeed what Haydon lacked, though he had been an inspiration to younger men like Peter Guillam, to whom he had seemed 'the torch-bearer of a certain kind of antiquated romanticism, a notion of English calling which—for the very reason that it was vague and understated and elusive—had made sense of Guillam's life till now.' This ideal is now tarnished by treachery, as are 'the plain, heroic standards [Guillam] wished to live by';[40] and we have the sense of reaching the end of an era when the traditional, upper-class, clubland hero is unmasked as a villain. There remains, however, the alternative of Smiley himself—unromantic, humdrum, but dependable. His ultimate beliefs remain uncertain, as do Haydon's. He is capable, at the moment he establishes Bill's guilt, of 'a surge of resentment against the institutions he was supposed to be protecting'; and once, when his guard is down, he reveals a basic scepticism about the moral-political claims of East and West. But we know him, as we know Bill Haydon, by his works. He lives in practice by a code of loyalty, of fidelity, of obligation—to his wife, his subordinates, his colleagues, his profession, ultimately his country; and the human value of this ethic is established fictionally, proved on our pulses, by the action of the novel. Its polarities tend ultimately to the allegorical: Smiley and Haydon are fully rendered, fully individualised characters, but in the roles of agent and double agent, hero and villain, they emerge as representatives of integrity and corruption in a world of crumbling values, which can be sustained, it seems, only by bleak courage and loyalty without much faith.

Yet the novel itself implies a faith—not so much in a country or political system (though Le Carré's preference is clear), as in man himself—in his capacity to live humbly, yet heroically and sacrificially, a life of service. ('The modern world,' observes Ralph Harper, 'has thought up many ways to diminish man, and the thriller is one way we have to affirm our belief in a human nature that, while menaced on all sides, has not withered beyond recognition and admiration.'[41]) It is true that Smiley's triumph is precarious, and the sequel to this novel is to end with his defeat. The power politics of Whitehall will soon relegate him to retirement, and reduce him to despair; his aides will once more be demoted; the C. I. A. will reap the benefit of his last great coup; and Ann will go on being unfaithful. All he has achieved is to stave off one specific danger—to keep the whole system running till another crisis supervenes; but perhaps that is the most that anyone can do. 'There *is* no product,' Bradfield exclaims near the end of *A Small Town in Germany*: 'There *is* no final day. This *is* the life we work for. Now. At this moment. Every night, as I go to sleep, I say to myself: another day achieved. Another day added to the unnatural life of a world on its death-bed. And if I never relax; if I never lift my eye, we may run on for another hundred years.'[42] The soldier's and the secret agent's work is more spectacular than his, but their claims would not be greater.

*   *   *

Human achievements are by their very nature ephemeral, but that does not mean they are worthless. Heroic virtue, like all other kinds, must ultimately be its own reward, but it can also be a proper object of our admiration. For all the authors whom I have considered it is not the hero's victory that establishes his greatness, but the qualities he shows in confronting ever-imminent defeat or death, and present tribulation. These things are, in a strict sense, sent to try him— whether by God or fate or history, or in the last analysis by the author playing God, fate and history in his own creation. All these heroes, from Parnesius to Smiley, are subjected to a trial by ordeal: they are tested by 'events . . . that show in the light of day the inner worth of a man, the edge of his temper, and the fibre of his stuff; that reveal the quality of his resistance and the secret truth of his pretences, not only to others but also to himself.'[43] Only through such a process can their true heroic virtue be made manifest. Hence Shakespeare's Agamemnon, though himself unworthy to be ranked with them, may serve as their spokesman in his discourse on the uses of adversity:

> Why then, you princes,
> Do you with cheeks abashed behold our works,

And call them shames, which are indeed nought else
But the protractive trials of great Jove
To find persistive constancy in men?
The fineness of which metal is not found
In fortune's love: for then the bold and coward,
The wise and fool, the artist and unread,
The hard and soft, seem all affined and kin;
But, in the wind and tempest of her frown,
Distinction, with a broad and powerful fan,
Puffing at all, winnows the light away,
And what hath mass or matter, by itself
Lies rich in virtue and unmingléd. [44]

Notes

1 INTRODUCTION

1 *The Collected Essays, Journalism and Letters of George Orwell*, ed. Sonia Orwell and Ian Angus, vol. II (London, 1968) pp. 163–4.
2 Arnold Kettle, *Introduction to the English Novel*, vol. II (London, 1953), p. 159.
3 Northrop Frye, *Anatomy of Criticism* (Princeton, 1957), pp. 33–4.
4 *The Variorum Edition of the Poems of W. B. Yeats*, ed. Peter Allt and R. K. Alspach (New York, 1957), p. 327.
5 F. R. Leavis, *The Common Pursuit* (London, 1952), p. 144.
6 Frye, *op. cit.*, p. 34.
7 *The Poems of John Milton*, ed. John Carey and Alastair Fowler (London, 1968), p. 1017.
8 T. E. Hulme, *Further Speculations*, ed. Sam Hynes (Minneapolis, 1955), pp. 199–200.
9 L. A. Fiedler, *Waiting for the End* (London, 1965), p. 30.
10 Alexander Solzhenitsyn, *Warning to the Western World* (London, 1976), pp. 20–1, 35.
11 Hulme, *op.cit.*, p. 200.
12 *The Works of John Ruskin*, ed. E. T. Cook and Alexander Wedderburn, vol. XII (London, 1904), pp. 55–6.
13 Richard Barber, *The Knight and Chivalry* (London, 1970), p. 60.
14 Matthew Arnold, 'On the Modern Element in Literature,' *On the Classical Tradition*, ed. R. H. Super (Ann Arbor, 1960), p. 23.
15 Harry Levin, *The Gates of Horn: A Study of Five French Realists* (New York, 1963), p. 40.
16 E. S. Dallas, *The Gay Science*, vol. II (London, 1866), pp. 325–6, 251, 323–4. Cf. Mario Praz, *The Hero in Eclipse in Victorian Fiction*, trans. Angus Davidson (London, 1956), *passim*.
17 *Rudyard Kipling's Verse*, Definitive Edition (London, 1960), p. 330.
18 *The Variorum Edition of the Poems of W. B. Yeats*, p. 429.
19 W. H. Auden, *Spain* (London, 1937), p. 11.
20 Vera Brittain, 'War Service in Perspective,' in *Promise of Greatness*, ed. G. A. Panichas (London, 1968), pp. 370–1.
21 Robert Graves, *Goodbye to All That* (London, 1929), p. 360.
22 Frank Kermode, *Modern Essays* (London, 1971), p. 83.
23 *The Poems of Tennyson*, ed. Christopher Ricks (London, 1969), p. 1575.
24 Graham Greene, *The Ministry of Fear* (London, 1943), pp. 89–90.

2 THE SUBALTERN AS HERO

1 Introduction to *Mine Own People* (New York, 1891). Quoted here from *Kipling:*

The Critical Heritage, ed. Roger Lancelyn Green (London, 1971), p. 166.

2 Correlli Barnett, *Britain and Her Army 1509–1970. A Military, Political and Social Survey* (London, 1970).

3 *Kipling: The Critical Heritage*, p. 98.

4 *The Works of Rudyard Kipling*, Sussex Edn. (London, 1937–9) [henceforth cited as Kipling, *Works*], vol. XXXI (*Something of Myself*), p. 99.

5 *Ibid.*, pp. 126–7.

6 *New Letters of Robert Southey*, ed. Kenneth Curry (New York and London, 1965), vol. II, p. 105.

7 *The Poems of Tennyson*, ed. Christopher Ricks (London, 1969), p. 584.

8 *Ibid.*, p. 1756.

9 E. M. Forster, *Aspects of the Novel* (London, 1927), p. 16.

10 W. M. Thackeray, *Vanity Fair*, ed. Geoffrey and Kathleen Tillotson (London, 1963), p. 290.

11 David Daiches, *Literary Essays* (Edinburgh and London, 1956), p. 88.

12 *The Collected Works of Walter Bagehot*, ed. Norman St. John-Stevas, vol. II (London, 1965), p. 187.

13 E. S. Creasy, *Fifteen Decisive Battles of the World, From Marathon to Waterloo* (London, 1851), vol. I, pp. iii–iv.

14 Andrew Lang, *Essays in Little* (London, 1891), p. 4.

15 Andrew Lang, 'Realism and Romance', *Contemporary Review*, vol. LII (1887), p. 693. Cf. George Saintsbury, 'The Present State of the Novel', *Fortnightly Review*, New Series, vol. XLII (1887), pp. 410–7. Cf. also Edmund Gosse's comment in 1891, quoted here from *Kipling: The Critical Heritage*, pp. 105–6: 'The fiction of the Anglo-Saxon world, in its more intellectual provinces, had become curiously feminized. . . . People who were not content to pursue the soul of their next-door neighbour through all the burrows of self-consciousness had no choice but to take ship with Mr. Rider Haggard for the "Mountains of the Moon." Between excess of psychological analysis and excess of superhuman romance, there was a great void in the world of Anglo-Saxon fiction. It is this void which Mr Kipling . . . has filled by his exotic realism and his vigorous rendering of unhackneyed experience.'

16 Kipling, *Works*, vol. V (*Many Inventions*), p. 30.

17 *Ibid.*, p. 31.

18 *Ibid.*, p. 33.

19 *Ibid.*, p. 43.

20 *Ibid.*, p. 45.

21 Kipling, *Works*, vol. XXXI, p. 224.

22 *Ibid.*, p. 132.

23 *Rudyard Kipling's Verse*, Definitive Edition. (London, 1960), p. 290.

24 L. C. Dunsterville, *Stalky's Reminiscences* (London, 1929), pp. 110–12.

25 Edmund Wilson, *The Wound and the Bow* (Cambridge: Mass., 1941), p. 114.

26 Kipling, *Works*, vol. XXXI, pp. 162–3.

27 Kipling, *Works*, vol. XVII (*Stalky & Co.*), pp. 406, 409, 414.

28 *Ibid.*, p. 404.

29 *Ibid.*, pp. 422–3.

30 *Ibid.*, p. 417.

31 Cf. *Rudyard Kipling's Verse*, p. 170:

'*Keep ye the Law—be swift in all obedience—*
Clear the land of evil, drive the road and bridge the ford.
Make ye sure to each his own
That he reap where he hath sown;
By the peace among Our peoples let men know we serve the Lord!'

It is a high, heroic endeavour to which Kipling summons his chosen people. But the activist ethic depends for its appeal on the sense of difficulties to be overcome, and one suspects that once the land *has* been cleared of evil, the roads and bridges built, peace and order established, things may seem rather dull. Only at times, for Kipling found something heroic in any work well done under arduous conditions, but crises and emergencies—floods, famines, or riots, for example— which test men's true quality measured in terms of ultimate breaking strain appealed to his imagination more than any smooth-running routine. Cf. my lecture 'Some Aspects of Kipling's Verse', *Proceedings of the British Academy*, vol. LI (1965), pp. 375–402.

32 Kipling, *Works*, vol. v, p. 37; vol. XIV (*Puck of Pook's Hill*), pp. 146–7.
33. J. M. S. Tompkins, *The Art of Rudyard Kipling* (London, 1959), pp. 72–3.
34 Kipling, *Works*, vol. XIV, pp. 135–6.
35 *Ibid.*, p. 136.
36 *Ibid.*, p. 164.
37 *Ibid.*, p. 183.
38 *Ibid.*, p. 161.
39 *Ibid.*, pp. 171–2.
40 Kipling, *Works*, vol. XXXI, p. 112.
41 *Rudyard Kipling's Verse*, p. 324.
42. Kipling, *Works*, vol. XXVII (*The Irish Guards in the Great War*), p. x.

3 THE INTELLECTUAL AS HERO

1 Wyndham Lewis, *Blasting and Bombardiering* (London, 1937), p. 244.
2 *Seven Pillars of Wisdom*, (London, 1935) [henceforth cited as *Seven Pillars*], p. 661; J. E. Mack, *A Prince of Our Disorder* (London, 1976), p. 189; T. E. Lawrence *to His Biographers Robert Graves and Liddell Hart* (London, 1963), I, p. 111.
3 E. M. Forster, *Abinger Harvest* (London, 1936), p. 143.
4 *Seven Pillars*, p. 192.
5 Republished in *Evolution of a Revolt: Early Post-War Writings of T. E. Lawrence*, ed. Stanley and Rodelle Weintraub (University Park and London, 1968), pp. 100–19.
6 *The Letters of T. E. Lawrence*, ed. David Garnett (London, 1938) [henceforth cited as *Letters*], p. 769.
7 *Ibid.*, pp. 768–9.
8 Reprinted in *Evolution of a Revolt*, ed. Weintraub, pp. 56–62.
9 *Letters*, p. 225.
10 See Mack, *op.cit.*, pp. 41–7.
11 *Letters*, p. 512.
12 *Ibid.*, p. 238.
13 *Ibid.*, p. 246; and see Mack, *op.cit.*, pp. 154–5.
14 *T. E. Lawrence By His Friends*, ed. A. W. Lawrence (London, 1937), p. 593;

Richard Meinertzhagen, *Middle East Diary 1917–1956* (London, 1959), p. 39.

15 Quoted in T. E. Lawrence, *Minorities*, ed. J. M. Wilson (London, 1971), p. 33.

16 T. E. Lawrence, *Oriental Assembly*, ed. A. W. Lawrence (London, 1939), p. 145.

17 *Letters*, pp. 263, 291.

18 *Seven Pillars*, p. 276n. Cf. *Letters*, pp. 345–6, 671–2, 684. For some criticisms of the settlement see H. St. John Philby, *Forty Years in the Wilderness* (London, 1957), pp. 82–109; and Suleiman Mousa, *T. E. Lawrence: An Arab View* (London, 1966), pp. 252–6, 265–70.

19 *Letters*, p. 853.

20 *Ibid.*, p. 358.

21 *Seven Pillars*, pp. 22–3.

22 *Ibid.*, p. 22. For a detailed study of his revisions, see Jeffrey Meyers, *The Wounded Spirit: A Study of 'Seven Pillars of Wisdom'* (London, 1973), pp. 45–78.

23 *Letters*, p. 360.

24 *Letters to T. E. Lawrence*, ed. A. W. Lawrence (London, 1962), p. 154.

25 *Letters*, p. 362.

26 *T. E. Lawrence to His Biographers*, I, p. 138.

27 *Letters to T. E. Lawrence*, p. 24.

28 Meinertzhagen, *op. cit.*, pp. 30–2.

29 *Letters*, pp. 549–50.

30 *Ibid.*, p. 455.

31 *Ibid.*, p. 603.

32 *Ibid.*, p. 559.

33 *Ibid.*, p. 521; *Oriental Assembly*, p. 139.

34 University of Texas: Humanities Research Center, *T. E. Lawrence: Fifty Letters, 1920–1935. An Exhibition* (Austin, 1962), p. 8.

35 *Seven Pillars*, p. 549.

36 Cf. R. M. Ogilvie, *Latin and Greek. A History of the Influence of the Classics on English Life from 1600 to 1918* (London, 1964), pp. 134–71.

37 J. A. Notopoulos, 'The Tragic and the Epic in T. E. Lawrence', *Yale Review*, vol. 54 (1964–5), p. 340. For examples of some minor episodes deliberately modelled on literary epic, see Desmond Stewart, *T. E. Lawrence* (London, 1977), pp. 235–9.

38 Robert Graves, *Lawrence and the Arabs* (London, 1927), p. 417.

39 *Evolution of a Revolt*, ed. Weintraub, pp. 70–1.

40 *Oriental Assembly*, p. 84.

41 *Ibid.*, p. 143.

42 *Ibid.*, p. 142.

43 *Ibid.*, p. 140.

44 The phrase is used in the Oxford text with reference to his much disputed journey to Damascus in May–June, 1917. See Meyers, *op.cit.*, p. 55.

45 *Seven Pillars*, p. 23.

46 *Ibid.*, p. 54.

47 *Oriental Assembly*, p. 142.

48 *Letters*, pp. 302, 621.

49 *T. E. Lawrence to His Biographers*, I, p. 117; *Letters*, p. 371.

50 *T. E. Lawrence to His Biographers*, II, pp. 54, 84.

51 Jean Beraud Villars, *T. E. Lawrence or The Search for the Absolute*, trans. Peter Dawnay (London, 1958), p. 296.

52 Janet Dunbar, *Mrs G. B. S. A Biographical Portrait of Charlotte Shaw* (London, 1963), p. 268.
53 *T. E. Lawrence to His Biographers*, I, p. 117.
54 *Letters*, p. 324.
55 *Ibid.*, pp. 533, 520, 542.
56 *Ibid.*, p. 370.
57 *Ibid.*, p. 358.
58 *Ibid.*, pp. 429, 672, 622.
59 *Ibid.*, pp. 813, 462, 366.
60 *Ibid.*, p. 692.
61 *Seven Pillars*, p. 29.
62 *Ibid.*, p. 29.
63 *Ibid.*, p. 31.
64 *Ibid.*, p. 412.
65 *Ibid.*, p. 445.
66 *Ibid.*, p. 447.
67 *Ibid.*, p. 181.
68 *Ibid.*, pp. 181–2.
69 *T. E. Lawrence, By His Friends*, p. 246.
70 *Seven Pillars*, pp. 367–8.
71 *Ibid.*, p. 305.
72 *Ibid.*, p. 308.
73 *Ibid.*, p. 655.
74 Meyers, *op.cit.*, p. 136.
75 *Seven Pillars*, p. 631.
76 *Ibid.*, p. 633.
77 *Ibid.*, p. 655.
78 *Ibid.*, p. 659.
79 *Ibid.*, 275–6.
80 *Ibid.*, pp. 276, 378, 441, 544, 550.
81 *Ibid.*, p. 562.
82 *Oriental Assembly*, p. 141.
83 *Seven Pillars*, p. 563.
84 *Ibid.*, p. 563.
85 *Ibid.*, p. 551.
86 *Letters*, p. 692.
87 *Seven Pillars*, p. 661.
88 *Ibid.*, pp. 646–7.
89 *Ibid.*, pp. 651–2.
90 *Letters*, p. 280.
91 *Seven Pillars*, p. 307.
92 *Ibid.*, p. 503.
93 *Ibid.*, p. 567.
94 *Ibid.*, p. 552.
95 *Letters*, p. 258.
96 *Seven Pillars*, p. 549.
97 *Ibid.*, p. 661.
98 Lord Moran, *The Anatomy of Courage* (London, 1945), p. 67.
99 *Letters*, p. 872.

100 E. R. Curtius, *European Literature and the Latin Middle Ages*, trans. W. R. Trask (London, 1953), p. 167.

101 *Seven Pillars*, p. 661.

4 THE COMMON MAN AS HERO

1 A. J. P. Taylor, *The First World War. An Illustrated History* (London, 1963), p. 9.

2 *The Collected Essays, Journalism and Letters of George Orwell*, ed. Sonia Orwell and Ian Angus, vol. II (London, 1968), p. 192.

3 See Correlli Barnett, *Britain and Her Army 1509–1970* (London, 1970), Chapters 15 and 16; Cyril Falls, 'The Army', *Edwardian England 1901–1914*, ed. Simon Nowell-Smith (London, 1964); and A. J. P. Taylor, *English History 1914–1945* (Oxford, 1965), pp. 20–1.

4 For authoritative treatments of this subject see J. F. C. Fuller, *The Conduct of War 1789–1961* (London, 1961); his earlier *Decisive Battles of the Western World*, vol. III (London, 1956); and John Terraine, *Douglas Haig, The Educated Soldier* (London, 1963).

5 Siegfried Sassoon, *Collected Poems 1908–1956* (London, 1961), p. 85.

6 Herbert Read, *A Coat of Many Colours* (London, 1945), pp. 25–6. Cf. T. E. Lawrence, *Letters*, pp. 547–51.

7 Richard Aldington, *Death of a Hero* (London, 1929), pp. 292–3.

8 H. V. Routh, *God, Man, and Epic Poetry* (Cambridge, 1927), vol. I, p. 27.

9 Siegfried Sassoon, *Memoirs of an Infantry Officer* (London, 1930), pp. 216–17.

10 Siegfried Sassoon, *Siegfried's Journey 1916–1920* (London, 1945), p. 53 (italics mine).

11 Siegfried Sassoon, *Memoirs of a Fox-Hunting Man* (London, 1928), p. 346; Robert Graves, *Goodbye to All That* (London, 1929), p. 240; Herbert Read, *The Contrary Experience* (London, 1963), p. 72 (letter of 17 July 1916).

12 'Charles Edmonds' [i.e. C. E. Carrington], *A Subaltern's War* (London, 1929), p. 195.

13 *The Collected Poems of Wilfred Owen*, ed. C. Day Lewis (London, 1963), p. 39.

14 Wilfred Owen, *Collected Letters*, ed. Harold Owen and John Bell (London, 1967), p. 591.

15 Edmund Blunden, *The Mind's Eye* (London, 1934), p. 85.

16 Herbert Read, *The Contrary Experience*, p. 97.

17 C. E. Montague, *Disenchantment* (London, 1922), pp. 35–6.

18 Frank Richards, *Old Soldiers Never Die* (London, 1933), pp. 98, 131, 285, 239, 101, 267.

19 *Ibid.*, p. 98., 'I found,' confirms Graves, 'that the only thing that the regiment respected in young officers was personal courage.' (*Goodbye to All That*, p. 174.)

20 C. M. Bowra, *Poetry and Politics 1900–1960* (Cambridge, 1966), p. 103.

21 *The Wipers Times*, ed. Patrick Beaver (London, 1973), p. xiii.

22 Siegfried Sassoon, *Collected Poems 1908–1956*, p. 87.

23 B. H. Liddell Hart, in *Promise of Greatness*, ed. G. A. Panichas (London, 1968), p. 108.

24 *Songs and Slang of the British Soldier: 1914–1918*, ed. John Brophy and Eric Partridge, 3rd edn. (London, 1931), p. 60.

25 *Ibid.*, p. 8.

26 A. J. P. Taylor, *English History 1914–1945*, p. 62. The tradition is, however, of

longer standing than Taylor suggests here: see Field Marshal Lord Wavell's comments on songs sung in the Boer War [*Other Men's Flowers* (London, 1944), pp. 76—7].

27 Correlli Barnett, 'A Military Historian's View of the Great War', *Essays by Divers Hands. Being the Transactions of the Royal Society of Literature*, New Series, vol. XXXVI (1970), p. 10.

28 Douglas Jerrold, *The Lie About the War* (London, 1930), p. 9.

29 Cyril Falls, *War Books: A Critical Guide* (London, 1930).

30 G. H. Greenwell, *An Infant in Arms: War Letters of a Company Officer 1914—18*, introd. John Terraine (London, 1972), p. xiii.

31 Cf. J. H. Johnston, *English Poetry of the First World War* (Princeton and London, 1964), *passim*.

32 *The Collected Poems of Wilfred Owen*, p. 31; Siegfried Sassoon, *Siegfried's Journey 1916—1920*, p. 40; Herbert Read, *Collected Poems* (London, 1966), p. 158.

33 Wilfred Owen, *Collected Letters*, p. 461.

34 *The Collected Poems of Wilfred Owen*, p. 39. Cf. his *Collected Letters*, p. 458.

35 Wilfred Owen, *Poems*, ed. Edmund Blunden (London, 1931), p. 41.

36 Wilfred Owen, *Collected Letters*, p. 461.

37 *Ibid.*, p. 580.

38 *Ibid.*

39 Jon Stallworthy, *Wilfred Owen* (London, 1974), p. 279n.

40 Wilfred Owen, *Collected Letters*, p. 573.

41 *Ibid.*, p. 498.

42 Robert Graves, *Goodbye to All That*, p. 326.

43 Frank Richards, *Old Soldiers Never Die*, p. 95. One rather sad exception is Arthur Graeme West: 'I do ill to go,' he wrote in a letter of 21 August 1916: 'I ought to fight no more. But death, I suppose, is the penalty; and public opinion and possible misunderstanding. . . .' *The Diary of a Dead Officer, being the Posthumous Papers of Arthur Graeme West* (London, 1918), p. 54.

44 *The Letters of Charles Sorley* (Cambridge, 1919), p. 229.

45 *Ibid.*, pp. 262—3; J. H. Johnston, *op. cit.*, pp. 67—70.

46 *The Letters of Charles Sorley*, p. 292, Cf. pp. 304—5.

47 *Ibid.*, pp. 253—5, 265, 274.

48 *Ibid.*, p. 276.

49 *Ibid.*, pp. 294—5, 305—6.

50 *Ibid.*, pp. 311, 312—3.

51 Herbert Read, *The Contrary Experience*, pp. 112—3.

52 *Ibid.*, p. 128.

53 Herbert Read, *Collected Poems*, p. 31.

54 *The Contrary Experience*, p. 123.

55 *Ibid.*, p. 122.

56 *Ibid.*, p. 99.

57 *Ibid.*, p. 62.

58 Siegfried Sassoon, *Sherston's Progress* (London, 1936), p. 242.

59 *Siegfried's Journey 1916—1920*, p. 64.

60 Vivian de Sola Pinto, 'My First War: Memoirs of a Spectacled Subaltern', in *Promise of Greatness*, ed. G. A. Panichas, pp. 80—1.

61 Robert Graves, *Goodbye to All That*, p. 339.

62 Henry Williamson, *The Linhay on the Downs* (London, 1934), p. 247.

63 *Poems by Wilfred Owen*, ed. Siegfried Sassoon (London, 1920), p. v.
64 *Siegfried's Journey 1916–1920*, pp. 70–1.
65 Edmund Blunden, *Undertones of War*, Penguin Edition (London, 1936), p. viii. (This edition incorporates all the minor but sometimes significant amendments which he made in the editions of 1928, 1929 and 1930.)
66 *Memoirs of an Infantry Officer*, p. 259.
67 Erich Maria Remarque, *All Quiet on the Western Front*, trans. A. W. Wheen (London, 1929), pp. 66, 154–5, 296–7 (my italics).
68 *Ibid.*, pp. 5, 317–18.
69 *Memoirs of an Infantry Officer*, p. 287.
70 Richard Aldington, *Death of a Hero*, pp. 295–6.
71 *Ibid.*, p. ix.
72 *Ibid.*, p. 253.
73 *Ibid.*, pp. 252, 31, 226.
74 *Ibid.*, pp. 436–7.
75 *Ibid.*, pp. 329–31.
76 *Ibid.*, pp. 351–3, 292–4.
77 Richard Aldington, *Roads to Glory* (London, 1930), pp. 269–70.
78 *Memoirs of a Fox-Hunting Man*, p. 335.
79 *Goodbye to All That*, p. 211.
80 *Ibid.*, p. 182.
81 *Ibid.*, p. 163.
82 *Memoirs of an Infantry Officer*, p. 152.
83 *Goodbye to All That*, pp. 202–3.
84 Robert Graves, *But It Still Goes On* (London, 1930), p. 17.
85 *Goodbye to All That*, pp. 210–11.
86 *Ibid.*, pp. 127, 408.
87 *Ibid.*, p. 437.
88 Edmund Blunden, *Undertones of War* (London, 1956), pp. vii–viii (my italics).
89 *Undertones of War* (London, 1936), p. 183.
90 *Undertones of War* (London, 1956), p. ix.
91 *Undertones of War* (London, 1936), pp. 67–8.
92 *Ibid.*, pp. 54–5.
93 *Ibid.*, p. 138.
94 *Ibid.*, pp. 20, 161, 220, 125, 73, 119, 204, 206, 143, 147.
95 *Ibid.*, p. 118.
96 *Ibid.*, pp. 208, 217.
97 *A Subaltern's War*, p. 200.
98 Edmund Blunden, *The Mind's Eye*, p. 43.
99 *Memoirs of an Infantry Officer*, p. 183; *Undertones of War* (London, 1936), p. vii.
100 *Siegfried's Journey 1916–1920*, p. 69.
101 *Goodbye to All That*, p. 440.
102 *Memoirs of an Infantry Officer*, pp. 233–4.
103 Edmund Blunden, *War Poets 1914–1918* (London, 1958), pp. 25–6.
104 Guy Chapman, *A Passionate Prodigality. Fragments of Autobiography* (London, 1933), p. 276–7.
105 Frederic Manning, *Her Privates We*, introd. Edmund Blunden (London, 1964), p. ix.
106 *The Mind's Eye*, p. 266.

107 *The Letters of Charles Sorley*, p. 284.
108 R. H. Tawney, *The Attack and Other Papers* (London, 1953), p. 14.
109 *Ibid.*, pp. 25−6.
110 *The Collected Poems of Wilfred Owen*, p. 80; *Memoirs of an Infantry Officer*, pp. 44−5.
111 Wilfred Owen, *Collected Letters*, p. 422.
112 *A Passionate Prodigality*, p. 60.
113 *War Books. A Critical Guide*, p. 292.
114 Frederic Manning, *The Middle Parts of Fortune* (London, 1929), p. 143.
115 *Ibid.*, pp. 27−9.
116 *Ibid.*, pp. 336, 369−70.
117 *Ibid.*, pp. 6−7.
118 *Ibid.*, pp. 16−17.
119 *Ibid.*, pp. 183, 144, 271−2, 124.
120 *Ibid.*, p. 377.
121 *Ibid.*, p. 147.
122 *Ibid.*, pp. 354−5.
123 *Ibid.*, pp. 255−6.
124 *Ibid.*, pp. 388−90.
125 *Ibid.*, pp. 394−5.
126 *Ibid.*, pp. 18−19.
127 *Ibid.*, p. 453.

5 THE CHRISTIAN AS HERO

1 *The Diaries of Evelyn Waugh*, ed. Michael Davie (London, 1976), p. 438.
2 Christopher Isherwood, *Lions and Shadows: An Education in the Twenties* (London, 1938), pp. 74−6.
3 *The Collected Essays, Journalism and Letters of George Orwell*, ed. Sonia Orwell and Ian Angus, vol. 1 (London, 1968), pp. 537−8.
4 Evelyn Waugh, *A Little Learning. The First Volume of an Autobiography* (London, 1964), pp. 59, 89.
5 *The Diaries of Evelyn Waugh*, p. 37.
6 *A Little Learning*, p. 132.
7 *Ibid.*, pp. 173−5; Christopher Sykes, *Evelyn Waugh. A Biography*, revised edn. (Harmondsworth, 1977), pp. 73−5.
8 Evelyn Waugh, *When the Going was Good* (London, 1946), p. 10.
9 *Evelyn Waugh and His World*, ed. David Pryce-Jones (London, 1973), p. 139.
10 Evelyn Waugh, *Brideshead Revisited* (London, 1945), p. 12.
11 *The Diaries of Evelyn Waugh*, p. 548.
12 Evelyn Waugh, *Helena* (London, 1950), p. 122.
13 A. E. Dyson, *The Crazy Fabric: Essays in Irony* (London, 1965), p. 187.
14 *Helena*, p. 120.
15 *Writers at Work. The 'Paris Review' Interviews*, 3rd series, introd. Alfred Kazin (London, 1968), p. 110.
16 Evelyn Waugh, *Officers and Gentlemen* (London, 1955), p. 97.
17 This statement appeared not in the volume itself, but on the dust-jacket.
18 *A Little Learning*, pp. 27−8.
19 Evelyn Waugh, *The Ordeal of Gilbert Pinfold* (London, 1957) p. 2.

20 *Sword of Honour* (London, 1965), p. 9.
21 Malcolm Bradbury, *Evelyn Waugh* (Edinburgh and London, 1964), p. 109.
22 *Sword of Honour*, p. 9.
23 F. J. Stopp, *Evelyn Waugh: Portrait of an Artist* (London, 1958), p. 32.
24 'Donat O'Donnell' [Conor Cruise O'Brien], *Maria Cross* (London, 1953), pp. 125–6.
25 Bernard Bergonzi, 'Evelyn Waugh's Gentleman', *The Critical Quarterly*, vol. v (1963), p. 23.
26 *Sword of Honour*, p. 9.
27 *Men at Arms* (London, 1952), p. 5.
28 F. J. Stopp, *op. cit.*, p. 168.
29 *Goodbye to All That* (London, 1929), pp. 117–22.
30 Rudyard Kipling, *Works*, vol. IV (*Life's Handicap*), p. 108.
31 *Men at Arms*, p. 87–8.
32 *Ibid.*, p. 91.
33 I. M. G. Stewart, *The Struggle for Crete* (London, 1966), p. 469.
34 *Officers and Gentlemen*, pp. 238–9, 276.
35 Edmund Wilson, *Classics and Commercials* (London, 1951), p. 302.
36 *Officers and Gentlemen*, pp. 146–7.
37 Cf. Bernard Bergonzi, *op. cit.*, p. 35.
38 *Officers and Gentlemen*, pp. 321–2.
39 Statement on the dust-jacket of the first edition of *Unconditional Surrender*.
40 *Unconditional Surrender* (London, 1961), p. 10.
41 *Ibid.*, p. 193.
42 F. J. Stopp, *op. cit.*, p. 46.
43 *Unconditional Surrender*, pp. 300–1.
44 Steven Marcus, 'Evelyn Waugh and the Art of Entertainment', *Partisan Review*, vol. 23 (1956), p. 354.
45 *Writers at Work. The 'Paris Review' Interviews*, 3rd series, pp. 112–13.
46 Fitzroy Maclean, *Eastern Approaches* (London, 1949), p. 499. Cf. also his comments in *The Diaries of Evelyn Waugh*, pp. 651–2.
47 The Earl of Birkenhead, 'Fiery Particles', *Evelyn Waugh and His World*, pp. 137–63.
48 Evelyn Waugh, *Scott-King's Modern Europe* (London, 1947), p. 2.

6 THE SPY AS HERO

1 Steven Marcus, 'Evelyn Waugh and the Art of Entertainment', *Partisan Review*, vol. 23 (1956), pp. 348–9.
2 Robert Louis Stevenson, 'The Morality of the Profession of Letters', *Essays Literary and Critical*, Tusitala Edition (London, 1924), p. 60. All subsequent quotations from Stevenson's works are from the Tusitala Edition.
3 Stevenson, *Letters*, vol. II (London, 1924), p. 104.
4 Stevenson, 'A Gossip on Romance', *Memories and Portraits*, pp. 122–3; 'A Humble Remonstrance', *ibid.*, p. 137.
5 *Memories and Portraits*, p. 138.
6 Stevenson, *Letters*, vol. II, pp. 298–9.
7 *Memories and Portraits*, p. 123. For a fuller discussion of Stevenson's theory and practice see my lectures on 'The Dominion of Romance', *Edinburgh University*

Journal, vol. 23 (1967–8), pp. 297–308; vol. 24 (1969–70), pp. 25–37.

8 Henry Fielding, *'Joseph Andrews' and 'Shamela'*, ed. Douglas Brooks (London, 1971), pp. 4–5.

9 *The Works of Charles and Mary Lamb*, ed. E. V. Lucas, vol. II (London, 1903), p. 142.

10 *Ibid.*, pp. 143–4.

11 Stevenson, *Memories and Portraits*, p. 129.

12 Sigmund Freud, 'Creative Writers and Day-Dreaming', cited from *20th Century Literary Criticism: A Reader*, ed. David Lodge (London, 1972), pp. 36–42.

13 *Ibid.*, pp. 36–7.

14 Gillian Beer, *The Romance* (London, 1970), p. 12.

15 Lionel Trilling, *The Liberal Imagination* (London, 1951), p. 56.

16 See H. W. C. Davis, 'The Great Game in Asia', *Proceedings of the British Academy*, vol. XII (1926), pp. 227–56.

17 John Buchan, *The Power House* (Edinburgh and London, 1916), pp. 64–5; Gertrude Himmelfarb, 'John Buchan: An Untimely Appreciation', *Encounter*, vol. 15 (1960), no. 3, p. 52.

18 John Buchan, *Mr Standfast* (London, 1919), pp. 242, 244.

19 M. R. D. Foot, *Resistance* (London, 1976), pp. 14–15.

20 William Garner, *The Us or Them War* (London, 1971), p. 22. (First published 1969.)

21 John Le Carré, *The Spy Who Came in from the Cold* (London, 1963), pp. 17–18.

22 *Ibid.*, p. 214.

23 *Ibid.*, pp. 9–10.

24 Cf. Mark Kinkead-Weekes, 'Vision in Kipling's Novels', *Kipling's Mind and Art*, ed. Andrew Rutherford (Edinburgh and London, 1964), pp. 197–234.

25 John Le Carré, *Call for the Dead* (London, 1961), p. 11.

26 *Ibid.*, p. 14; *A Murder of Quality* (London, 1962), p. 29.

27 *Call for the Dead*, pp. 12–13.

28 *The Spy Who Came in from the Cold*, p. 221.

29 Hugh Trevor-Roper, *The Philby Affair* (London, 1968), p. 61.

30 John Le Carré, *The Honourable Schoolboy* (London, 1977), p. 461.

31 John Le Carré, *Tinker Tailor Soldier Spy* (London, 1974), pp. 12–13.

32 *Ibid.*, pp. 19, 345.

33 *Ibid.*, pp. 348–9.

34 *Ibid.*, p. 326.

35 E. M. Forster, 'What I Believe', *Two Cheers for Democracy* (London, 1951), p. 78.

36 George Eliot, *Felix Holt* (Edinburgh and London, 1866), vol. I, p. 88.

37 Henry James, Preface to *The American*, cited here from *The Art of the Novel: Critical Prefaces by Henry James*, ed. R. P. Blackmur (New York, 1935), p. 33.

38 See his introduction to Bruce Page, David Leitch and Phillip Knightley, *Philby: The Spy Who Betrayed a Generation* (London, 1968).

39 Joseph Conrad, *Notes on Life and Letters* (London, 1921), p. 255.

40 *Tinker Tailor Soldier Spy*, p. 328.

41 Ralph Harper, *The World of the Thriller* (Cleveland, Ohio, 1969), p. 98.

42 John Le Carré, *A Small Town in Germany* (London, 1968), p. 287.

43 Joseph Conrad, *Lord Jim* (London, 1900), p. 9.

44 *Troilus and Cressida*, ed. Alice Walker (Cambridge, 1957), p. 18.

Bibliography

This bibliography is necessarily selective, but the main omission is an extensive list of thriller titles relevant to the first part of Chapter 6, but familiar, I assume, to most readers.

Alexander Aitken, *Gallipoli to the Somme. Recollections of a New Zealand Infantryman* (London, 1963).
Richard Aldington, *Collected Poems* (London, 1929).
——, *Death of a Hero* (London, 1929).
——, *Death of a Hero*, unexpurgated edn. (London, 1965).
——, *Lawrence of Arabia. A Biographical Inquiry*, 2nd edn. (London, 1969).
——, *Life for Life's Sake* (London, 1968).
——, *Roads to Glory* (London, 1930).
Kingsley Amis, *The James Bond Dossier* (London, 1965).
Richard Barber, *The Knight and Chivalry* (London, 1970).
Henri Barbusse, *Under Fire*, trans. F. Wray (London, 1917).
Correlli Barnett, *Britain and Her Army 1509–1970. A Military, Political and Social Survey* (London, 1970).
——, 'A Military Historian's View of the Great War', *Essays by Divers Hands. Being the Transactions of the Royal Society of Literature*, New Series, vol. XXXVI (1970).
——, *The Sword-Bearers. Studies in Supreme Command in the First World War* (London, 1963).
John Baynes, *Morale: A Study of Men and Courage* (London, 1967).
Patrick Beaver, ed., *The Wipers Times* (London, 1973).
Gillian Beer, *The Romance* (London, 1970).
Bernard Bergonzi, 'Evelyn Waugh's Gentleman', *The Critical Quarterly*, vol. V (1963).
——, *Heroes' Twilight. A Study of the Literature of the Great War* (London, 1965).
R. P. Blackmur, 'The Everlasting Effort. A Citation of T. E. Lawrence', *The Lion and the Honeycomb* (London, 1956).
Edmund Blunden, *The Mind's Eye* (London, 1934).
——, *Poems, 1914–30* (London, 1930).
——, *Undertones of War* (London, 1928).
——, *Undertones of War* (London, 1936).
——, *Undertones of War* (London, 1956).
——, *War Poets 1914–1918* (London, 1958).
C. A. Bodelsen, *Aspects of Kipling's Art* (Manchester, 1964).
Colonel Sir Hugh Boustead, *The Wind of Morning* (London, 1971).
C. M. Bowra, *Poetry and Politics 1900–1960* (Cambridge, 1966).

Malcolm Bradbury, *Evelyn Waugh* (Edinburgh and London, 1964).

Vera Brittain, *Testament of Youth* (London, 1933).

John Brophy and Eric Partridge, eds., *Songs and Slang of the British Soldier 1914–1918*, 3rd edn. (London, 1931).

J. H. Buckley, *William Ernest Henley: A Study in the 'Counter-Decadence' of the 'Nineties* (Princeton, 1945).

Jenni Calder, *Heroes. From Byron to Guevara* (London, 1977).

Charles Carrington, *Rudyard Kipling. His Life and Work* (London, 1955).

——, *Soldier From the Wars Returning* (London, 1965).

——, *A Subaltern's War* (London, 1929), under pseudonym 'Charles Edmonds'.

Guy Chapman, *A Passionate Prodigality. Fragments of Autobiography* (London, 1933).

——, ed., *Vain Glory: A Miscellany of the Great War 1914–18* (London, 1937).

Joseph Cohen, *Journey to the Trenches. The Life of Isaac Rosenberg 1890–1918* (London, 1975).

Morton Cohen, *Rider Haggard, His Life and Works* (London, 1960).

——, ed., *Rudyard Kipling to Rider Haggard. The Record of a Friendship* (London, 1965).

E. S. Creasy, *Fifteen Decisive Battles of the World. From Marathon to Waterloo* (London, 1851).

E. R. Curtius, *European Literature and the Latin Middle Ages*, trans. W. R. Trask (London, 1953).

E. S. Dallas, *The Gay Science* (London, 1866).

Bonamy Dobrée, *Rudyard Kipling. Realist and Fabulist* (London, 1967).

L. C. Dunsterville, *Stalky's Reminiscences* (London, 1929).

Cyril Falls, 'The Army', in *Edwardian England 1901–1914*, ed. Simon Nowell-Smith (London, 1964).

——, *War Books: A Critical Guide* (London, 1930).

L. A. Fiedler, *Waiting for the End* (London, 1965).

M. R. D. Foot, *Resistance* (London, 1976).

——, *S.O.E. in France* (London, 1966).

Ford Madox Ford, *No More Parades* (London, 1925).

——, *A Man Could Stand Up* (London, 1926).

——, *Some Do Not* (London, 1924).

John Fraser, *Violence in the Arts* (Cambridge, 1974).

Northrop Frye, *Anatomy of Criticism* (Princeton, 1957).

Paul Fussell, *The Great War and Modern Memory* (London, 1975).

J. F. C. Fuller, *The Conduct of War 1789–1961* (London, 1961).

——, *Decisive Battles of the Western World* (London, 1954—6).

Brian Gardner, ed., *Up the Line to Death. The War Poets: 1914–1918* (London, 1964).

Brigadier J. B. Glubb, *The Story of the Arab Legion* (London, 1948).

Robert Graves, *But It Still Goes On* (London, 1930).

——, *Fairies and Fusiliers* (London, 1917).

——, *Goodbye to All That* (London, 1929).

——, *Goodbye to All That*, revised edn. (London, 1957).

——, *Lawrence and the Arabs* (London 1927).

Roger Lancelyn Greene, *Kipling and the Children* (London, 1965).

——, ed., *Kipling: The Critical Heritage* (London, 1971).

Ralph Harper, *The World of the Thriller* (Cleveland, Ohio, 1969).

Ian Hay, *The First Hundred Thousand* (Edinburgh and London, 1915).

W. E. Henley, ed., *Lyra Heroica. A Book of Verse for Boys* (London, 1892).

A. P. Herbert, *The Secret Battle*, 3rd edn. (London, 1928).

Richard Hillary, *The Last Enemy* (London, 1942).

W. E. Houghton, *The Victorian Frame of Mind* (New Haven, 1957).

Irving Howe, 'T. E. Lawrence: The Problem of Heroism,' *The Hudson Review*, vol. 15 (1962–3).

T. E. Hulme, *Further Speculations*, ed. Sam Hynes (Minneapolis, 1955).

——, *Speculations* (London, 1936).

Douglas Jerrold, *The Lie About the War. A Note on Some Contemporary War Books* (London, 1930).

J. H. Johnston, *English Poetry of the First World War* (Princeton and London, 1964).

David Jones, *In Parenthesis* (London, 1937).

Alfred Kazin, introd., *Writers at Work. The 'Paris Review' Interviews*, 3rd Series (London, 1968).

Robert Kiely, *Robert Louis Stevenson and the Fiction of Adventure* (Cambridge, Mass., 1964).

Rudyard Kipling, *Rudyard Kipling's Verse*, Definitive Edn. (London, 1960).

——, *The Works of Rudyard Kipling*, Sussex Edn. (London, 1937–9).

Holger Klein, ed., *The First World War in Fiction* (London, 1976).

Phillip Knightley and Colin Simpson, *The Secret Lives of Lawrence of Arabia* (London, 1969).

A. W. Lawrence, ed., *Letters to T. E. Lawrence* (London, 1962).

——, ed., *T. E. Lawrence. By His Friends* (London, 1937).

T. E. Lawrence, *Evolution of a Revolt. Early Post-War Writings of T. E. Lawrence*, ed. Stanley and Rodelle Wientraub (University Park and London, 1968).

——, *The Letters of T. E. Lawrence*, ed. David Garnett (London, 1938).

——, *Men in Print: Essays in Literary Criticism*, ed. A. W. Lawrence (London, 1940).

——, *Minorities*, ed. J. M. Wilson (London, 1971).

——, *The Mint* (London, 1973).

——, *Oriental Assembly*, ed. A. W. Lawrence (London, 1939).

——, *Revolt in the Desert* (London, 1927).

——, *Secret Despatches from Arabia*, ed. A. W. Lawrence (London, 1939).

——, *Seven Pillars of Wisdom* (London, 1935).

——, *T. E. Lawrence: Fifty Letters, 1920–1935* (Austin, 1962).

——, *T. E. Lawrence's Letters to H. S. Ede 1927–1935*, ed. H. S. Ede (London, 1942).

——, *T. E. Lawrence to His Biographers Robert Graves and Liddell Hart* (London, 1963).

M. R. Lawrence, ed., *The Home Letters of T. E. Lawrence and His Brothers* (Oxford, 1954).

'John Le Carré' [David Cornwell], *Call for the Dead* (London, 1961).

——, *The Honourable Schoolboy* (London, 1977).

——, *The Looking-Glass War* (London, 1965).

——, *A Murder of Quality* (London, 1962).

——, *A Small Town in Germany* (London, 1968).

——, *The Spy Who Came in from the Cold* (London, 1963).

——, *Tinker Tailor Soldier Spy* (London, 1974).

Bibliography 171

Harry Levin, *The Gates of Horn: A Study of Five French Realists* (New York, 1963).

B. H. Liddell Hart, *A History of the First World War, 1914–1918* (London, 1970).

——, *A History of the Second World War, 1939–1945* (London, 1970).

——, 'Lawrence and Lloyd George', *Memoirs* (London, 1965).

——, *'T. E. Lawrence': In Arabia and After* (London, 1934).

David Lodge, ed., *20th Century Literary Criticism: A Reader* (London, 1972).

J. E. Mack, *A Prince of Our Disorder. The Life of T. E. Lawrence* (London, 1976).

Fitzroy Maclean, *Eastern Approaches* (London, 1949).

André Malraux, 'Lawrence and the Demon of the Absolute', *Hudson Review*, vol. 8 (1956).

Frederic Manning, *Eidola* (London, 1917).

——, *Her Privates We* (London, 1930).

——, *Her Privates We*, introd. Edmund Blunden (London, 1964).

——, *The Middle Parts of Fortune* (London, 1929).

——, *The Middle Parts of Fortune*, new edn. (London, 1977).

——, *Scenes and Portraits*, revised edn. (London, 1930).

Steven Marcus, 'Evelyn Waugh and the Art of Entertainment', *Partisan Review*, vol. 23 (1956).

Philip Mason, *A Matter of Honour. An Account of the Indian Army, Its Officers and Men* (London, 1974).

——, *The Men Who Ruled India* (London, 1953–4) under the pseudonym 'Philip Woodruff'.

Richard Meinertzhagen, *Middle East Diary 1917–1956* (London, 1959).

Jeffrey Meyers, *The Wounded Spirit: A Study of 'Seven Pillars of Wisdom'* (London, 1973).

C. E. Montague, *Disenchantment* (London, 1922).

——, *Fiery Particles* (London, 1923).

——, *Rough Justice* (London, 1926).

Lord Moran, *The Anatomy of Courage* (London, 1945).

R. H. Mottram, *The Spanish Farm Trilogy* (London, 1927).

Nicholas Mosley, *Julian Grenfell* (London, 1976).

Suleiman Mousa, *T. E. Lawrence: An Arab View* (London, 1966).

J. A. Notopoulos, 'The Tragic and the Epic in T. E. Lawrence', *Yale Review*, vol. 54 (1964—5).

George Orwell, *The Collected Essays, Journalism and Letters of George Orwell*, ed. Sonia Orwell and Ian Angus (London, 1968).

Wilfred Owen, *Collected Letters*, ed. Harold Owen and John Bell (London, 1967).

——, *Collected Poems*, ed. C. Day Lewis (London, 1963).

Bruce Page, David Leitch, and Phillip Knightley, *Philby. The Spy Who Betrayed a Generation*, introd. John Le Carré (London, 1968).

G. A. Panichas, ed., *Promise of Greatness. The War of 1914–1918* (London, 1968).

I. M. Parsons, ed., *Men Who March Away* (London, 1965).

H. St. John Philby, 'T. E. Lawrence and His Critics', *Forty Years in the Wilderness* (London, 1957).

H. A. R. ('Kim') Philby, *My Silent War* (London, 1968).

David Piper, *Trial by Battle* (London, 1966).

Mario Praz, *The Hero in Eclipse in Victorian Fiction*, trans. Angus Davidson (London, 1956).

David Pryce-Jones, ed., *Evelyn Waugh and His World* (London, 1973).

Herbert Read, *Ambush* (London, 1930).
——, *A Coat of Many Colours* (London, 1945).
——, *Collected Poems* (London, 1966).
——, *The Contrary Experience* (London, 1963).
E. M. Remarque, *All Quiet on the Western Front*, trans. A. W. Wheen (London, 1929).
Frank Richards, *Old Soldiers Never Die* (London, 1933).
——, *Old Soldiers Never Die*, introd. Robert Graves (London, 1964).
Isaac Rosenberg, *Collected Works*, ed. G. Bottomley and D. Harding (London, 1937).
Andrew Rutherford, 'The Dominion of Romance', *Edinburgh University Journal*, vol. 23 (1967–8) and vol. 24 (1969–70).
——, ed., *Kipling's Mind and Art* (Edinburgh and London, 1964).
——, 'Some Aspects of Kipling's Verse', *Proceedings of the British Academy*, vol. LI. (1965).
Siegfried Sassoon, *Collected Poems 1908–1956* (London, 1961).
——, *Letters to a Critic* (Nettlestead, 1976).
——, *Memoirs of a Fox-Hunting Man* (London, 1928).
——, *Memoirs of an Infantry Officer* (London, 1930).
——, *Sherston's Progress* (London, 1936).
——, *Siegfried's Journey 1916–1920* (London, 1945).
R. C. Sherriff, *Journey's End* (London, 1929).
Jon Silkin, *Out of Battle: The Poetry of the Great War* (London, 1972).
Field Marshal Sir William Slim, *Unofficial History* (London, 1959).
Janet Adam Smith, *John Buchan. A Biography* (London, 1965).
C. H. Sorley, *The Letters of Charles Sorley* (Cambridge, 1919).
——, *Marlborough, and Other Poems* (Cambridge, 1916).
Jon Stallworthy, *Wilfred Owen*. (London, 1974).
Robert Louis Stevenson, *Works*, Tusitala Edn. (London, 1924).
Desmond Stewart, *T. E. Lawrence* (London, 1977).
I. M. G. Stewart, *The Struggle for Crete* (London, 1966).
F. J. Stopp, *Evelyn Waugh: Portrait of an Artist* (London, 1958).
Christopher Sykes, *Evelyn Waugh. A Biography*, revised edn. (Harmondsworth, 1977).
R. H. Tawney, *The Attack and Other Papers* (London, 1953).
A. J. P. Taylor, *English History 1914–1945* (Oxford, 1965).
——, *The First World War. An Illustrated History* (London, 1963).
John Terraine, *Douglas Haig. The Educated Soldier* (London, 1963).
——, *The Great War 1914–1918* (London, 1965).
——, ed., *General Jack's Diary 1914–1918* (London, 1964).
——, ed., G. H. Greenwell, *An Infant in Arms: War Letters of a Company Officer 1914–18* (London, 1972).
Lowell Thomas, *With Lawrence in Arabia* (London, 1924).
Michael Thorpe, *Siegfried Sassoon: A Critical Study* (London, 1966).
J. M. S. Tompkins, *The Art of Rudyard Kipling* (London, 1959).
Hugh Trevor-Roper, *The Philby Affair* (London, 1968).
Lionel Trilling, *The Liberal Imagination* (London, 1951).
Richard Usborne, *Clubland Heroes*, revised edn. (London, 1974).
Evelyn Waugh, *The Diaries of Evelyn Waugh*, ed. Michael Davie (London, 1976).
——, *A Little Learning. The First Volume of an Autobiography* (London, 1964).

——, *Waugh in Abyssinia* (London, 1936).

——, *When the Going Was Good* (London, 1946).

——, *Brideshead Revisited* (London, 1945).

——, *Men at Arms* (London, 1952).

——, *Officers and Gentlemen* (London, 1955).

——, *Unconditional Surrender* (London, 1961).

——, *Sword of Honour* (London, 1965).

  Other novels as cited in Notes, pp. 165–6 above.

Stanley and Rodelle Weintraub, *Lawrence of Arabia: The Literary Impulse* (Baton Rouge, 1975).

D. S. R. Welland, *Wilfred Owen: A Critical Study* (London, 1960).

Arthur Graeme West, *Diary of a Dead Officer, Being the Posthumous Papers of Arthur Graeme West* (London, 1918).

H. V. F. Winston, *Captain Shakespear. A Portrait* (London, 1976).

Henry Williamson, 'Reality in War Literature', *The Linhay on the Downs* (London, 1934).

Index

Abd el Kadir, 61
Abdulla (brother of Feisal), 42, 61
Aldington, Richard, 68, 72 (*Death of a Hero*), 87, 88—91
Allenby, Field-Marshal Lord, 49, 61, 62
Arnold, Matthew, 6
Astor, Nancy, Lady, 62
Auda ben Tayi, 47
Auden, W. H., 8

Bagehot, Walter, 15
Bairnsfather, Bruce, 101
Balzac, Honoré de, 136
Barbusse, Henri, 69, 86—7, 96
Barnett, Correlli, 12, 75
Bayard, Seigneur de, 5
Baynes, John, xi
Beer, Gillian, 141
Bergonzi, Bernard, 128
Birkenhead, Earl of, 116, 132
Blake, William, 139
Blunden, Edmund, 64—5, 70, 71, 72 (*Undertones of War*), 86, 88, 93—7, 98, 100
Bonaparte, Napoleon, 5—6, 26
Bowra, C. M., 73
Bradbury, Malcolm, 120
Brittain, Vera, 8
Brooke, Rupert, 65, 80
Brophy, John, 74—5
Buchan, John, 142—4
Butler, Samuel, 88
Byron, George Gordon, Lord, 5, 15, 48, 59

Carlyle, Thomas, 6, 11, 15
Carrington, Charles, 70, 72 (*A Subaltern's War*), 96
Cervantes, Miguel de, 1, 2 (*Don Quixote*), 5

Chandler, Raymond, 9
Chapman, Guy, 99, 102
Chaucer, Geoffrey, 3
Churchill, Randolph, 116
Churchill, Winston, 11, 42—3, 45
Clarendon, Earl of, 46
Clayton, General Sir Gilbert, 40
Congreve, William, 139
Conrad, Joseph, 14, 29, 49, 51 (*Heart of Darkness*), 53, 79 (*Lord Jim*), 118, 135, 154
Creasy, E. S., 15
Cruttwell, C. R. M. F., 115—16
Curtius, E. R., 1, 62—3

Daiches, David, 14
Dallas, E. S., 6—7
Davies, Peter, 100
Deighton, Len, 149
Dibdin, Charles, 12
Dickens, Charles, 6, 132
Dostoevsky, F. M., 44 (*The Brothers Karamazov*)
Doughty, C. M., 38
Dumas, Alexandre, 136
Dunsterville, L. C., 22
Dyson, A. E., 118

Eliot, George, 6, 136, 152

Falls, Cyril, 76, 102
Feisal, 42, 46, 60, 62
Fiedler, L. A., 4
Fielding, Henry, 138
Fleming, Ian, 10 (James Bond), 144
Foch, Marshal, 89
Foot, M. R. D., 143—4
Ford, Ford Madox, 72 (*Parade's End*), 120
Forster, E. M., 14, 39, 45, 46, 152

Franco, General, 124
Freud, Sigmund, 140–1, 151
Frye, Northrop, 3
Fuller, General J. F. C., 67

Garner, William, 144 (*The Us or Them War*)
Garnett, Edward, 43, 44, 51
Gibbon, Lewis Grassic, 120
Gide, André, 50
Goethe, J. W. von, 59
Gosse, Edmund, 158
Grant, James, 16
Graves, Robert, 8–9, 39, 44–5, 47, 50, 59, 64, 70, 72 (*Goodbye to All That*), 77, 79, 85, 87, 91–4, 97, 125, 162
Greene, Graham, 10, 142, 146, 149
Grenfell, Julian, 69, 81, 85

Haggard, H. Rider, 16, 158
Haggard, William, 149
Hall, Adam, 149
Hardy, Thomas, 45, 94 (*The Dynasts*)
Harper, Ralph, 135, 155
Hašek, Jaroslav, 1 (*The Good Soldier Schweik*)
Heller, Joseph, 3
Hemingway, Ernest, 24, 80
Hillary, Richard, 3
Hitler, Adolf, 5, 128
Hogarth, D. G., 40
Homer, 13, 40, 47, 49 (*Iliad*)
Howe, Irving, 38
Hulme, T. E., 4, 5
Hunt, William, 7
Huxley, Aldous, xi

Isherwood, Christopher, 114

Jack, General J. L., 64
James, Henry, 11–12, 153
Jerrold, Douglas, 75–6
Johnson, Lionel, 12, 15
Johnson, Samuel, 1
Jones, David, 72 (*In Parenthesis*), 88, 109
Jünger, Ernst, 69

Kazin, Alfred, 113
Kennington, Eric, 47

Kermode, Frank, 9
Kettle, Arnold, 2
Kingsley, Charles, 16 (*Westward Ho!*)
Kipling, Rudyard, 7, 11–37, 38–9, 49, 54 (*Puck of Pook's Hill*), 89, 125–6, 142 (*Kim*), 146, 155, 159
Kitchener, Field-Marshal Lord, 66, 115

Lamb, Charles, 137, 138–40
Lang, Andrew, 16
Lartéguy, Jean, 32
Lawrence, D. H., 25
Lawrence, T. E., 38–63, 68 (*Seven Pillars of Wisdom*), 105, 154
Laycock, General Sir Robert, 116, 119, 132 ('Layforce')
Leavis, F. R., 3
Le Carré, John (David Cornwell), 135–55
Lever, C. J., 16
Lewis, Wyndham, 38
Liddell Hart, B. H., 40, 59, 67, 74
Linklater, Eric, 113
Littlewood, Joan, 73
Longinus, 44
Ludendorff, General, 67

Macaulay, T. B., 15, 30 ('Horatius')
MacLean, Fitzroy, 132
Malory, Sir Thomas, 40, 47
Manning, Frederic, 51, 72 (*Her Privates We*), 88, 99–100, 102–12, 113
Marcus, Steven, 131, 135
Marryat, Frederick, 16
Maugham, W. Somerset, 144
Meinertzhagen, Richard, 41, 45–6
Melville, Herman, 44 (*Moby Dick*)
Meyers, Jeffrey, 57, 160
Miller, Arthur, 3 (*Death of a Salesman*)
Milton, John, 4 (*Paradise Lost*), 138 (*Il Penseroso*)
Montague, C. E., 71, 72 (*Disenchantment*), 87, 88
Moran, Lord, 62
Mottram, R. H., 72 (*The Spanish Farm Trilogy*)
Muir, Edwin, 8
Mussolini, Benito, 124

Nietzsche, F. W., 44 (*Thus Spake Za-rathustra*), 84
Notopoulos, J. A., 47

O'Donnell, Donat (Conor Cruse O'Brien), 122—3
Orwell, George, 1—2, 65, 114—15
Owen, Wilfred, 65, 67, 69, 70, 76, 77—80, 86, 101—2

Partridge, Eric, 74
Philby, H. A. R. ('Kim'), 149, 150, 153
Piper, David, 4
Plumer, Field-Marshal Lord, 67
Pope, Alexander, 133
Proust, Marcel, 50, 122

Rawlinson, General Lord, 67
Read, Herbert, 46, 68, 70, 71, 72 (*In Retreat*), 77, 82—4
Reade, Charles, 136
Remarque, E. M., 69, 87, 88, 91, 104
Richards, Frank, 64, 72, 80, 107
Roberts, Field-Marshal Lord, 12
Routh, H. V., 69
Ruskin, John, 5
Russell, William, 15

Sassoon, Siegfried, 44, 45, 47, 65, 67, 69, 70, 76, 77, 81, 84—5, 86, 87, 88, 91, 92, 97—9, 101
Scott, Sir Walter, 14, 136
Shakespeare, William, 1 (*Henry IV*, Part 1), 3 (*Othello*), 106, 135 (*Hamlet*), 136, 150, 155—6 (*Troilus and Cressida*)
Shaw, G. B., 1 (*Arms and the Man*), 43, 44, 45, 46, 55
Shaw, Mrs. G. B., 50
Sherriff, R. C., 72 (*Journey's End*), 87, 91
Sinclair, Andrew, 1
Smollett, Tobias, 12
Solzhenitsyn, Alexander, 4—5
Sophocles, 150 (*Oedipus Rex*)
Sorley, Charles, 80—2, 100

Southey, Robert, 13
Spenser, Edmund, 3, 9 (*The Faerie Queene*)
Stevenson, R. L., 16, 85, 136—8, 140
Stewart, Desmond, 55, 160
Stopp, F. J., 124
Strachey, Lytton, 3
Swinburne, A. C., 59
Sykes, Christopher, 119

Tawney, R. H., 101
Taylor, A. J. P., 65 (quoted), 75, 162—3
Tennyson, Alfred, Lord, 3, 6, 9 (*Idylls of the King*), 12 ('Ode on the Death of the Duke of Wellington'), 13—14, 124 (*Maud*)
Terraine, John, 64, 76
Thackeray W. M., 6, 14, 15 (*Henry Esmond*), 25
Thomas, Lowell, 59
Thucydides, 46
Tillotson, Kathleen, 120
Tito, Marshal, 132
Todi, Jacopone da, 35
Tolstoy, Count Leo, 14, 65
Tompkins, J. M. S., 28—9
Trilling, Lionel, 142
Trollope, Anthony, 6

Villars, J. B., 50
Virgil, 3 (*Aeneid*), 47, 49
Voltaire, 5
Vonnegut, Kurt, 4 (*Slaughterhouse Five*)

Waugh, Evelyn, 8, 22, 113—34
Wavell, Field-Marshal Lord, 163
West, A. Graeme, 163
Williamson, Henry, 85, 102
Wilson, Edmund, 23, 127
Wordsworth, William, 3, 12, 49 (*The Prelude*), 59
Wycherley, William, 137 (*The Country Wife*), 139

Yeats, W. B., 3, 7—8, 73, 77
Yonge, Charlotte M., 16